TODAY'S IMMIGRANTS, THEIR STORIES

Today's Immigrants, Their Stories

A NEW LOOK AT THE NEWEST AMERICANS

Thomas Kessner
Betty Boyd Caroli

New York   Oxford
OXFORD UNIVERSITY PRESS
1981

Library of Congress Cataloging in Publication Data

Kessner, Thomas.
  Today's immigrants, their stories.

  Bibliography: p.
  Includes index.
  1. United States—Emigration and immigration—
History. I. Caroli, Betty Boyd. II. Title.
JV6455.K46   325.73   81-4004
ISBN 0-19-503000-1   AACR2

Acknowledgment is made for permission to reprint the
excerpt from *Babi Yar*, translated by Max Hayward.
Copyright, The Warden and Fellows of St. Antony's
College, Oxford. Reprinted by permission of Dr.
R. K. Kindersley, Executor.

  For permission to use their photographs we wish to
thank: Be'er Hagolah Institutes; Helga Buseman; Mar-
garet Defina; Federation of Jewish Philanthropies;
Greater New York Conference on Soviet Jewry; Greek
Orthodox Archdiocese of North and South America;
Yuri and Golda Gershkovich; *The Hartford Courant*;
Hong Kong Christian Service; Irish Arts Center; *The
Korea News* (of New York)/*Hankook Ilbo*; Margaret
Latimer and Brooklyn Rediscovery, a program of the
Brooklyn Educational and Cultural Alliance, sup-
ported by the National Endowment for the
Humanities; Herbert Mack and the Neighborhood
Documentation Project of Community Studies Inc.;
Reportorio Espanol; Three Hierarchs Church; Lidio
Tomasi and the Center for Migration Studies;
Tomche Shabbos D'Boro Park; United Nations;
United Nations High Commissioner for Refugees;
G. V. Wurtemburg.

Printing (last digit): 9 8 7 6 5 4 3 2 1

Printed in the United States of America

For
Eugene and Livia Kessner
and
Livio Caroli

Preface

When President Lyndon Johnson signed into law the Immigration Act of 1965, he put an end to fifty years of immigration restriction based on racial considerations. Although many legislators assumed at the time that the new law would not materially increase the numbers admitted or alter the overall character of American immigration, they would be proved wrong. Over the past decade and a half, not only has the total number of annual arrivals soared, but the range of cultures represented has been significantly broadened.

The historic immigrant port, New York, continues to receive a major share of the nation's newcomers. Its ability to respond to the special needs and hopes of this newest immigrant population has no doubt been altered from what it was nearly a century ago when New York was a city of limitless industrial expansion with a voracious need for low skilled workers. But so too have the needs of those who come here now.

Most of those people who chose to leave their homeland in the 1960s and 1970s did not make the journey with dreams of gold in the streets. Many did not need to. A number stepped off gleaming jets seeking only more attractive outlets for their developed skills and professional training; calculating known quantities, these immigrants made sober judgments to join the massive numbers traveling the world for a better place and greater opportunity. Of course, others were not so lucky; some had been plucked from death on the South China Sea; others had entered surreptitiously or had overstayed the time alloted them on student or tourist visas, thus creating a special population of millions of undocumented aliens. For these the city no longer offers boundless commercial opportunities. For a few, it holds out welfare entitlements and a broad range of social services to ease the transition to a new life, but for most, these services are not available or are a poor substitute for opportunity. For others seeking to live as earlier immigrants did in neighborhoods of their co-ethnics, the transition is also difficult; the voluntary and fraternal organizations that used to lend special support to these enclaves have been replaced by government programs administered by bureaucrats.

Facing its own crises, New York has, perhaps, paid less attention than it might have to the implications of its steady evolution from a city of Irishmen, Italians, Jews, and Germans to a city with a substantial immigrant population from a variety of Third World countries. In these changed circumstances, these modern immigrants must make their accommodations with America and with New York. But they come nonetheless, for reasons as varied as the lands they left, seeking political freedom, opportunities for wealth, a less restrictive atmosphere (a particular bonus for today's women immigrants), and, perhaps, one day, a stake with which to return home and enjoy the life of a landowner.

This book, then, tells their stories, adding new chapters to America's immigration history and new depth to America's immigrant heritage.*

In preparing this book, we have had the help of many people who generously shared their time and knowledge with us. We cannot acknowledge everyone here but some deserve special mention. Many individuals provided special insight into the broader immigration picture by telling us their stories. Since we promised all our subjects anonymity, we cannot name them but we gratefully acknowledge their assistance. We also wish to thank the staffs of the Kingsborough Community College library and the New York Public Library at 42nd Street, especially for the use of the Wertheim Study. John Tenhula and Mel Lehman of the Church World Service, David Ment, Sidney Saffer, Sheldon Epstein, Winsome Downey, Jack Tchen, and Ann Fleisher all provided important help. Several people read portions of the manuscript and shared their reactions with us. We would particularly like to thank the members of the Immigration Study Group of the Institute for Research in History for their comments and suggestions.

Susan Rabiner, of Oxford University Press, midwifed this book into publication with firm support and a kindly, experienced editorial hand. She has made our association with Oxford an exceptionally pleasant one. Elizabeth Fox and Margaret Joyner, also of Oxford, have been consistently generous with their help.

Our parents played very important but different roles in preparing us to collaborate on this book. Eugene and Livia Kessner lived the immigrant

---

* For those who wish to look beyond these narratives, at the broader statistical picture of American immigration, the appendix includes several tables. There is also a selected bibliography for readers who wish to pursue their study of immigration.

experience, having arrived in New York City in 1950 after having been torn loose from Europe by the special intolerance that marked the 1930s and 1940s. Clyde and Edna Boyd, whose American roots reach back 250 years earlier, have nevertheless, maintained the firm belief that the familiar is not always the best and that change is not necessarily bad. Their attitudes helped shape ours, causing us to look at immigration not just in national but in human terms.

Our spouses have been drawn into this project in many ways. To Rachel Kessner and Livio Caroli, whose good humor, hard work, and continuous support helped get this book finished, we owe a very special debt.

Contents

TODAY'S IMMIGRANTS, THEIR STORIES

Introduction

Reopening the Doors

On October 3, 1965, the thirty-sixth president of the United States, Lyndon B. Johnson, journeyed to New York City to sign a new immigration law. Those who knew the tall Texas politician knew that his deep commitment to liberal ideals was also matched by an equally acute appreciation of the symbolic. His campaign for the passage of the Civil Rights Act of 1964 had included phrases from the anthem "We Shall Overcome," and his War on Poverty speeches contained references to his own roots in rural poverty. Thus, it did not surprise many that when he signed the new immigration law, Lyndon Johnson chose to do so in the shadow of the Statue of Liberty, the most famous symbol of New York's unique role in American immigration.

The bill Johnson signed very much reflected the dominant, liberal spirit of the 1960s, a spirit that recognized past failures of action but remained committed to the ideal that government could play a decisive role in making opportunity available to those for whom it still remained elusive. The 1965 immigration law also emphasized concern for the weak and respect for equality and individual differences. President Johnson made special mention of these aspects of the new law in his address:

> This is one of the most important acts of this Congress and this administration. For it repairs deep and painful flaws in the fabric of American justice. It corrects a cruel and enduring wrong in the conduct of the American nation. It will make us truer to ourselves both as a country and as a people. It will strengthen us in a hundred unseen ways. . . . This Bill says simply that from this day forth those wishing to immigrate to America shall be admitted on the basis of their skills and their close relationship to those already here. . . . America was built by a nation of strangers. From a

3

What about the Indians your people annihilated?

hundred different places they have poured forth into an empty land, joining and blending in one mighty and irresistible tide. The land flourished because it was fed from so many sources—because it was nourished by so many cultures and traditions and peoples. And from this experience, almost unique in the history of nations, has come America's attitude toward the world. We, because of what we are, feel safer and stronger in a world as varied as the people who make it up.

President Johnson noted the uncommonness of the United States experiment in making one country out of many peoples, an experiment he judged "almost unique in the history of nations." Other countries, born out of largely homogeneous native populations, simply kept newcomers on the fringes, without offering them much hope that they might easily become part of the country's fabric. Still today in Japan, non-Japanese, even if they are Asians, are not welcome. Germany's millions of foreign workers remain "guest workers," clearly not part of the *volk*. In Sweden, foreigners can be found, but again they are plainly marked *invandrare*, much as the ancients once rejected foreigners as "barbarians." Newspaper accounts occasionally document the ease with which unfriendly feelings can turn into violence: a neighborhood brawl in Switzerland leads to death for Italian workers; Turks fight local Germans in the town where these Turks have lived in a precarious, set-off way for years. London streets reverberate with cries of "Foreigner, go home," directed at nonwhites who were born there of immigrant parents. Reports from Mandai, India, in the summer of 1980, vividly underscored the point. In a village near Agartala, the capital of Tripura state, adjoining the eastern border with Bangladesh, indigenous tribal groups massacred three hundred and fifty people, including men, women, and children. Armed with guns, spears, swords, and scythes, they spiked children, crushed the skulls of adults, and littered the scene with randomly severed limbs. The simple reason for the massacre—to be rid of foreigners, of resented outsiders.

The United States never separated out a pure stock whose germ plasm contained us all. America's founding fathers were of varied ethnic strains and their children made America more diverse still. Hector St. Jean de Crèvecoeur's eighteenth-century "Letters of an American Farmer" tells the story: "I could point out to you a family whose grandfather was an Englishman, whose wife was Dutch, whose son married a French woman and whose four sons have now four wives of different nations."

As a result it quickly became a truism of American life that as varied groups came to settle, they had to learn to get along and respect each other's differences or, as one observer noted, they would provide the Indians with the satisfaction of seeing European antagonisms play themselves out in bloody conflicts. With less to agree about than other societies, Americans

Is this really true when some have not truly been accepted?

When Ellis Island opened for tourists in 1976, the rooms where millions of immigrants had been processed had fallen into disrepair. (*Peter J. Harris*)

focused on their political ideas, on their commitment to a fresh vision of government, and, by making a virtue of a necessity, on an ideology of liberty, tolerance, and diversity.

The revolutionary generation felt sufficiently confident about this formula for diversity within a nation to offer America as a haven for all, regardless of national origin. Tom Paine declared in 1776: "The old world is overrun with oppression." The new nation-in-making was therefore, "obliged to receive the fugitive, and prepare in time an asylum for mankind." The apotheosis of America's struggle for independence, George Washington, viewed his America in the same terms: "The bosom of America is open to receive . . . the oppressed and persecuted of all nations and 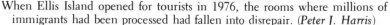 religions."

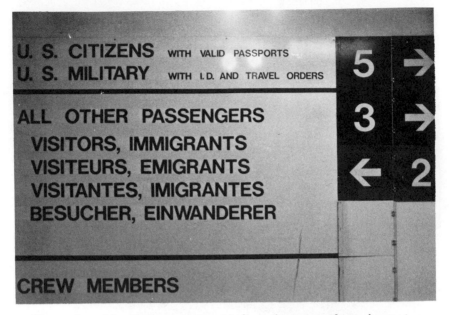

Signs at busy John F. Kennedy airport indicate the variety of arrivals entering
New York City. (*Betty Boyd Caroli*)

Americans were relatively comfortable with the notion of building unity
from diversity and they used it as the formula for a federal political system
in which states kept their individual identities in a loose national framework.
E Pluribus Unum—Out of the Many One—became the national slogan,
and American history has plumbed the phrase's ambiguities: Did it mean a
strong central government, a "one" in which the many would gradually
recede? Or did it imply that the many might remain separate and yet be as
one in all that is important? This issue became most important when diversity produced its discontents and North fought South in a Civil War over
such issues as union, secession, and states rights. Manifestly the many had
not become one in too many things.

America's varied social geography also gave rise to periodic nativist conflicts, religious feuds, and transplanted Old World antagonisms. Even before
the Civil War, the inventor Samuel F. B. Morse showed how fervid such
biases could become:

> How is it possible that foreign turbulence imported by shiploads, that riot,
> and ignorance in hundreds of thousands of human priest-controlled ma-
> chines should suddenly be thrown into our society and not produce turbu-
> lence and excess? Can one throw mud into pure water and not disturb its
> cleanness?

Pride!.

Morse wrote in an era when the United States had not yet agreed on a national immigration policy. Each locality was free to devise its own admission standards. When jobs became scarce, for instance, New York City restricted immigration. The federal government was so uninvolved in this issue that it did not even require ship captains transporting immigrants to file an account of their passengers, future American inhabitants, until 1819.

By the time of the Civil War, a nationwide policy seemed desirable to avoid contradictions and circumventions. In 1864, under the Department of State, the Immigration Bureau was established, but Congress did not pass a comprehensive federal immigration law until 1882. Convicts, persons deemed mentally incompetent, those likely to become public charges, and, reflecting the intense prejudices against non-European immigrants, Chinese workers were barred entirely. A tax of fifty cents on each arrival provided funds for administering the law and processing the immigrants. Three years later Congress passed a law designed to limit the importation of low-paid contract labor and forbade the immigration of people who held work contracts. While this Foran Act, as it was called, did not completely halt the efforts of recruiters to ensnare unsuspecting emigrants in unfair contracts, it did make the process more difficult.

Immigration soared in these years, as the United States grew to industrial maturity. Between 1880 and 1920, 23 million Europeans arrived in the United States. As never before, immigration came to dominate American thinking. When France presented the United States with the Statue of Liberty her call was phrased in global terms. "Give me your tired, your poor. . . . Send these, the homeless, tempest tost, to me. . . ." Yet by the time Emma Lazarus's sonnet was duly bronzed and fastened to the great statue's base in New York harbor in 1903, Congress had already begun to view immigration and the American mission in narrower, nativist terms. Americans were already speaking of limits to their land of plenty. In the 1790s, Thomas Jefferson had predicted that the continent would require two centuries to fill up, but by 1890 the Bureau of the Census reported that the era of the open frontier had come to an end. In 1893 Frederick Jackson Turner addressed his fellow historians and warned of the deeper implications of this development. Attributing great significance to the frontier experience in creating a freer, more democratic America, Turner viewed the end of the frontier with misgiving. Others took it as a sign to close our doors to immigrants.

The forces that brought about industrialization and urbanization were not set in motion simply by the availability of cheap immigrant labor, yet the new Americans became convenient scapegoats for all the ills brought about by rapid economic, cultural, and social change. These were also years of great debate over such issues as the relative superiority of the various races and ethnic strains. Sentiment continued to grow for a more general ban that would regulate both the number and the quality of new arrivals. By 1917 most Asians were barred, along with those who could not read and comprehend some language or dialect.

The poet's concern for the tired, huddled, and hurt began to compete with the fear of being overrun by inferior men. A quickly expanding nation, Americans argued, had to concern itself with the problem of overpopulation, especially in the congested urban immigrant Meccas. Did not Americans already here have priority in the competition for jobs? Could the American social order absorb so many poor, needy, uneducated? Was it fair to visit such inevitable effects as higher crime and disease on the communities in which immigrants chose to settle? Did Americans not have a right to maintain the integrity of the dominant Anglo-Protestant culture; would not an even more diverse religio-cultural kaleidoscope result in a harshly fragmented society incapable of defining a common national identity? Could the United States, in its maturity, still absorb thieves, malcontents, adventurers and dissidents with the equanimity of its colonial infancy?

Elected by constituencies that favored a hardened pragmatism over the poet's idealism, Congress in the 1920s passed a series of immigration laws establishing an absolute quota on entries, locking out Orientals and implementing a national origins system of preferences designed to make more room for immigrants from the Nordic countries of Europe while discouraging those from Southern and Eastern Europe. The laws allocated quotas based on the national origins of the then-current American population, consciously favoring those groups that had arrived earlier—the English, Germans, and Irish—with the largest quotas. The new invitation was muted and hedged about with qualifications. John F. Kennedy noted in his short history of American immigration that the needy were now welcome only "as long as they come from Northern Europe, are not too tired or too poor, or slightly ill, never stole a loaf of bread, never joined a questionable organization and can document their activities for the past two years."

This new mood found its laureate in Thomas Bailey Aldrich:

> Wide and unguarded stand our gates
> And through them press a wild, a motley throng—
> Men from the Volga and the Tartar steppes,
> Featureless figures of the Hoang-Ho,
> Malayan, Scythian, Teuton, Kelt, and Slav,
> Flying the Old World's poverty and scorn;
> These bringing with them unknown gods and rites,
> Those tiger passions, here to stretch their claws,
> In street and alley what strange tongues are these,
> Accents of menace alien to our air. . . .

In passing its national-origins act, the United States projected a period of retrenchment, a time for the Americanization process to have an effect on the many immigrants already here. Elwood Cubberly, the noted historian of education, described the procedure's goals:

> Everywhere these people [immigrants] tend to settle in groups or settlements, and to set up here their national manners, customs and observations. Our task is to break up these groups or settlements, to assimilate and amalgamate these people as a part of our American race, and to implant in their children, so far as can be done, the Anglo-Saxon conception of righteousness, law and order, and popular government, and to awaken in them a reverence for our democratic institutions and for those things in our national life which we as a people hold to be of abiding worth.

White supremacist attitude

Cubberly's thinking and that of like-minded people prevailed in the immigration acts of the 1920s. Immigration slowed to a trickle. Between 1901 and 1910 almost 9 million immigrants arrived in the United States, about 1 each year for every 100 Americans already here. In the 1920s total immigration dropped to slightly more than 4 million, or roughly 1 in 300 of the native population. Thereafter, the restrictive quotas, the Depression, and World War II kept the numbers low. For the decade of the 1940s only 1 million newcomers settled in the United States, adding each year fewer than 1 new resident to every 1,400 Americans. Attempts to modify the restriction during World War II, to grant haven to European refugees, foundered.

In 1952 Congress passed a lengthy new immigration law, the McCarran-Walter Act. A by-product of Cold War attitudes, it set forth many grounds for exclusion and deportation. Although it claimed to reject the theory of Nordic superiority, the law upheld the national-origins quotas for reasons of "cultural and sociological balance." Western Hemisphere nations continued to be exempt from the quotas (the view prevailed that any change might upset delicate bilateral relations and complicate the patrolling of borders with Mexico and Canada) though some Congressmen felt they too should be included. Under the new law, Asians were no longer barred entirely—every country received a minimum quota of one hundred persons. Invidious criteria did, however, persist. Under the Asia-Pacific Triangle provisions, any alien whose ancestry was one-half or more Oriental would be charged to one of the Asia-Pacific countries, even if he came from another part of the world.

The 1952 law established a preference system to operate within the national-origins quotas. Half of each country's quota went to people with skills or education particularly needed in the United States. Three other categories allocated priority to close relatives of American citizens and permanent residents. Anyone who examined the law closely realized that as long as the national-origins quotas were in effect, an Italian engineer had less chance of getting a visa to settle in the United States than did an Irish unskilled worker.*

In vetoing the act, President Harry Truman had argued that the continuation of national-origins quotas would be a gratuitous insult to friends and allies:

> Today we have entered into an alliance, the North Atlantic Treaty Organization, with Italy, Greece and Turkey, against one of the most terrible threats mankind has ever faced. We are asking them to join us in protecting the peace of the world. We are helping them to build their defenses and train their men in the common cause. But through this bill we say to their people: you are less worthy to come to this country than Englishmen or Irishmen.

But Congress apparently felt differently, overriding the presidential veto. Some legislators may have voted their prejudices; others emphasized the need for the law's exclusion of aliens who belonged to proscribed political organizations, primarily the Communist Party and affiliated groups.

Truman, however, proved to have been more foresighted than Congress. The McCarran-Walter bill demonstrated itself to be inadequate for the needs of the fluid world situation of the 1950s. Immigration policy for the rest of the decade was characterized by a tension between the restrictive-quota limits of the 1952 law and a more humanitarian proclivity toward the granting of asylum for political refugees. Several laws, including the Refugee Relief Act of 1953, the Refugee Escape Act of 1957, and the Fair Share Refugee Law of 1960 all made provisions for additional admissions beyond the quota limits. Other newcomers, including residents of the Western Hemisphere and members of the immediate families of American citizens, continued to enter outside the quotas. Of the 2.5 million immigrants admitted between 1951 and 1960, more than half were in excess of the formal quota numbers. Over the years the amendments, refugee laws, and special provisions for nonquota immigration effectively shifted the standard of entry from national origins to an *ad hoc* use of preference categories and refugee parole (a special power granted to the attorney general for admitting aliens on an emergency basis). The system, shot through with so many exceptions, special cases, and emergency provisions, stood in need of major recasting.

The search for a set of guidelines that would yield a valid, reasonable, and fair immigration policy was not conducted only by the United States.

---

* In 1964, Italy had a list of about 250,000 people hoping to get visas, many of them brothers and sisters of American citizens and residents. The same year, Great Britain filled less than half of its 65,361 quota slots. The McCarran-Walter Act did not provide for one country to pass on its unused quota places to another.

Canada also repeatedly revised its entry rules in response to changed national attitudes regarding desirable immigration policies. In fact, the history of Canada's immigration legislation roughly parallels that of the United States. In 1878, for example, four years before the United States passed the Chinese Exclusion Act, Canada barred Asians. In 1910 Canada reinforced its earlier exclusion provision and passed measures giving preferential treatment to people from Northwestern Europe, much as the United States quotas of the 1920s would later do. After lifting racial barriers in 1962, Canada began admitting newcomers on the basis of a point system, a system that underwent revision in 1977 to give preference to those with needed skills and education.

Under Canada's current point system, family reunification counts for very little, securing a possible five points of one hundred for people with relatives in Canada able to assist them. Age,* education, and a willingness to settle in unpopulated areas bring far more points. Most important of all, however, is Canada's current economic health, since not even a score of one hundred points guarantees admission. Canada annually alters its limits on admissions to reflect the country's economic needs.

Australia, the other large immigrant-receiving nation, also rewrote its immigration laws, making them more responsive to the country's employment needs. A Numerical Multi-Factor Assessment System, which went into effect in January 1979, assigns more weight to employee skills than to family reunification. Emphasizing its century-old policy of permanent immigration, Australia provides few incentives for guest workers. Under the 1979 law, Australia aims to admit the equivalent of about 1 percent of its population each year, but provisions exist for changing that figure if the economy worsens.

In the United States, John F. Kennedy spearheaded a campaign to alter the old immigration law when he introduced in July 1963 a new framework to abolish the national-origins standard. His assassination a few months later ended his efforts but his successor, Lyndon Johnson, gave unqualified support to the measure. He noted:

> We must lift by legislation the bar of discrimination against those who seek entry into our country, particularly those with much-needed skills and those joining their families. In establishing preferences, a nation that was built by the immigrants of all lands can ask those who now seek admission, "What can you do for your country?" But we should not be asking "In what country were you born?"

The first years of Johnson's presidency marked a good time for change. A heavily Democratic Congress, interested in reform, drew support from

---

* Those between the ages of eighteen and thirty-five are most favored.

many private organizations in favor of modifications. Americans who sometimes turned shrill and defensive of their own interests when confronting
efforts to liberalize immigration policy were muted in the early 1960s by a
pervasive spirit of optimism. Their confidence was relatively untempered,
not yet having faced the destructive race riots or the unsettling questioning
about the Vietnam War that would come later in the decade. Most Americans remained convinced that they lived in the richest, most powerful, best-
intentioned country in the world. Shortages of oil and concerns about clean
air lay in the future. Talk of limits and restrictions would have been seriously out of place in the predominantly generous mood.

Opinion was by no means unanimous on the dropping of national-
origins quotas but debate circled around the racial issue rather than hitting
it directly. Those favoring the maintenance of quotas talked of preserving
the existing population mix. Sam J. Ervin, Jr., Democrat from North Carolina and a member of the Senate Judiciary Committee at that time, called
the national-origins quotas system "a mirror reflecting the United States."
He judged this a "rational and uniform formula for the admission of immigrants."

Mrs. Robert V. H. Duncan, president of the Daughters of the American
Revolution, also favored the old quotas "wisely giving preference to those
nations whose composite culture—Anglo-Saxon from northern and western
European countries—has been responsible for and actually produced the
American heritage as we know it today."

But the major argument against the quotas proved difficult to refute: it
no longer reflected the image most Americans held of themselves or wished
to convey to others. Secretary of State Dean Rusk, testifying at subcommittee hearings on the proposed 1965 bill, urged passage so that the United
States "as a leader in the struggle for freedom . . . [could] exemplify all
that freedom means." Attorney General Nicholas deB. Katzenbach spoke of
the need to pass the bill "as simple humanity." Congressman Bernard Gra-
bowski of Connecticut advocated "increasing our attention to matters of
equality and justice for all under the law."

For one man, the fight against the national-origins quotas was a
long one. Emanuel Celler, Democratic congressman from Brooklyn, had
spent much of his four decades in the House of Representatives advocating
the dropping of the quotas but, he said, "My efforts were about as useless as
trying to make a tiger eat grass or a cow eat meat." For Celler, the dropping
of quotas would result in an increased diversity in the country's population,
a change he believed to be for the better. He boasted of his own Jewish
neighborhood in Brooklyn where he could enter a Chinese restaurant and
be served pizza by a black waiter.

When Celler's colleagues remained unimpressed, he reassured them that even if the law dropped national-origins quotas it would not seriously alter the immigrant composition. Since preference would be given to family members of those already in the country, people without families would have little chance of entering. Celler noted: "There will not be comparatively many Asians and Africans entering the country . . . since [they] have very few relatives here." He seemed to be offering to his opponents family preferences as an alternative to national-origins quotas.

Economics emerged as the most important consideration in the debates on the 1965 law. William E. Miller, vice-presidential candidate on the Republican ticket in 1964, kicked off his campaign on Labor Day with a speech charging President Johnson with attempting to abolish selective immigration rules to "open the floodgates for virtually any and all who would wish to come and find work in this country. . . . These people need jobs, but where will they find them? Are you willing to give them yours?"

Lyndon Johnson responded that unskilled workers (the segment of the economy most glutted) would not enter in greater numbers than previously and that those who did come to the United States would fall predominantly into the thirty-five–forty-four age group, the one whose size had been affected by the low birth rate of the 1930s. Congressman Celler was specific and adamant on the point that the law would not adversely affect the labor market: "There will be practically no increase in authorized immigration. Therefore, there will be practically no workers coming in beyond the number that now come in. . . . Under the present law, the number of additional workers that now come in is microscopic in relation to the United States working force, that is about 24,000 as against 80 million. That is less than one for each 3,000 workers, hardly a drop in the bucket." Other Congressmen added their own assurances that the law would not adversely affect job opportunities for other Americans.

Many of those opposing the bill feared, however, that changing conditions in the Western Hemisphere, primarily in the Caribbean and parts of South America where Congress had never set limits, would yield significantly increased immigration in the 1960s. Congressman Clark MacGregor of Minnesota, introducing an amendment to initiate a Western Hemisphere limit, stressed that immediate action was necessary since "it will be almost impossible from a policy standpoint to take action 3 or 5 or 7 years hence."

MacGregor's colleague, Emanuel Celler, whose polyglot Brooklyn district already included many West Indians, rejected this line of reasoning: "This is not the time," he said, "to muddy the waters of foreign affairs. . . . We need all the friends we can muster. We cannot afford to have any nations turn against us, particularly our neighbors to the south of us." Celler refused, however, to promise that he would never favor limits on Latin America, saying, "You do not roll up your pants until you get to the river."

In the end a compromise bill was worked out. A Western Hemisphere ceiling was accepted in return for the abolition of national-origins quotas. The final bill limited the Eastern Hemisphere countries to 170,000 and the Western to 120,000 places. The latter, however, had no individual country limits while no more than 20,000 individuals could enter from any one country in the Eastern Hemisphere.

Lyndon Johnson, in signing the bill, stressed that it favored those applicants with the skills and training the United States most needed. In fact, only two preference categories, out of a total of seven, dealt with education or applicant abilities. Individual members of Congress, seeking to get the bill through, had singled out these two categories, however, and had predicted that passage of the bill would bring highly skilled and professional immigrants into the country. Congressman Michael Feighan of Ohio spoke of the "physicians, surgeons, scientists and teachers . . . able to come to many of our hospitals, universities and private institutions urgently in need of their services."

In the years that followed "brain drain" became part of the national vocabulary, although it described a phenomenon that was not altogether new. After World War II, American universities and private research laboratories began to attract many British and German nationals. (Perhaps one of the most pointed supporting arguments for immigration lay in the fact that among American Nobel Prize winners in these years, more than 40 percent were foreign born.) After 1965 it became the developing nations, not the highly industrialized countries of Europe, who lost their most prized citizens to the greater relative attractiveness of America. More than one-quarter of those Africans and one-third of those Asians arriving in the United States after 1965 were professionals.

In some professions, the impact was immense. By 1972 more than 63,000 graduates of foreign medical schools were serving as doctors in the United States. This represented more than one-fifth of all practicing physicians in the country. In some states, such as New York, foreign graduates represented almost 40 percent of the state's medical doctors, and in New York City, 90 and even 100 percent of some hospital staffs were foreign trained. At the same time the home countries of these professionals were in far more desperate need of their services. In 1970, 70 percent of the foreign medical graduates in the United States came from Asia, primarily India, the Philippines, and Korea. The doctor-patient ratio in these countries stood at 1:5,000; 1:1,300 and 1:2,700 respectively; in America the ratio stood at 1:600.

Medical groups, complaining that this heavy reliance on foreign medical graduates also had effects closer to home, charged that these doctors did poorly on medical examinations, often had not overcome severe language difficulties, and, in general, depressed the quality of American medical care. On the strength of such arguments, Congress, in 1976, fashioned the Health Professions Act, limiting the number of residency positions open to foreign medical school graduates and distributing them over a broad geographical area to prevent a concentration of foreign medical personnel in any one area of the country.

The medical profession was not the only one in which people played geographical hopscotch in order to improve their careers. Immigration had always been partly employment-induced. In the late 1800s and early 1900s immigrants often constituted a floating proletariat of temporary, unskilled workers, moving to improve their day's earnings. By the age of the multinational corporation, economic immigration continued but the career orientation of the immigrants had changed. Many were business executives, engineers, scientists, and nurses. The 1965 law, giving advantage in its third preference category to professionals and the highly skilled, facilitated international mobility at the higher status levels. In 1960 fewer than 20 percent of arriving immigrants brought professional or technical qualifications. A decade later the number stood at 30 percent.

The other preference category established to attract needed skills, the sixth preference, gave 10 percent of the total slots available to those persons with blue-collar skills in short supply in the United States, such as mechanics, repairmen, tailors, cooks, and especially private household workers. Employers were to demonstrate sincere attempts to hire from the available pool, but if they were unable to acquire qualified help, they could secure preference to bring in immigrants to fill the jobs. In practice foreigners circumvented the law, however, entering as tourists, finding work and then securing sponsorship.

Although President Johnson emphasized the attention to skills and professions in the 1965 law, the bulk of the slots available went to those whose admission would help reunite families. Of the four categories for family reunification, first preference went to unmarried adult sons and daughters of citizens; second preference to unmarried children and spouses of legal residents. After the third preference for the professions, the fourth favored married children of citizens. Fifth preference dealt with brothers and sisters of citizens. Closer family members (spouses, minor children, and parents) did not have to compete for limited visas—their applications were considered outside the ceilings.

Loopholes in the family reunification measures were not difficult to locate, and some of the uses of the preferences mocked the intended purpose. Geraldo Diaz,* a Honduran who sought to enter the United States in 1978,

---

* All immigrants described in this book have been assigned pseudonyms.

is one example. When his immigration lawyer in New York reviewed the narrow grounds for legally entering the country, Diaz volunteered that he had a half-sister whom he had not seen in thirty-five years. Living in California and married to an American citizen, the sister was surprised to receive a telephone call from a brother of whom she had completely lost track. Unfortunately for Diaz, she had not become a citizen and could not help. Had she been a citizen, she would have willingly sponsored Diaz, and thereby been able to spare her half-brother the several years of waiting for a visa that followed. Other people tailored fictive relationships, often for nieces and nephews, godparents and godchildren, who in many countries form part of close family but who have no consideration as family under United States law.

The last preference category was reserved for refugees. As a country that is convinced that it has a special mission to help the refugee, but understandably finds it difficult to bear that open-ended responsibility wholeheartedly, America has always had the greatest difficulty squaring its immigration policies with the special responsibility it has assumed for itself regarding victims of political oppression. Under the 1965 law, 6 percent of the total number of admissions went to refugees, a number later supplemented by the Refugee Act of 1980, which allowed as many as 50,000 homeless to enter the country each year. Refugees entered under somewhat different rules than other immigrants. For the first two years of their American residence they lived under parole status and then, at the end of that time, they were allowed to apply for legal alien resident status.

Until 1980 the United States granted refugee status on an *ad hoc* basis, often without system or consistency. Thus, those oppressed by Communist regimes generally received greater attention than those suffering under pro-American rightist dictatorships. The 1980 law adopted virtually intact the United Nations definition of refugees: individuals rendered homeless by racial, religious, political, or social persecution. By this definition 10 million of the world's peoples, according to UN estimates, were eligible. The American experience with Cubans and Vietnamese represented merely a beginning. Entire populations seldom seen or known in the United States now began to compete for slots as qualified refugees. People from Afghanistan, Ethiopia, Eritrea, Namibia, Uganda, Libya, Lebanon, and every other land ruled by a dictator became potential newcomers under the revised law.

And the word spread quickly. In Peshawar and Islamabad, Pakistan, Afghan citizens on the run petitioned the American embassy for visas. In Kenya, Sudan, and Djibouti exiles from Ethiopia's volatile Eritrean region filled out the long forms as the first step to a possible American life. In Botswana, Lesotho, Zambia and Swaziland, South Africa, dissidents pointed to their tenuous home status as an argument for the much-envied visa.

If this trend toward refugees from less well-known countries was just beginning, American immigration patterns had already been substantially transformed by the early 1970s. Of the twenty-one countries responsible for the bulk of American immigration since 1965—Canada, Mexico, Costa Rica, El Salvador, Guatamala, Honduras, Nicaragua, Colombia, Ecuador, Peru, Dominican Republic, Haiti, Jamaica, Nigeria, India, Iran, Korea, Philippines, Thailand, Greece, and Italy—only the last two had been traditional sources of large numbers of immigrants. Citizens of extremely poor countries, such as Bangladesh, had never shown much interest in immigration and individuals who did leave such nations generally came from the well-educated, upper-class minority. The lifting of national-origins quotas however, ushered in a new era of greater diversity in immigrants than the United States had ever known before.

Of those top twenty-one countries contributing the greatest number of immigrants, many had rapidly developing economies in which the increase in national production had outstripped the rise in individual income. All showed the pressures of high population growth with some expecting doubled populations by the year 2000. Moreover, the relative youth of their citizenry suggested that these pressures would continue. In the absence of immediate easy solutions at home, emigration remained strong.

As further inducements, average incomes reported in the United States were often many times what most workers earned in the high emigration nations. (Canada was the notable exception.) And this information was communicated quickly, even down to towns and villages that knew little else about the United States. Central America, for example, received about one-third of its television programming from the United States. Double-car garages, gadget-filled kitchens and elegantly clothed TV characters also conveyed the message of American affluence.

Americans responded to immigration growth and change with ambiguous feelings. Keenly aware that increased immigration often carried steep costs both in dollars and social problems, they were stung by reports of refugee Cubans rioting on American soil and of others hijacking airplanes to go back home. Some Americans had doubts rooted in ecological concerns. During the late sixties and early seventies, Zero Population Growth became a principal concern of liberal social reformers. But continued immigration, especially of child-bearing women, threatened to keep pushing national Z.P.G. further into the future.

Plainly, immigration did add to the population, although little consensus developed on exactly how much. Estimates ran between 17 and 25 percent of the annual population growth. At the upper limit, accepted by the Immigration and Naturalization Service, documented immigration accounted for one-fourth of the country's increase in the seventies and would result in an additional 15 million people by the year 2000.

Further, this estimate reflected legal immigration only. The inclusion of persons entering without legal documentation would greatly increase, probably double, the figure. For many Americans "illegal alien" read "Mexican" because most of the people apprehended by the Immigration and Naturalization Service were Mexicans. Most entered without going through the inspection process but others (145,000 in 1970) carried fraudulent documents.

From interviews with those apprehended, observers and government officials believe that illegals come largely from the rural areas of Mexico, areas of high unemployment, the same regions that used to furnish legal workers to the Southwestern United States from 1942 to 1964 under the bracero program. The bracero program, in turn, merely formalized a long-standing practice of Mexicans working in the United States. After the United States defeated Mexico in the 1848 Mexican-American War, the United States permitted any Mexican national living in what now had become United States territory to be repatriated. But only a few thousand chose to do so, leaving the American Southwest with a significant Mexican minority. Over the years Mexicans living both south and north of the border crossed at will, either in search of jobs or to visit relatives on the other side. As the two countries underwent very different economic development, the flow of workers north surged.

The exchange served the interests of both sides, draining Mexico's surfeit of unemployed to the labor-thirsty farms of the Southwest. Cheap labor was especially in demand after the Chinese Exclusion Act of 1882 barred Chinese workers, and again after the drop in immigration following the restrictive 1924 law. In 1942, when war needs made the labor shortage particularly pressing, the bracero program began, and in the twenty-two years of its operation, 5 million Mexicans came under contract to work on American wheat fields, truck farms, and orchards. Another 5 million are estimated to have come outside the program. During the 1950s, Operation Wetback, a major effort to apprehend these illegals and return them to Mexico, made "wetback" a synonym for illegal alien.

Under pressure from American labor unions, who complained of competition for jobs, the government ended the bracero program but Mexican workers continued to operate much as they had earlier. One legislative act could hardly cancel aspirations developed over decades. Workers from Mexico relied on old contacts and information networks to lead them to jobs that they could not find at home. The Mexican government, faced with rapid population growth and high unemployment, saw little reason to stop them.

That the men continued to cross over was not surprising. The relatively unpatrolled two thousand-mile border separated countries of great differences, with the United States reporting an average income roughly seven times that of Mexico. No other border in the world marks such great disparities in wealth and standard of living. To facilitate the crossing, profiteers ("coyotes") provided guide services and employment tips. Teenagers, some barely fifteen, drove illegal immigrants across the line, expecting to be treated leniently if they were caught because of their youth. Youngsters, some only ten years old, earned pocket money by walking others over the line. An intricate, highly developed network of employers, employment agencies, and government officials sustained the movement.

The United States was not unique in attracting labor from outside its boundaries. Many industrialized countries have been in a similar position at one time or another. During the post-World War II reindustrialization, when France, Switzerland, and Germany all sought Southern Europeans to run their factories and build new roadways, Western Europe relied heavily on guest workers. In the decades that followed, Western Europe became involved with these workers in ways not anticipated. As the men became politically active, they demanded the same services as those given all citizens, and in bad times they did not go home. Men who had earlier been encouraged to change their residences, temporarily renounce family ties and personal pleasures, and work at backbreaking jobs when they were needed did not automatically forget all that when demand for their work fell off. They developed ties, friends, and habits that were not easily broken. One scholar, describing what happened in Western Europe, explained: "The countries wanted workers but they got men."

Other Latins, besides the Mexicans, have crossed the vulnerable southern border to work and live, although many have underestimated the risk associated with the crossing. A group of middle-class Salvadorans found out in the summer of 1980 how dangerous the process could be. Forty-five of them, aged thirteen to thirty-five, boarded an air-conditioned bus on the first leg of a trip out of their violence-torn homeland. They paid between $1,200 and $2,000 to "coyotes" to fly them to Los Angeles. But no plane was waiting for them in San Luis Rio Colorado, Mexico, and fourteen of the group decided to stay behind. The remaining thirty-one, believing new arrangements had been made for trucks to pick them up, set out on foot to cross the Mexican border. They climbed the barbed wire fence and touched American soil on July 3. Again they were disappointed to find no trucks or vans. They started to trek across the desert equipped with only twenty gallons of water among them and suitcases filled with money, jewelry, per-

fume, and assorted clothing. By noon on this July 4, American Independence Day, a broiling sun pushed the temperature to 115 degrees. Before
they were found by American border patrol officials, thirteen of the group
had died after drinking cologne, deodorant, and finally their own urine.
Some of the dead, apparently hallucinating, had also gobbled sand.

Immigration officers, no matter how numerous or well-intentioned, can
hardly block a path that millions have already risked death to travel. By late
1980 headlines about Haitian refugees drowning no longer made the front
pages of the country's newspapers; they were relegated to inside sections,
mere updatings of continuing horror. People from the Dominican Republic,
who applied for visas in much larger numbers than could be accommodated, heard in September 1980 of the Regina Express, a tanker that would
take them to Miami for $1,800 to $3,000. For many the trip north represented their last hope for work and they had scraped together the price of
the journey by selling all they had and by borrowing as much as they could.
Thirty-four men paid, some more than once, for the privilege of hiding in
the ship's ballast tank. When it filled with water before they left Santo Dom-
ingo, twenty-two of them died.

Nor has the Immigration and Naturalization Service, charged with processing newcomers, been immune to temptation, and people intent on entering the United States at almost any cost have offered plenty of temptation.
Unscrupulous, greedy immigration inspectors have by no means been the
rule, but neither have they been the exception. In the spring of 1980 newspapers across the country carried details of a new clean-up within INS. An
earlier investigation in 1974, called Operation Cleansweep, had concentrated on the records of one hundred and fifty employees, including several
top officials, accused of smuggling illegal aliens and drugs, taking bribes and
kickbacks, physically abusing aliens, and engaging in perjury and fraud.
Fewer than a dozen were indicted and only seven were subsequently convicted, although one investigator said: "The only crime we didn't find was
bank robbery." The allegations had not changed in 1980. Women aliens
complained that they were required to have sexual relations with border
patrol officers and men told of blackmail and extortion.

Thousands of those who did make it into the country were not much
better off. Shackled to unreasonable bills for smuggling "services," aliens
without proper documents often became hostages to their ever-rising debt.
Coyotes transferred these "indentures" to labor contractors who welcomed
the opportunity to buy a voiceless, nonunion labor force that could be
trucked around the country at will. Reduced to peonage and afraid to talk
because of their fear of being arrested and deported, many undocumented
aliens were trapped in virtual slavery.

No real figure has existed for the number of aliens in the United States at any one time without legal status. In 1974 the INS Commissioner Leonard Chapman estimated 6 or 7 million, a considerable increase over the 1 million suggested by his predecessor in 1972. By 1975 district directors of INS offices jointly proposed a total figure of 6,299,750 although they were unable to explain exactly how they had arrived at this figure. The same year a consulting firm presented a figure of 8 million. In 1976 district directors dropped their estimates a bit to 6,036,500, of whom 3.8 million were employed. Whatever the exact figures, nobody has predicted that the totals will decrease in the near future. In fact, most observers expect illegal immigration to increase under a law that, they say, refuses to recognize realities about the desirability of American jobs.

Scholars who have attempted to study the broader, economy-wide impact of immigration typically have concluded their reports with qualified recommendations and predictions. One government Task Force summarized its survey of such studies: "Perhaps the clearest consensus . . . among those . . . analyzing the economic effects of immigration is that these effects are impossible to measure, or if they are measurable in principle, are extremely difficult to quantify in practice."

Complicating the problem of prediction is the increasing awareness of scholars and politicians that many immigrants—both legal and illegal—come with only a tentative commitment to remain. On the basis of census records and mortality tables, two demographers have estimated that about 1 million foreign-born persons chose to leave the United States in the 1960s to reside elsewhere. Other students of the subject refined the figure slightly to about 113,000 repatriates per year. Another 50,000 or so American citizens decided to emigrate each year, according to records of receiving countries. Studies done in 1973 showed that expatriation became more popular for Americans after World War II, especially in the 1960s when more people had the money to experiment with living elsewhere and political discontent caused others to leave. In 1972 one American left for every seven legal immigrants who arrived.

Many immigrants who did remain in the United States let decades pass without transferring their citizenship. In January 1976, the first month of America's two hundredth birthday, 4.3 million aliens registered as permanent legal residents, joining several million others who failed to register because of their illegal status. Thus, two hundred years into America's history, perhaps 1 in 20 of her inhabitants was not a citizen.

Many aliens did eventually apply for citizenship. One Brooklyn courtroom, decorated with murals salvaged from Ellis Island, annually witnessed the swearing in of over 30,000 immigrants as naturalized American citizens. The murals depicted an industrializing America endlessly fueled by brawny foreign laborers come to do pick and shovel labor. One spring day in 1979, a crowd of 329 petitioners for naturalization were obviously very far removed from the mural scenes. Modern immigrants, members of a computer-chip society, they were more middle class, younger, better educated, more confident, and less awed by officials and literacy tests than their predecessors had been. They had not come in steerage but in airplanes, and many had not seen the Statue of Liberty up close. From more than fifty different nations, few of those being sworn in were manual laborers and none appeared to be experienced in wielding a pick and shovel. An Armenian was president of his own computer firm; other soon-to-be-sworn-in Americans included a doctor, a music publisher, a lawyer, and a doctoral candidate in anthropology.

The judge who swore them into a new national identity was himself the New York-raised son of immigrants. He seemed genuinely touched by the occasion. His speech bore the message of a tolerant new America. He instructed them to be loyal to their adopted homeland, to love it for its willingness to have them, but not at the cost of cutting themselves off from their old cultures. America, he suggested, did not mean to impose an exclusive idea or culture—it prized diversity.

Despite a more skeptical attitude on the part of many Americans about the specialness of American society and its democratic processes, the United States continues to impress the newly arrived. A Joseph's coat of nationalities, the country remains, in relative terms, the most open and socially permissive of the world's developed nations. It still attracts the world's tired, its ambitious, and its bored, all eager to improve their own lives.

A symbol of this continued magnetism—as varied and troubled as the land itself—is the tarnished but still-inviting immigrant city of New York. Dragged down by a decade of fiscal crises and assorted social problems, New York City continues to attract and acculturize still more recent immigrant arrivals. Of the more than one thousand newcomers arriving in the United States daily, one-fifth settle in New York. "New York," explains Auxiliary Bishop Anthony J. Bevilaqua of the Brooklyn Catholic Diocese, "is probably the best known city in the world." From television, magazines, and movies the world knows of New York as it does not know of Charleston or Houston, for example, or even of Philadelphia, Chicago, or Los Angeles. New York's contrasts continue to attract and amaze: poor but munificent, sophisticated but pocked with severe illiteracy, three hundred-year-old Dutch-named streets fading into overnight slums.

New York has remained a city in process. In the 1920s French historian Bernard Fäy wrote of New York that it was the "only city rich enough in money, vitality and men . . . to rebuild itself." Public money ceased to be plentiful by the 1970s but the vitality and manpower have endured. Other cities stopped receiving newcomers in the first quarter of the century. New

Orleans, San Francisco, and hundreds of other American communities were allowed to develop into matured immigrant cities with characteristic styles and personalities. New York was never given an extended breathing period. Three great twentieth-century influxes shaped, reshaped, and continue to shape her now.

The first great migration brought millions of Italians and Jews to New York in the years preceding World War I. The second, in the years of curtailed immigration, 1924–1965, witnessed a major resettlement of Puerto Ricans and southern blacks molding a multiracial New York. And after 1965, the third wave, comparable in magnitude and importance to the others, began bringing to New York the many peoples whose stories are the subject of this book.

By the early 1970s, Asian immigration from this third wave had so swelled Chinatown's traditional borders that the community spilled over into Little Italy, and Brooklyn's Eastern Parkway, an old Jewish neighborhood, found it necessary to pocket its colorful remnant of Chassidic Jews among a recently arrived Caribbean multitude. In Brooklyn's blighted Brighton Beach area, Russian émigrés reclaimed the boardwalk-lined neighborhood and made of its ocean-sprayed streets an "Odessa by the Sea." In North Queens, in an area designated Zip Code 11373, is the most diversely populated immigrant neighborhood in the world. Much like early twentieth-century Harlem, this neighborhood in the early 1970s had so great an abundance of unrented family housing that realtors in search of renters were forced to be less rigid in the selection of tenants. In January 1979, 18,000 individuals, more than one-quarter of the postal zone, completed alien registration cards. Included in the varied assembly were large numbers of Colombians, Chinese, Cubans, Filipinos, Indians, Koreans, and smaller groups from the Dominican Republic, Argentina, and Hong Kong. This polyglot community also provided a natural haven for illegal aliens estimated to equal in number the legal alien community.

From the beginning of its settlement, New York City has been more diverse than other American cities and in 1980 it accepted more than 100,000 new immigrants, as well as an uncertain number of illegal aliens. Their uprooted psyches, their language problems, the immense complications in their lives, all made them part of New York's problem. But they also contributed to its solution, infusing as they did immense energy, ambition, and youth into the city. They enlivened its concert halls and galleries, mopped up its hotel rooms, and hawked wares on the smallest profit margins.

In 1963 Nathan Glazer and Daniel P. Moynihan published what became a classic study of ethnic groups in New York City. *Beyond the Melting Pot* announced in its title a thesis that was, at the time, unexplored if not entirely novel. That the melting pot had never really existed, hard as Americans had labored at various recipes, had not before been so decisively and authoritatively argued. The book became the first of many proclamations in the 1960s of a new kind of pluralism, sometimes approaching separateness.

In part this reflected a long-range trend toward the liberalization of American society, making less awkward the cultivation of an ethnic identity. Moreover, the rhetoric of liberalism, freedom, and civil rights so typical of the sixties loosened restrictive cultural styles and proclaimed for all the right to do one's "own thing." It bred new respect for and recognition of the authentic folkways and values of immigrants. The election of the great-grandson of an Irish immigrant farmer from County Wexford as America's first Catholic president symbolized the fall of some barriers; John Kennedy's clear independence from the Church toppled others.

Moreover, in the late 1960s, Americans learned to doubt some of their old loyalties. Amidst violent racial confrontations, bitter generational conflict and agonized debates over Vietnam and American foreign policy, few were certain enough to thump their chests at newcomers and declare, "You came here because America was better than your homeland, now do it our way." Americans themselves, less proud of their primary national identity, and less confident in its righteousness, found satisfaction and a broader dimension in their ethnic backgrounds.

Blacks, well advanced toward an ethnic identity (in part, because society forced them into a racial niche), set the model. They transformed race and color into a broader ideology based on a mixture of race, class, and African ethnicity. The ideology served effectively to gather political and economic benefits for them, and in the manner of such social movements it exploded beyond its original formulation into a mass consciousness, taking the label "Black Power." Other groups, partially in reaction, rushed to espouse their own ethnicities. Italians, Jews, Irish, Greeks, Puerto Ricans, Poles, and others already joined into their own distinct groupings, now began demanding respect, government funds, political patronage, ethnic college courses, and a host of other rights and favors. Ethnicity in this age of cultural relativism became unassailable, a shibboleth that has served politicians, immigrants, ethnics, indeed, practically all constituents except WASPs.

An old thesis advanced by the pioneer immigration historian Marcus Hansen appeared to be substantiated. He had suggested that ethnicity and assimilation followed a regular pattern in which the early generations suffer their identity as outsiders in quiet, all-the-while trying to gain acceptance as loyal Americans. But the third generation, confident of its American credentials, handles its past with greater ease, demanding the right as Americans to be proud both of its American nationality and of its ethnic heritage.

When Moynihan and Glazer produced a second edition of *Beyond the*

Melting Pot in 1969, they needed a lengthy preface to revise many of their predictions, even their observations, although not the major thesis, of course. That they underlined. But the choice was no longer, they wrote in 1969, between assimilation and ethnic-group status. The choice lay between separatism and ethnic-group status. The authors noted that during the 1960s, ethnicity and race, as they had predicted, had increased rather than diminished their hold on the city. Religion, on the other hand, came to have even less influence than the authors had predicted. Assumptions about blacks had proved particularly wrong; in 1963 Glazer and Moynihan had discounted the effects of racism and had assumed that blacks from the South would move into the mainstream of New York City life along the same course traveled by European immigrants earlier in the century. They were wrong and although they gave several reasons for their error, they failed to note their disregard of immigration's continued impact on the city, or even the existence of an exodus out of the city. Glazer and Moynihan assigned the city a static quality that it had never had. And New York's population became even more transient with the 1965 immigration law and the development of faster, cheaper transportation and communication.

This phenomenon of an urban population in transit has been part of New York City's character since the arrival of its earliest immigrants. After settling and achieving some success, many New Yorkers have moved on, fortified to meet the demands of America as Americans. Others, worn down by the pace, moved out to seek gentler, quieter lives outside the city. New York's Jewish population declined by more than half from its 2.1 million in the late fifties. Large numbers of Irish and Italians continued to depart from the city. In the seventies for the first time blacks too began moving out to "Sun Belt" jobs, life in the suburbs, or to the South (higher educated blacks were the most likely to migrate South, hoping to cash in on the New South's burgeoning economic promise). A New York bank survey found that between 1975 and 1978 the city's white (excluding Puerto Rican) population dropped 13 percent and its black population, despite a heavy West Indian influx, remained static. Puerto Ricans, a significant element of New York's ethnic mosaic also declined as a percentage of the population by 6 percent over the four years of the survey.

But while many have left, many still come, and the city, ever sensitive to world currents, continues to be refashioned. The jobs and apartments earlier arrivals leave behind are filled by other men and women, this year's political refugees or economically deprived. New York City's population flow has always been a finger on the pulse of the world. The appearance of Indochinese in Queens signaled the fall of Vietnam; South Korean instability in the 1970s could be read in the appearance of a new corps of greengrocers setting up fruit and vegetable stands; fear of the dreaded Tontons Ma-

New faces and new costumes in American supermarkets signaled the change
in the country's immigration after 1965. (*Courtesy United Nations High
Commission for Refugees*)

coutes in the spread of Haitian voodoo ritual and charm stores; Russian
persecution in a fleet of new immigrant taxi drivers; Italian economic woes
and political difficulties in the "New Italians" of Bay Ridge and Bensonhurst
and in the string of luxury shops along Fifth Avenue's "Italian Row."

Each group, in its time, arrived by means of transportation as varied as
the reasons for their having come. Some traveled on ocean liners and
gleaming 747s; others stowed in the holds of cargo ships berthed in seedy
New York piers. They came on Greyhound buses and by way of open boats
crossing the South American seas and they came illegally on foot and in
stifling closed vans. They came in army transports and coast guard vessels,
saved from certain death on the high seas.

Ahmad Ali arrived in New York from Karachi, Pakistan in 1978 in the
soft luxury of a first-class airplane trip. His relocation expenses were paid by
his company, an international bank. Fluent in several languages including
English, he relished the opportunity and challenge that his New York appointment represented; the city stood at the hub of world finance and the
experience, he was sure, would enhance his résumé. He knew that New
York operated at several social levels. There were the ethnic enclaves that
usually became home for immigrant workers and their families. But other
immigrants such as he joined different, separate circles, communities of

professionals, intellectuals, and artists. A society peopled by other bankers, by lawyers, international investors, and translators—people at home anywhere in the world—provided Ahmad Ali's social network. He and his wife considered this just one more move in a career that could go all over the world without much social dislocation.

The Haretopolous family arrived in more modest circumstances from the Greek isle of Cephalonia. Locked into the low-paying position of a small town policeman, Dimitri Haretopolous was disillusioned by the limited futures Greece promised his five children. Meager savings forced the family to emigrate piecemeal. In March 1977, Mrs. Haretopolous, with her two oldest sons, came to New York and settled in the Astoria section of Queens, the largest Greek community outside Athens.

Her two sons, Theo, twenty, and Alex, eighteen, went to work as busboys in a local restaurant. Every week a hefty slice of their earnings went back to Greece. Within a year and a half Dimitri and the remaining three children joined the family.

Two days after he arrived in New York, Dimitri Haretopolous took a job with his two sons in the restaurant in which they worked as busboys. His weekly pay was $140. Within a few months a local Greek organization placed him in a bakery. A year later the entire family had jobs—a working immigrant's American dream. Son Joseph was a grill man for a delicatessen; John made sandwiches for a local Astoria fast food store; daughter Mary was a beautician, and Mrs. Haretopolous worked too, for the first time out of the home (although she was not sure this was a good idea, she did enjoy the sense of freedom and independence) as a paint mixer for a Queens manufacturer.

Haitians such as Jay Volney typify a significant portion of the people who come to the United States as undocumented aliens. Fleeing the lowest per capita income in the Western Hemisphere and two generations of Duvalier rule—with its repressive Tontons Macoutes—Jay Volney recalled in 1979 how his father was "shot for laughs" by Duvalier's police. For his own reaction to this murder, Jay Volney was clapped in jail for months. The American shadow began to loom so large in his mind that very little, certainly not the unavailability of a visa, could keep him out. With a few friends he boarded a fishing boat and, without a compass, set sail for Miami. After mistakenly landing in Cuba, the group set out again, and this time reached Florida. There they were immediately arrested. Given friendly American relations with the Duvalier regime, American officials did not grant political asylum. Jay Volney and his fellow Haitians were shipped to an El Paso, Texas jail and detained until a group of local Catholic nuns became interested in their plight and raised $500 for bond.

From Texas, Jay Volney and the others made their way to New York where a Haitian priest provided them with a room in Brooklyn's dilapidated Bushwick section. Despite the odds against him, Volney petitioned for asylum. While officials weighed his fate, he reflected, "I don't care if I am in a poor place. I am free." His first job paid him $73 a week and within a few months it rose to $90. Amidst the ruins of Bushwick's burned-out houses, he says, "At least I am living. It's a life."

And it could get better. Individual success stories have abounded. The realization that in New York it is possible to shake off one's old status is sometimes as important as the validity of the Horatio Alger rags-to-riches inspirational tales. Some people who in their old countries would rather die poor than work poor, are changed. "I could not have dug ditches before, it would have been beneath my dignity. You could have put gold bricks at the bottom of those ditches, and I wouldn't have dug them out. But people here are not ashamed to do any work," one Korean reported. Others brought their expectations and hoped that the city would fill them. "You foolish to ask silly questions about why we want to go . . . ," a newcomer exclaimed. "I go to New York to get good work, not just $20 a week. You ask foolish questions."

Perhaps the question was not so foolish. There was crime, much of it irrational and brutal—torched buildings, subway riders thrown in front of oncoming trains for no reason, elderly people not merely robbed but terrorized. Drug pushers converted green patches into needle parks, creating dangers that New York's immigrants never faced at home. One Russian family, arriving in the city after years of trying to leave the Soviet Union, was stunned when their sixteen-year-old son leaped out of a twenty-four-story building, an apparent suicide hallucinating on LSD. To this family and others, the city appeared wide open, loose, too tolerant of eccentricity, nonconformity and crime. Others suggested that it was a necessary price, that a society must be loose and ragged at its edges to reach the levels of tolerance one finds in New York, a tolerance essential to change.

Still in the making, New York is ever changing. During the seventies, as New York pitched between bankruptcy and social disorder, some complained that the city had gone to pieces (of course they meant only that again it was changing), that the whole had become fragmented, the center unable to hold. But others, more percipient, understood better. New York had always been in pieces. Created unassembled, it had always suffered from the fact that some parts had been poorly joined while others lay side by side without fitting together at all. What kept the entire city operating was not its tight fit but its dynamic energy. Its diverse parts spun so quickly that they were held together not by organic unity but the sheer force and speed of its momentum.

A good part of the momentum and constant change came from immi-

Moondog, the tall Norse-dressed man who became a common sight in midtown Manhattan in the late 1960s, symbolized for many the city's tolerance
of eccentricity. Some found that tolerance excessive. (*Peter J. Harris*)

gration to the city. The stories that make up this book represent an effort to
understand elements of the major immigration movement to the United
States since 1965 and particularly, the interaction of these newest arrivals
with the "Immigrant City." We have attempted to find out what drove these
individuals to leave their homelands, travel to America, and settle in
New York. Convinced that the immigrant story begins at home and not on
the road we have cast each individual's story within a broader historical
perspective. None of the individuals (all have pseudonyms) discussed in this
book are prototypical nor are the specific groups profiled strictly representative. There is no formula, we are convinced, for reducing the immigrant
experience to one or a handful of lives, but certain patterns of commonality
do seem to emerge and, taken together, these chapters provide a fair example of immigrants' lives, casting varied angles of illumination on a phenomenon of both historical and contemporary significance.

Oral testimonies play a significant part in the following chapters. As
much as possible we have sought to allow the subjects to tell their stories in
their own style, but within a disciplined range of questions and issues.

New York, we understand, is not America, but it is New York, and in
itself deserves to be understood. Moreover, rather than select diverse com-

munities around the nation offering no single point of focused reference, we believe it is more useful to fix these immigrant stories in one set of surroundings, each one helping to shed light on the other, so that, in the end, we have learned something about how the place and the experience interact, what it is that attracts immigrants to New York, and how varied newcomers react to their surroundings. In some chapters New York plays a very small role, in others it is larger, but we consider a fixed location with a changing cast an appropriate strategy.

Immigrants, we have found as we suspected, do not undergo a uniform purifying, liberalizing process, making them more acutely sensitive to the needs of others. They are often as bigoted or even more so than native Americans. Many come from societies that have few competing ethnic groups and no racial minorities. Perhaps then it should not be surprising that they reflect many of the common prejudices about America's racial minorities. We found no special tolerance among these people as a group. This is not what makes them special. It is their relationship to the immigration process we wanted to know about and that is why we present their stories.

These modern immigrants are by and large neither bitter nor broken or uprooted. Like the nation they come to, they are in process and the process is in some ways easier for them than it was for their predecessors. They come to a society no longer committed to the individualism and ideals of laissez-faire of the early 1900s. Social Darwinism holds little sway and scientific racism none at all. There is welfare, unemployment insurance, job placement, housing and rent subsidies, food stamps, and assorted other aids and services. But the economy they come to is different too. It has less need for unskilled and low-skilled labor: brawn often earns more pay elsewhere. But it is still New York—Walt Whitman's "visor'd, vast, unspeakable show and lesson"—that attracts. The following chapters aim to make that lesson less mysterious.

1

I Get Homesick Every Day

Refugees from Indochina

The road is difficult not because it is blocked by a mountain or a river. It is difficult because people are afraid of the river and the mountain.

Old Vietnamese Saying

June 1977. The Tin family sits disconsolately in a Flushing, Queens apartment in New York City. They are refugees from Vietnam. In Saigon, Mrs. Tin had worked for The Chase Manhattan Bank. As did several other American companies in Saigon when the city began to fall to the Communists in April 1975, Chase Manhattan had its employees and their families evacuated whenever possible. The Tins had looked forward to starting new lives in the United States far from the terror and insecurity of war. But the long conflict in Vietnam affected not only Vietnamese; its backwash touched America in many ways and on the streets of New York it would deeply wound the Tin family by playing a role in the murder of their young daughter.

The murder would be committed by a burly veteran. Like so many other American males of his generation, Michael Crident had his teenage years interrupted by a national call to arms; he would spend months hunting "gooks" in Indochinese forests. Under these conditions other men had

31

snapped. The massacre of civilian Vietnamese at My Lai was only the most infamous result of training men to hate and kill with few questions or qualms. Americans, so concerned to raise a generation of gentle children, sent their Dr. Spock-raised sons to war. Of those so sent, many returned disfigured—missing arms or legs. Others were wounded in other ways—crippled in spirit and psyche. ✓

Michael Crident is one of these physically-whole wounded. He admits to raping and murdering a seventeen-year-old Vietnamese girl, Mrs. Tin's daughter, on a Queens street. The girl had become after only two years in this country a much-liked honors student in the local high school. She had adapted well to the new city, mastering the language with ease and making many friends among her classmates. But Crident perceived her through a surrealist prism. As he walked down a city street undergoing renovation his cruelly distorted brain flashed to Vietnam and it showed him bunkers. The young girl walking to her apartment was a Viet Cong "gook."

He grabbed her and (he later told psychiatrists) began to interrogate her. She would not admit her complicity with the enemy. He raped her, a fair spoil of war. And then he strangled the Queens girl in the forests projected by his brain. My Lai in Queens.

Mr. Tin, a slight, distinguished looking gentleman, is a victim again. He ponders the irony. His daughter, My Duc, was the one most excited about coming to America. "For her it was everything." For him? Well, he must sort it out. It will take time. The United States had promised to save his homeland and then lost it; then it promised to shield those Vietnamese who had sided with America and left many behind. Now its courts accept a plea of insanity from the soldier who killed his daughter because she did not respond to interrogation after the veteran took her prisoner in Queens.

Tin does not want to give in to bitterness. He wants to believe that Crident is crazy, and he hopes that he can eventually accept the court's verdict. He will remain in New York, to lay the foundation for a new life, studying for a Ph.D. in education while earning his livelihood as a night watchman. Despite his loss he speaks feelingly about American freedom. He does not regret the long hours he and his wife work or even the effort his other children put into studying American society in school. "The effort is good. We have to pay a price for freedom."

"Look," says a pleasant young man whose face quickly becomes a darkened cloud, his voice heavily emotional, his eyes narrow, his visage clenched. "I know Americans are not pleased to think about Vietnam. On Veteran's Day I hear once a Vietnam veteran say just what I feel. If he was a veteran of World War I or World War II or even Korea he could march proud.

The people be proud of him. But Americans try to forget the Vietnam war and forget him. They also want to forget me and my people. Those movies—*The Deer Hunter* and *Coming Home*—it's terrible; the men who made them don't know Vietnam. Do you think my country terrible like that? See my hand. It has two sides. But when I show it to you and you see only the back of it you do not see my hand. It's like if I make a movie of New York City, two hours of poor people and race fights. It's part true, but also not true. These movies make me sad. They make us so poor, so bad, so ugly, so low. If Americans see a decent picture of my people they will want to help. But they only see uneducated poor people. Tell the people. I am a worthy, proud person. I will do by myself. Give me a chance. I want to work. I want to help my people and to develop your country. This is my desire. I will do everything I can to show that my people are good, worthy people. Not a garbage people, to throw away."

Duong, like the members of the Tin family, is made vulnerable by history. Speaking on this calm summer day in 1979 he earnestly and with great feeling defends his people. The ignominy frequently heaped on Vietnam wounds him deeply. But it is not merely a matter of hurt feelings. He knows that a reductionism that makes all Vietnamese "gooks" can be deadly. It can kill on Queens streets. And it can kill on the South China Sea, by ignoring the pleas of hundreds of thousands of Indochinese refugee "boat people" for a home. An American mood that blames the American defeat on the South Vietnamese will also affect his chances here and the chances of his parents, still in Vietnam, to come here. His demand is a simple one: Don't take us for what you describe us; don't saddle us with sole responsibility for the loss in Vietnam; and don't stop being our ally now that we really need you, not to fight on our soil, but to show magnanimity on yours.

Like refugees of the past, Duong knew that the United States lacked an explicit refugee policy and that without a positive public response the United States might do nothing. With quotas in place, such inaction, as those who tried to seek refuge from Hitler in the thirties had learned, can kill. In those years, after Germany annexed Austria and Czechoslovakia, carved out Western Poland, conquered Norway, Denmark, the Netherlands, Belgium, and France, the world spun with homeless, threatened millions. Unmoved, Congress refused to tamper with the gates at America's door. The quotas stood fast. All who arrived in the United States during the holocaust years, including such eminent refugees as Albert Einstein, were admitted under existing quotas. The United States accepted no special responsibility, and refugees were not recognized as a separate or special class of immigrants. It was an era, Harvard historian Oscar Handlin has noted, "when no one was his brother's keeper."

By 1945, however, the war's end found millions displaced from their homes. Concentration camp survivors, forced laborers brought to Germany from occupied regions, and those who fled the Baltic States before the Russian advance of the winter 1944–45, all needed help and a place to settle. Antisemitic outbreaks in Poland and Romania following the war increased the number of homeless and stateless. Moreover, the descending Iron Curtain spurred the flight of many others from Czechoslovakia, Yugoslavia, and Poland. Prosperity and the sobering evidence of genocide disposed America toward greater tolerance.

President Harry Truman, while acknowledging the international dimension of the problem, urged Congress to extend a generous hand to the victims of war. He asked Americans to be true to their tradition of asylum and to shoulder the considerable burdens of world leadership. But Congress would not be persuaded. Veterans groups and isolationists combined to forestall timely action. Not until 1948 was a Displaced Persons Act passed providing for the admission of 400,000 people over the following four years. The bill expressly confirmed the quota system, however, ruling that any refugees brought in must be charged against future quotas.

By the time this program ended, the Cold War produced a new flood of refugees streaming out of Communist countries, adding to the considerable number of displaced persons still homeless. Citing both humanitarian concern and "international political considerations," the president supported and Congress passed a new Refugee Relief Act in 1953, authorizing the entry of 214,000 refugees over the next four years, this time above and beyond individual country quota limitations. This was the first in a series of emergency refugee enactments that would establish an *ad hoc* political approach on this issue over the next two decades.

The brutal Soviet suppression of Hungary's revolution in 1956 opened the next chapter in American refugee policy. Again laws defined how helpful the United States would be. About 6,500 persons were immediately accommodated with visas still available under the 1953 Refugee Relief Act. President Dwight D. Eisenhower then directed his attorney general to use a special parole power, which eventually brought in 30,000 more Hungarians. Initially designed for emergencies, the parole provision empowered the attorney general to respond with dispatch to requests for asylum. At his discretion he could permit individuals to enter the country and settle temporarily. Parole, however, offered no grounds for permanent settlement. For the next two decades this parole provision became the basic tool of refugee policy, a flexible device for thwarting quotas. Nevertheless, because its degree of administrative discretion was unusually wide and threatened the spirit of congressional control over immigration policy, it was sparingly used.

After the United States severed relations with Cuba, and particularly after President Lyndon Johnson inaugurated "Operation Airlift" in 1965 to bring out those disaffected with Fidel Castro's rule, the parole power was employed anew to welcome large numbers of Cubans into the country outside the regular quotas. By the late seventies, more than 750,000 Cubans lived in the United States, mostly in Florida's Miami area. New York City, with its large Hispanic community, also attracted a Cuban population of more than 100,000.

These émigrés from Castro's rule illustrate the unique nature of refugee migration. Other Hispanic American populations, especially Mexican Americans and Puerto Ricans, have tended to come for economic reasons. Drawn from lower occupational ranks, they struggled in less than decent jobs with few skills. But the Cuban refugees generally came for political reasons. Many brought substantial economic experience, good education, and significant business skills. It did not take very long for them to find entrepreneurial opportunities. In the Miami, Florida area alone, they opened over 10,000 stores, including pharmacies, bakeries, groceries, and many other types. More than half the Cuban population of Miami owned private homes after living here a few years; nine in ten had cars.

Prior to the Cuban refugee program, the United States had never articulated a consistent policy on mass refugee assistance. Traditionally, voluntary agencies preferred aid to coreligionists, fellow nationals, and so forth. But the Cuban migration produced massive inflows of displaced persons in an era of heightened governmental involvement in social welfare matters. Under President Eisenhower the government for the first time opened an emergency Cuban Refugee Center in Miami. The level of operations expanded under President Kennedy. Both Eisenhower and Kennedy drew on presidential contingency funds to pay for the assistance until 1962 when, with no end to the flow of Cuban refugees in sight, Congress appropriated funds through the Migration and Refugee Assistance Act. This law provided needy refugees with a range of services in health, education, and vocational and professional retraining. Refugees could also claim transportation and resettlement allowances. In addition to helping those fleeing Castro, these programs produced an important side effect: an established official bureaucracy with a vested professional and vocational interest in obtaining high levels of funding for programs to provide liberal refugee allowances, and in obtaining enabling legislation to authorize the continued admittance of rising numbers of dependent refugees.

The United States government spent well over 1 billion dollars for Cuban refugee help. Despite repeated notices to state and local governments that these programs would be phased out in 1973 and 1974, refugee political

power, combined with pressure from voluntary agencies and the bureaucracy that administered these refugee programs, brought continued funding-
ing until 1978, when Congress finally initiated a six-year phase-out.

By this time the United States faced a far more critical refugee problem.
On January 20, 1961, John F. Kennedy presented America with his vision
for a new frontier in the 1960s.

> Let the word go forth from this time and place to friend and foe alike.
> That the torch has been passed to a new generation of Americans—born in
> this century, tempered by war, disciplined by a hard and bitter peace, proud
> of our ancient heritage, and unwilling to witness or permit the slow undoing
> of those human rights to which this Nation has always been committed and
> to which we are committed today at home and around the world.
>
> Let every nation know whether it wishes us well or ill, that we shall pay
> any price, bear any burden, meet any hardship, support any friend, oppose
> any foe to assure the success and survival of liberty. . . .
>
> To those people in the huts and villages of half the globe struggling to
> break the bonds of mass misery, we pledge our best efforts to help them help
> themselves, for whatever period is required—not because the Communists
> may be doing it, not because we seek their votes, but because it is right. If
> a free society cannot help the many who are poor, it cannot save the few
> who are rich.

When the vigorous young President spoke of burdens and of the price of
liberty, he caught America's mood well. In part this tendency to worry about
others helped produce the well-meaning efforts at helping Cubans, at con-
tainment of Communism, and at saving South Vietnam.

Duong Van Minh came to the United States from Vietnam in 1975 at age
twenty-five. "I was born in the North, but when I'm three years old my
family moved to South Vietnam in 1954. By that time Communists took
over the North and we could not live there."

In 1954 the Communist Viet Minh defeated the French colonial forces
at Dienbienphu and after the French withdrew, a million Vietnamese fled
from North to South Vietnam. Most were either Catholics, businessmen,
or former officials who feared reprisals from the Communist government.
So anti-Communist was the Vietnam Catholic Church that the faithful
spoke of the Virgin Mary leading the flight to South Vietnam. If this was
hyperbole it was nonetheless not uncommon to see parish priests leading
their flocks south. Entire southern villages like Ho-Nai and Phuoc-Tuy developed as Catholic villages transplanted from the North.

"My parents in 1954 come to Saigon. I am a city boy. My parents have
a grocery and I study in school. I'm a Catholic person so I go to a Catholic
school, but most of the children in Saigon attend public school.

"Saigon looks like New York very much. It is busy with a lot of people. When I came there it was smaller. Even in 1961 its population was 300,000, but when I leave it has maybe 4 or 5 million.

"Most Vietnamese in Saigon own a private house. I did not know about an apartment house there. If you do not have much money you have a small house. If you have more you have a bigger house. It was important to have a big house, if you could, because that keeps the family together. In my father's generation in the North Vietnam the family includes grandfather, grandmother, and others. But this is very expensive, so now in Saigon only rich families could afford it. It makes a family strong and their children grow up the way they want them to. But poor families don't have finances and they have to live separately if they cannot support a big family.

"I have a friend with fifty persons in the family. They have a business company. So they have fifty persons live together. Very nice. Always like a party. I like very much.

"By the time I grow up you know I think if I can get an education, a good job, or run my own business well and get money, I think I like my children live with me, even after they get married. And if they live with me they get support from me, money and advice.

"My parents had no trouble with money. They support me and I live with them. I was twenty-four and they still support me so I should get a well education. I got a Master's degree from Ming Duc University in economics and continue for my Ph.D. degree. This same thing I want to do for my children. Keep the family together.

"One thing . . . very important. I am oldest son. I have obligation to take care of my parents. I get a lot of help from them; my education, my support until I get married. So I have obligations. So when I get married I have to take care of them. When they are old they don't work anymore and I care for them and the family. Oldest son is responsible. If second son for some reason doesn't like to live with his brother so he can move to his wife's family. Parents will live with oldest son or maybe youngest. They are sensitive to him so sometimes they want to live with him, but if not, oldest son. Very important.

"Between 1954 and 1963 my country was run by Mr. Ngo Dinh Diem. Not so much trouble. We do not feel war so much and many still live on countryside. But after Mr. Diem is killed in 1963 the war gets worse and people on countryside scared. They move to city and Saigon becomes very populated. Also other cities. Schools and government offices moved out from the countryside, also for security. Teachers who usually come from city were afraid after 1963 to go to the small towns or far out where Viet Cong attack and many schools closed.

"I'm a Catholic person and we be proud of Mr. Diem [also a Catholic], maybe for religious reasons. When he was there I know that I can get a good education. One time, when Mr. Diem came to the United States I remember that—I think it was Mr. Eisenhower—somebody said he is the 'Churchill of Asia.'

"Up to Mr. Kennedy United States back him. I still today trying to find out why Kennedy turned against him. Why they get so much bad information about Mr. Diem. Yes Diem did put a lot of his family to run the country. His brothers had big jobs, archbishop, ambassador, governor. But . . . one thing. You cannot compare my people with Americans. In United States you can have a freedom. But on countryside we had enemy. Communist and Viet Cong. So government ordered people living there to move out to isolate the Communists. So Kennedy thought Mr. Diem did wrong. Later a lot of people found he was not so wrong. The Buddhist also make Americans think he was wrong."

Duong Van Minh speaks of "my country" with an intense seriousness. His emotions run high and his voice cracks often. Duong is too Vietnamese to appear openly critical of his host country, but after a series of questions his feelings of violation surface. In a frank moment he delivers his hard judgement: Vietnam served as a staging area for a monumental war game between the superpowers.

"Americans came to test their weapons—aircraft, tanks, guns—in my country. Very important point. Industrial companies who make the guns convince United States to go to Vietnam." He is not comfortable with this simplistic rendering of a complex situation. "Maybe is true, Maybe no." But he is not willing to see the United States as a hapless savior.

"No. No. No. My country did not want Americans to come. Mr. Diem was happy to run my country alone. We need help and equipment, not a lot of advisers and army telling us what to do. When was my country destroyed? After America came with a big hand.

"Vietnam was not a civil war because weapons not from Vietnam. It was an international war for Russia, China, and United States to test their weapons and make war on someone else's territory. North and South wanted to be united, not separated and kept separate by big hands. I want to explain to you when I go to summer camp after school is over we all join hands and everybody sings a very hopeful song: 'We hope someday to open our eyes to see no more war, not hear more bombs and see when everybody will hand in hand together rebuild the country.' Buddhism, Catholic, and others, everybody sing this. My relatives from North Vietnam wrote me a letter. The first sentence is 'we hope some day the war over and we see each other.' I and other young men we want to do something for my country. We can do nothing when United States, Russia, and China fight in our land.

"I get high emotion when I tell you this—we get education. For what?

Not for me, not for my family, for my people. I had ambition that someday when the war over I can do something for my country. Now there is no chance. I see all destroyed, many families and places.

"After 1972, Americans do 'Vietnamization.' Help me until I am almost able to win and then after the other side becomes strong, withdraw and let me fall. The amount of Chinese and Soviet help became larger because of American involvement. This made North Vietnam strong. So if you get involved stay there till you help me win. Don't withdraw while China and Soviet are still on other side, for then you kill me.

"Then in Spring, 1975 we get information from friend in United States that every day American television and newspapers talk about Vietnam. My friend write: 'Don't hope anything. Try to find a way to go away. Any way you can go, leave. The United States gave up on the war. They try to forget it. They don't care.' I depend on you—South Vietnam depend on United States. When United States say we cannot help you anymore, I fall.

"In Saigon the rumors were so much. Nobody knows what is really happening. President Thieu gives no information. People do not know what to do. Finally he goes on TV and tells of the situation. No help from America. A lot of people all come to Saigon. From Dalath to Danang they came because they think that at least Saigon would be defended."

But in Hanoi, by early 1975, North Vietnamese officials had already concluded that even an attack on Saigon would not bring about new intervention by the United States. In Saigon, President Thieu, wholly unprepared for the major offensive about to come, did not have a clear contingency policy. Over the weeks from March to April he changed plans and military leaders, often erratically. Not incidentally he also spent a fair amount of time planning to ward off plots hatched by former Vice-President and arch-nemesis Nguyen Cao Ky. In the United States, Secretary of Defense James Schlesinger predicted that there would be no major Northern attack on the South, Congress made clear its intention to draw a firm line on American assistance, and Secretary of State Henry Kissinger told a news conference that Indochina would test "what kind of people we are."

By mid-March, Pleiku, Kontum, and Ban Me Thuot had been overrun. Poorly led, dispirited, and ill-equipped, the South Vietnamese quickly fell back. But rather than stop at some point and shore up defenses, Thieu decided to collapse the resistance and build a defense perimeter around Saigon. By March 26, the Provisional Communist flag was unfurled above Hue, the old imperial capital. Only then did American consular officials begin to make serious plans for evacuating Americans and selected Vietnamese.

In Danang displaced-persons camps like this one sprang up overnight in parks and along roadsides. This photo was taken March 10, 1975; by the end of April all South Vietnam had been overrun by the Communists. (*Courtesy UNHCR*)

As cities fell one could see the planless, catch-as-catch-can evacuation unfolding. In some cases American officials fled without evacuating local Vietnamese who had worked with them. It did not take much to imagine the fate awaiting these friends of America under the Communists. Other Americans were heroes. Frank Snepp's *Decent Interval* describes the courageous work of Edward Daly, President of World Airways. He would not be persuaded to stop his evacuation flights from Danang despite the great dangers. At his own expense, on his own authority, and under harrowing conditions he continued to ferry people out on his planes.

Conditions turned chaotic on his last trip. Two planes, the first piloted by Daly, came back for their loads. As the first plane touched down thousands swarmed forth on the tarmac. The plane quickly filled to capacity, jammed with 267 soldiers, 2 women and 1 child. As the craft pulled away one trooper who had not made it threw a grenade, ripping the wing and dropping the landing flaps into open position. In this "flight out of hell" Snepp writes, "scores of people clung to the wings and the landing gear as

the plane took off and many were crushed under the wheels. Others fell off after it was airborne, and several bodies were later found mashed in the wheel wells themselves. The center aisle in the cabin glistened with blood." The second plane did not even land. Thousands, among them translators, office workers, CIA contacts and consular functionaries associated with the United States, were left behind.

By month's end Communist forces held the coastal cities and Saigon made ready to defend itself, alone. As the situation deteriorated President Gerald Ford tried to persuade Congress to send more arms. Ambassador to South Vietnam Graham Martin, effectively shielded from reality by a screen of self-delusion, sought desperately to win more American military aid. He suggested that an "operation babylift" to bring Vietnamese orphans to America might capture sentiment for the beleaguered ally. Although this operation eventually brought over two thousand orphans to the United States it did not soften congressional opposition to more aid. This was not its only failure. Tragically, the initial transport on April 4, a World Airways C–5A, crashed, killing two hundred children and fifty adults.

The rapidity with which South Vietnam buckled caught all by surprise. Only on April 8 had State Department officials begun a week-long series of meetings with House and Senate committees to set policy for using the attorney general's parole power to evacuate selected Vietnamese. No clear standards existed to determine who had priority for evacuation. How and where these parolees would be taken also had to be resolved. Finally parole was authorized for dependents of American citizens still in Vietnam and eventually also for those who had worked for or with the American government.

Not until April 18 did President Ford establish a task force of twelve federal agencies to "coordinate . . . . all United States Government activities." The President also directed this group to plan and administer the resettlement of the evacuees.

In Vietnam rumor and disorder reigned. Thieu fled his government after he had taken care to ship his personal fortune to Taiwan and Canada. Fears of Communist reprisals terrified Saigon's inhabitants. Gail Paradise Kelley interviewed scores of Vietnamese who left Saigon in its last days. One woman, typical of many others, told her:

> They said that they (the Communists) are going to give each girl a huge sack containing a sick or handicapped Communist soldier to take care of him, and to marry him, or if the men soldiers "need," the single girls have to give. The children born will belong to the government. I rather die. . . .

As gracefully as possible Americans averted their eyes from Vietnam. They concentrated on domestic economic issues closer to home. Vietnam had come to be weighted down with controversy, ideological passion, and the frustration of American defeat. In several 1975 opinion polls more than 50 percent of the American public opposed bringing Vietnamese to the United States. One congressman from California expressed his opposition in crisply racist tones: "Damn it, we have too many Orientals." Even George McGovern, liberal peace candidate of the Democratic party in 1972, allowed that the Vietnamese "are better off in Vietnam, including the orphans."

Nevertheless, the evacuation effort proceeded, but with distressing disorder. Americans watched on TV as over a decade of effort collapsed with thousands of terrified Indochinese scrambling to board Huey choppers to safety. Although local American officials did try to set some priorities, trying to select those most involved with the American effort, the process was haphazard and rife with pay-offs. Many paid dearly for the privilege of leaving home. Vietnamese pilots did a flourishing business filling the empty seats of their air force jets as they made their last flights out of Vietnam. Available shipping vessels were filled on a first-come basis with soldiers often bullying their way aboard at gunpoint. Willy-nilly, families split as some made it to a departing vessel and others did not. Later, many would suffer burdens of guilt for their hasty departure, but irrevocable decisions had to be made quickly, often in panic.

In the largest evacuation effort in American history, seventy helicopters flew 630 sorties on April 29–30 bringing out 7,053 individuals in eighteen hours. In all 51,888 persons were flown out of Saigon in April. Others departed by barge or commercial carrier bringing the total to 65,000. According to Frank Snepp, however, only a fraction of those who had worked with the Americans got out with their families. Also left behind was over $5 billion in United States hardware, including 550 tanks, 73 F–5 jet fighters, 1,300 artillery pieces, and 1,600,000 rifles.

To escape by sea, one had to be very lucky. If the vessel were not seaworthy or were without sufficient provisions the trip could be a wet hell. Amidst the chaos of helicopters landing on streets, with pushing, gouging crowds trying to board while mortar fire claimed victims indiscriminately from among those clustered, one survivor decided to try the sea. Le Thuc, his wife, child, sister, and nephew joined others making their way up the river to reach a small boat. His sister lost her fifteen-year-old son on the way, but turning back was impossible. After the boat departed all aboard took stock. They found one man, one woman and two children missing. On the ocean "we lost many people. If you had luggage you put it on the ocean. There was no need for enemies," recalls Le Thuc, "we died ourselves."

Families often traded a lifetime of savings to secure permission and passage out of Vietnam on flimsy crafts such as this one after the Communist take-over. (*Courtesy Hong Kong Christian Service*)

Duong Van Minh tried to plan for himself and his family, to make the decisions that could save them.

"From 15 of March people who worked with Americans begin to apply to get out. 'Big hands' helped take out Thieu and some others, but most of the people don't have a way to leave. By middle April I know Communists will come. Everybody is coming to Saigon so I went opposite to the countryside, about thirty miles north. Me and my family decided that Communists will go straight to Saigon to have a big battle there and that countryside will be safer.

"After Communists come to Saigon it is very mixed up, everybody is busy and no control so we come back. My father is sick and my mother said she does not want to leave him alone. She will not leave Saigon. Three sisters also stay. Then my mother said 'O.K. you're able to take care of your young brother and your sister go ahead to go.' We don't have time to discuss about that. My mother order to go and I just obey. She stay in Saigon. So now my family with eight persons, five in Vietnam and three go.

"My friend's family was making plans to go and I join. They drive car to Saigon river. By that time have a lot of ships prepared to go. Communists control Saigon but they don't know everything, cannot control everything. They just came in and have to do everything, have to run whole city and they do not have so many men, so they do not stop us.

"So we got a private ship . . . not for money. The owner left Saigon already and everybody—maybe three thousand people, oh my!—just got on the ship. A lot of soldiers force themselves on. One of the people on the ship was a ship captain so he took the ship on the ocean. Others helped. Many times engine stopped. Stop. Stop. Stop. On the sea we run out of food and water. When people left they did not think to bring a lot of food and water, only for two or three days. Some people jump over to kill themself. Others kill self with guns. The soldiers have guns. No food no water but a lot of guns. Some who jump on ship to go feel very sorry, very depressed for leaving family and kill themself.

"We see a lot of small ships but they cannot help. We send message. Nobody answer. The engine was finished and ship almost sinking. Then we pretty lucky a Denmark ship see us and take us to Hong Kong. Queen Elizabeth was coming to visit Hong Kong that time. We sent message to every country. She got message and she is willing to help us. She ordered Hong Kong government to welcome us and we have permission to land. I heard she gives us 500,000 pounds. She think we just stay in Hong Kong for about a couple of weeks. She think in two weeks we will go to United States. But United States took in already more than 130,000 and no more now. So we stay in Hong Kong first week, second week—.

"Americans come to Hong Kong to interview. Everybody fill out a form and everybody happy, think that next day we go to United States. But after that United States embassy don't come anymore to camp. A week later, a month later, nobody come. Everybody very depressed. We lucky, but we not very lucky. Then they change to let more people in and again they interview. By then a lot of people give up and go to Australia, England, Denmark, France. Half the people from the ship go to other countries."

By mid-May, 130,000 Vietnamese entered United States territory with 60,000 still in refugee camps in Hong Kong and Thailand seeking parole for entry into the United States. In the fall, 10,000 more received parole and by spring 1976 another 11,000 entered.

Initially American officials planned to process the refugees overseas in order to avoid setting up refugee camps on American soil. But Guam and other resettlement areas quickly overflowed and the massive nature of the evacuation made it necessary to establish way stations in the United States. Camp Pendleton in Southern California opened as the first such processing

Refugees occupying the gunwales of a ship arriving in Hong Kong. (*Courtesy Hong Kong Christian Service*)

center on April 29, the same day that the American embassy was closed down in Saigon. With only a week to get ready, its staff gathered as much equipment as possible and prepared to welcome the Vietnamese. By mid-May, convoys of military buses were discharging the refugees into their new surroundings. Their faces etched with fatigue and uncertainty, they took the mattresses, bed clothes, toilet articles, and sandals, along with the single candy bar that each person was issued, to their quonset huts where finally they could uncoil from the anxiety and travail of their recent experience.

Within a month three additional reception centers opened at Fort Chafee, Arkansas; Eglin Air Force Base in Florida; and Fort Indian Town Gap, Pennsylvania. By June 15, the seven-week-old system had welcomed 131,399 refugees and completed processing 36,077 into American society.

Because of the nature of the refugee population—most were evacuees who had worked with Americans—officials expected immigrants who knew some English and were familiar with Americans ways. Planning assumed that these refugees would quickly fit into American society. They would, officials confidently told each other, adapt even more readily than the Hungarians and Cubans had. Indeed, despite the fact that almost half of all the refugees were under age eighteen, and 65 percent knew no English, the

In the camps the refugees were often crowded into triple-tier bunks. From these crowded and makeshift conditions they tried to link up with one of the receiving nations. (*Courtesy Hong Kong Christian Service*)

household heads among these Vietnamese did carry impressive credentials. Many came from white-collar occupations; there were professionals, managers, and officials among them. More than 70 percent spoke English and over one-third spoke it well. Half had at least some secondary education, one-quarter had attended college and quite a few had done some postgraduate work. This was clearly a select group, not a random cross-section of Vietnam. Most were city folk, largely Catholic (Catholics represented 10 percent of South Vietnam's population but about 40 percent of the refugees), and a disproportionate number, perhaps even a majority, had fled North Vietnam before 1955.

At the centers they exerted little control over their own destinies. Remarked a refugee psychologist quartered at Pendleton, "I never know what will happen to me, I know only what has happened to me." They could only hope that the future would be kind. "I believe I have a good future here. I think the Americans in the end are good people. I think. I hope."

Refugees could leave the camp in one of four ways. They might choose to resettle outside the United States. Camp officials encouraged this, with

The movement out of Vietnam was often one of several generations traveling together. (*Courtesy Hong Kong Christian Service*)

one camp newspaper running a banner across the front page reading "And why not Malawi." Of the seven thousand who chose this option, half went to Canada and others to France, Australia, Taiwan, or the Philippines. But most of the receiving countries were highly selective. France, for instance, accepted only those who had relatives in the country, spoke French, and had a job waiting for them. Canada took only highly skilled professionals or those with Canadian relatives. Taiwan limited entry to ethnic Chinese.

A second choice was repatriation. Some of those who got to the United States had second thoughts, or had been unwitting passengers on commandeered vessels. By the end of 1975 slightly more than fifteen hundred returned to Vietnam.

Another group came directly to jobs and required no sponsorship. If the refugee could show $4,000 cash on hand or a good job waiting for him he could leave on his own. As many as ten thousand left the camps to settle independently.

The rest, the vast majority, required sponsors who assumed responsibility for the refugees and for easing their way into the new society. A handful of states undertook a few thousand sponsorships, and a few local benevolent agencies also accepted several hundred sponsorships, but most Vietnamese acquired sponsors from a pool of seven voluntary agencies (volags*) that received government contracts and stipends to arrange appropriate local sponsorships. The volags in turn appealed to local parishes and communities to undertake such a project. "Why should Presbyterians be concerned about refugees?" asked a Church World Service pamphlet. "The answer is human need. Refugees are the victims of persecution, oppression or calamity. . . ." The same pamphlet instructed potential local sponsors that such an undertaking involved welcoming the new family, providing adequate temporary housing, accepting financial responsibility for an initial period, accepting the foreigners as equals, finding them jobs, placing their children in schools and orienting them to the community.

Officials did not want Vietnamese forming refugee pockets in the several states that they favored and the high costs of sponsorship did make it unlikely that large numbers would initially be brought into any one locale. Organizational sponsorship was considered the most desirable. It gave a group responsibility that they could reasonably share far better than any one individual could be expected to bear. Moreover, except for the pressure of proselytizing ("sponsorship: 'what will it cost'?" asked another Church World Service pamphlet, "A fair question . . . on the other hand if sponsorship is a face to face ministry. . . ."), as some churches pursued the opportunity to attract new members, this method limited the likelihood of exploitation, a distinct possibility with individual sponsorships.

In more than a few cases individual sponsors sought to purchase indentured servants, wives, mistresses, or cheap labor. Enterprising small businessmen took ads in the Vietnam language camp newspapers offering specifically to sponsor mechanics, fishermen or chicken farmers. Some ads asked for entire crews of twenty and thirty. Camp officials ruled many of these out, observing that they were poorly disguised efforts at contract labor, below the minimum wage.

The Vietnamese did not always find it easy to live with the notion that

---

* The seven organizations, which had previous resettlement experience, were: International Rescue Committee; Church World Service; Lutheran World Council; Hebrew Immigrant Aid Society; United States Catholic Conference; Tolstoy Foundation; American Fund for Czech Relief.

others managed their lives. A large seventeen-member family at Fort Indian Town Gap refused to be broken up for the pictures to be sent to prospective sponsors. The volag representative, realizing that a seventeen-member family could not easily be placed, wanted them photographed in groups of three and four. The refugees knew what this meant and refused to accept what they perceived might be a first step in disrupting their extended family simply to make the American happy. They agreed to pose only after they were assured that they would all be photographed together.

To prevent the development of a dependency syndrome, government officials insisted that the centers be closed as soon as possible. An informal deadline allowed forty-five days at maximum for securing sponsorship, pushing the refugees into American society as soon as possible. Haste did produce some mismatches but the complex task was accomplished with dispatch. By December 1975, when the task force ceased operations and the last of the reception centers closed its doors, over 130,000 refugees had been relocated around the United States under supervised sponsorships. ✓

"I got a lot of help from American sponsor," says Duong Van Minh. "I came to Pennsylvania by plane in October and they take me to Indian Town Gap. I live over there about one month and I want to get out. No, not because it's bad. It's good but I'm worry it will close [it closed December 15, 1975] in a month so I must find a sponsor. The volags help me . . . they work very hard to find places for the refugees, and in Indian Town every family got a sponsor.

"I had a very wonderful sponsor in El Paso, Texas. The Ashbury United Methodist Church sponsor my family with three persons. They provide everything—house, transportation, food, health, clothing. The minister of the church asked the people to help the Vietnamese. The church was ready to sponsor a family with eight people, but nobody like to come to El Paso. They want to live in a big city with Americans, not to live in El Paso, with about 70 percent Mexican. And they want better weather and sometimes it's 110 degrees there. I'm a person who doesn't mind about that point. I don't mind who they are. I don't mind where it is. I just want to have sponsor in order to get out of camp as soon as I could. I go anywhere, Hawaii or Alaska or even my sponsor black or white or Mexican American. I just want people who will help me and show me how to rent an apartment, to get a job.

"We go to El Paso. Church prepare everything for us. They have a house belong to church. They repaint that, bring in some furniture and clothing for us. Some people take care of painting, some take care of furniture, like committees. One committee for transportation, one for food, one for health and one committee care for education. I stay with church sponsor

four months and I learn English. They do everything for us. I don't have to
worry how to live. They give us some money and also show me how to get
a high school equivalency diploma. I have a Master Degree in Economics,
but I try to forget about that. I get an equivalency diploma and start college.
I go for two semesters to University of Texas and work part-time in the
library.

"I talk to my friends at University of Texas: "Tell me what you do in
1972?' We talk about that. They join the antiwar movement. Why? 'I don't
want me or my friend to be killed in Vietnam. We try to help them for
nothing.' This hurt me. I cannot explain to him when he talks about so
many changes in Vietnam government, maybe twelve or sixteen coups and
new governments after Mr. Diem is dead, but who helped to kill Mr. Diem?

"In the summer I go to Nevada [Duong pronounces it Nay-va-da]. They
say there is work for young people there. I work as busboy, money changer,
washer. I want to make money. I need much money to get rest of my family
out of Vietnam. I save my money and I send to my parents in Vietnam
through France. They get the money and contact some people and they
plan to get a ship. They give the money, but still the Communists come
and take the ship and we lose the money.

"I don't give up. I try to work more on this, to get more information. I
talk to Vietnamese in America to find out who is helping bring out families.
I tell my parents to contact with them. But four years already and my parents still live there. I write every week and they write every month. Every
letter they say 'we will meet someday in America.' They can't write this
open, but with hidden meaning. Like they say next week they go to New
Economic Zone in Vietnam to see my friend, but he is here in the United
States; this means they will come here. I try to work with the Vietnam
community to find out what they can do for my parents through reunification program but programs not work so well and for me no success.

"After we settle in El Paso we try to be in touch with friends and relatives from Vietnam. We know some people left but we do not know where
they are. So we write note in the newspaper. 'Duong Van Minh is here in
El Paso, Texas, wants to be in contact with you. . . . please answer.' My
sister had a friend from Vietnam and we know he is in the Western United
States but not where exactly. She wrote a letter in the paper and he answered from Albuquerque, New Mexico. That is how I found my cousins
also.

"Soon my sister's friend came from Albuquerque every week to see her.
First he has a low pay job because of English barrier. But he works hard. I
see he is a good worker, try very hard to make success and he will take good
care of my sister. About ten months after we come to El Paso they want to

get married. My parents not here so I think about it and give my permission. Now they both work and he gets steady upgrade. Very good."

When they began to arrive in 1975 the Vietnamese encountered a gashed economy. Not many weeks before the denouément in Saigon, Gerald Ford introduced his stillborn WIN (Whip Inflation Now) program to rally Americans. More than 9 percent unemployment, uncharacteristic shortages, and a staggering inflation crippled the economy. Nativists, turned inward by these concerns, called for measures to keep out foreigners. Strident voices predicted that the Vietnamese would compete for jobs, depress wages, and overburden welfare budgets.

But by December 1975, many of the newly arrived Vietnamese held jobs. Admittedly, the jobs scraped the bottom level of the economy in status and pay. Professionals were doing menial labor. Of those in white-collar occupations in Vietnam, only one in ten could secure similar employment here. The others donned blue collars and accepted substandard wages. A former Director General of the South Vietnamese Ministry of Interior did yard work. The flamboyant ex-premier and conspirator of the last days, Nguyen Cao Ky, ran a liquor store in a Los Angeles suburb. A medical doctor found work driving a corporation limousine, another washed dishes for a local diner. The floor sweeper of a Houston bank had been a bank manager in Saigon and a South Vietnamese general served diners in a Pennsylvania restaurant.

A newspaper profiles Nguyen Van Huong. He has twelve citations including one from Major General Homer D. Smith declaring that he worked courageously to help evacuate Americans amid rocket fire as Saigon fell in 1975. In Vietnam he owned a large house and two cars and lived lavishly. He knew English and computer science. Now he worked in Maryland as an assistant cook at the only restaurant in a small town. Painful as such reductions in status undoubtedly were, they showed a willingness to face new realities and to try to work within the limitations they imposed.

In November of 1978, as Americans debated the desirability of a second Vietnamese influx, this time of "boat people," the Department of Health, Education, and Welfare conducted an economic survey of the 1975 refugees. The results showed a remarkable immigrant pattern. Of those in the labor force, 95 percent (slightly higher than native Americans) held jobs, as compared with some 60 percent in 1975. These were not part-time jobs undercutting American wages. Fully 86 percent of the male refugees contributed forty hours or more a week to the economy. Approximately 70 percent of the families reported monthly incomes above $800 (in 1975 only 15 percent earned as much) and 96 percent of the refugees earned at least $100 a week. Despite the availability of funding for cash and medical assistance (to ease the burden on local budgets the federal government reimbursed state outlays), nine of every ten dollars spent by Vietnamese refugees came from productive labor and not public funds.

This success produced envy and bitterness in some. After That Din Le found all his automobile windows smashed, he felt he understood the message all too clearly. "The Americans are jealous. . . . We have little here but they think we're stealing their jobs." In New York City an HEW official still shakes her head recalling an incident in 1976. One day after the newspapers had run a feature on the help being provided by federal and local authorities for Indochinese refugees, a Vietnamese walked into the warehouse where he worked within a largely minority work crew. The others had been talking and were agitated by the news item. The next thing he knew they had attacked him and heaved him over a forklift. In 1979 he was still recovering from a ruptured spleen and multiple injuries.

Some of the sharpest feelings come from Vietnam veterans. A black veteran interrupts a speaker discussing the problems of the refugees: "Don't tell me about their problems. And don't tell me about North or South. Both sides were killing us in Nam. Now they're [the United States government] doing more for them than us. I left a part of me there while they were apathetic. I can't take them."

Duong Van Minh is sensitive to these hatreds, but he cannot understand them. "Some people are so selfish. Some people say the Indochinese come here and create a lot of economic problems like inflation and unemployment. The American family lives on the highest standard in the world and the Indochinese need help to survive. Maybe they make some economic problems, but they are human beings who need help, a place to live and food and eat. Some people think Indochinese come without education, without job skills and just take welfare. I think—I have two years experience with Vietnamese in New Mexico, California and New York—that after they learn some English and about job opportunities they work very hard.

"I'm proud of myself here. I go to university, work part-time, earn enough to care for my family. When my sister gets married both she and her husband work very hard. Now they have children, own their own home with furniture and a car. They contribute to the welfare of the system, not depend on welfare.

"Or for example Mr. Chu. Second day in New York after leaving the camp he got a job for $1.90 an hour. He didn't speak English or even know the streets. Just how to go to work and go home. Now he speaks English, earns good pay, has a beautiful house in Queens and he helps other Vietnamese who are coming. He is a good citizen and everybody likes him at work and in the neighborhood. He keeps the laws, pays the taxes, teaches his children to be good. Isn't America happy to have him?"

Duong's question is perhaps fair but sometimes beside the point. Hard Yankee competitiveness and dramatic success stories do not always win admirers. In Florida, where refugees quickly moved into the fishing business, a Florida legislator bitterly accused them of "raping the waters." In 1976, Vietnamese began arriving in the small Texas town of Seadrift (population: 1,000). Local fisherman viewed them as intruders and relations quickly soured. After working a while for others, a number of the thrifty refugees bought their own boats with their combined savings, further stoking resentment. Seadrift's shrimp, crab, and oyster fishermen accused them of violating local agreements aimed at limiting competition on the seas. Reaction turned churlish. Most whites would have nothing to do with them. Incidents multiplied. Finally one summer afternoon a disagreement turned particularly ugly and a local fisherman was shot; two Vietnamese were charged. A few hours later three refugee boats were torched, a home firebombed, and the principal processing plant serving the Vietnamese burned to the ground. Within days Seadrift's one hundred fifty Vietnamese had packed up and fled en masse.

With many eyes upon them the refugees found themselves in an uncomfortable predicament—between the hard place of antagonism if they added to welfare costs and unemployment and the rock of resentment if they worked hard and succeeded. Resentment grew strongest in small towns. Even under the best of circumstances it is not always easy to carry on your back the good grace of a community intent on doing good works. The big city provided anonymity and isolation, a private space to work out the new situation without the overwhelming attention of others. Duong Van Minh grew tired of El Paso's small-town focus.

"I like to travel. I want to know other people in the United States. I quit New Mexico and I go to New York. I heard New York is biggest city in United States; there is Vietnamese community in New York. I have no idea how big New York is, but only that it is very big. I drive my car for six weeks from New Mexico and I arrive in April 1979. I stop in Kansas City, Missouri, Oklahoma, Ohio, Pennsylvania. Then New York.

"First thing. I remember that New York have Empire State Building. I come to New York, park my car in the Bronx, and ask someone how to get to Empire State Building. He said, 'What for?' I said I am newcomer and I want to see the big building. He shows me where to get on subway. I buy a token and I travel to the city. I asked a man on the train where to get off and I see the Empire State Building. I buy a ticket to the top and I see how New York City looks like. Then I think about where to stay in New York. I open a phone book and . . . I get a trouble. I get a trouble because they don't have a resident phone book, only yellow phone book.

"I have experience when I travel—like when I went to Oklahoma and look for Vietnamese people. I open the telephone book I look for Vietnamese. I look for the name. In Vietnam there are few last names like, for instance, Nguyen is the most popular last name, so if I find Nguyen in the phone book I know he is a Vietnamese. I found it easily in Oklahoma. I call up and explain I am a student, I like to travel, I am over here. I do not know anyone here. Are you willing to help me? Would you let me come to your house to visit? I meet very nice people from my people.

"Usually I call up five o'clock in the afternoon before supper and many times they say come. When I traveled in 1976 it was very easy. Vietnamese felt close. Now it is harder. People have a good life and they hesitate more. Some do not want to be disturbed. Not so sympathetic. In 1976 I call and they let me stay four days, even a week with meals for free. So when I come somewhere I open telephone book, find a Vietnamese name, and call to them.

"In Empire State Building I lose patience I can't find anything in the yellow telephone book. I go back to Bronx and go to supermarket to buy something to eat. There I find a white paper telephone book and see a Vietnam name. I call to him. He says he cannot help me but give me to somebody else. I call and I get a good call. Mr. Thong, he is single and have a room in the hotel. He says, 'Go ahead, come to my room and if you don't mind you can sleep in my bed. I can't guarantee food but you can sleep here for a few days.' I stay there.

"He give me a number and I call VACO [Vietnamese American Cultural Organization]—a social service agency for Indochinese. The lady on the phone said go ahead come to my office and she interview me. She sent me to a watch company. I get a job that day. But it is a hard job. I have no experience. I don't like it; I quit.

"I go back to the office. The lady very busy in the office, she need help. I tell her my background and that I work in New Mexico and California in social work. She hire me to work for her.

"Every afternoon when I get off the job I ride a subway to find out the stations and how to travel in this city. Then I can tell people how to get to government offices. I help people get social security numbers, get children into school, get jobs, get benefits, get food stamps, get welfare.

"One reason people come to New York is if they have a sponsor here. They want to live in California or Texas but they come to the sponsor. Such a people find a lot of difficulty in New York. Everything takes so long time. I have to go to hospital for my leg, I broke it. I must wait to have x-rays and wait to have analysis and wait to see doctor. From nine o'clock to three o'clock I must wait. In New Mexico it's right away and finished. It is so big here. It is difficult to send kids to school. Other places a principal will discuss problems; in New York they do not have time. For example, you

A family giving a party in December, 1979 to help furnish their new apartment. All who came to the party brought an appropriate housewarming gift.
(*Courtesy Hartford Courant, John Long*)

need a vaccination to get into school. Many do not understand and no one has the time to explain. It's crowded and busy and the kids get lost.

"Here in Queens I have many good neighbors but others who live in apartments do not have close neighbors. Other people in the apartment come home, lock the door, and they don't care what everybody does.

"Another problem, jobs. For poor people who do not have experience or a skill it is very hard. In New Mexico my sister and her husband both have good jobs and they only have a high school education. There you can start on a low level and upgrade. In New York you have to be very rich or must have a skill and an education.

"In Texas, there are more industrial jobs, but New York is more commercial and for commercial you need English. In Lancaster, Pennsylvania about one hundred Vietnamese work for RCA making TVs. They start at $4.25 entry level. After three months they make $5.25 and $6.00 an hour. It's very difficult to get such good-paying industrial jobs in New York. Here a college degree or experience in banking and computer is good.

"New York is harder place. Lots of people competing, all looking for jobs at the same time. But it is a twenty-four-hour city. You can work in the afternoon and look for another job in the morning or you can take two jobs.

"Before I came to New York I create a picture for myself. In the picture I show myself you come to New York to have good life. You have to work hard. It is good, exciting. New York gives you a lot of experience. Live here three years it's like you live somewhere ten years. I like to learn a lot. I get a good job and experience. In a couple years if something good somewhere else, I am ready to go. No problem.

"When I came here I was willing to take any job to pay for food. The same week when I know already more about New York my eyes open and I look for a better job. I always advise people: 'If you are willing to work I can get you a job right now. Then for several weeks learn about New York and then you can get a better job. First right away you can be a dishwasher or sweep floor, minimum wage jobs.'

"But we must talk about welfare system. Like a family of seven persons. They willing to go to work and I send them to work to a company. His job to carry something and he get about $3.50 an hour, $140 a week, $560 a month. For people like this welfare system make more sense. If they get welfare they get medicaid, cash, food stamps, everything. Add up to $700. So why go to work for $560 a month and maybe some food stamps?

"It does not take them long to find out about public assistance in New York. But this is bad. Once they get public assistance it is hard to quit. They compare how much they get from work with the welfare.

"In my country we learn when you have a lot of free time you do nothing and it is easy to think about bad things. When you do not work, not study, nothing, it is trouble. Children have to be in school, mother and father have to work. Must be like that. When you work you save your money and before you spend you think about how much do you work for this much money. It is money from your hands, from your labor, so you do not want to throw it away. People on public assistance do not have that feeling.

"If you go to work you learn English. You must. Stay home and you don't learn. I sent a client to his first job. The employer asked him, 'What is your name?' He couldn't answer. But the next week he could chat with the employer. Would you believe it?

"I must talk about crime. In small cities you don't worry about that. In El Paso I open my door. In summer at night I keep it open to sleep with cool breeze. No one come in to take everything. Here I live in my hotel. Second week someone came and take everything. Then I park my car one time and I lose my battery. Later someone takes my suitcase. Three times I get robbed in three months. ✓

"The people I live with here they advise, don't come home after nine, ten o'clock. I like to learn, to go out in the streets so sometimes I get home two or three in the morning. But I must be very careful. You know what I do if I get on the train late at night? I get a can of beer and I keep it in my hand; open my shirt. I show I'm a person who doesn't care so they will not hurt me. I look like a drunk. If a police comes I explain to him why I do that.

"People are very afraid. I know a family lived in Coney Island in a housing project. It's a very nice apartment. Very, very, nice. You can see people swim on beach. Also it is cheap, very cheap. And they were comfortable with six children. But they have to quit. Because his wife was cut up few times by blacks. They take her money. She very scared. Get nightmares, almost get sick. Every hour they knock on her door. They even put fire to her door. It's terrible. Nobody—no neighbors—come to help.

"Even here. This house. Two months ago the lady here was attacked by a man. He came to the door and ask for money. She said, 'Please I have a house but I do not have money.' He started to walk and then turned around and attacked her. She lose two teeth. Now they must build expensive fence. The house is beautiful, with fence not look so beautiful.

"In Vietnam we were never afraid about that. We always think if we have trouble the neighbor or the police will help us. Not in New York. No neighbor. No police. One time another man was stealing a car in front of the house. I call police. Tell them I see a guy doing it. The police say O.K., O.K. I wait half-hour; one-half hour and nobody came. I can't believe it. I give my name, my phone number, my address, everything he ask me on the phone. What he think, I make it up? Or maybe he doesn't care. No one came all night.

"Most people who come here really do not know the New York situation. My first week here I not afraid. I have nothing. First week I live in motel. Nothing happen. I think this is O.K., nothing bad. Why people talk about crime? The second week it happened. They take everything. My clothes. My camera. Everything.

"I see that a lot of young people don't care. One time after I pick up a hitchhiker. He force me. He says, 'Give me money'. I said 'Listen to me, think about it. I don't have money to give you. I'm so nice I stop to take you. If you need a cigarette I give. If you need food, share with me from my bag. But don't ask me for money, I don't have. I care nothing about money. I take you in my car for nothing. Look at me. I'm not a rich person. Go ahead.' It makes me feel bad. I still believe if I do a nice thing people should not hurt me. He quit with no money and leave me.

"I learn from all people. But I see people here don't care so much about their children. Then they grow up and don't obey you. When I get older,

The more rapid assimilation of the young, such as these two girls shopping in mid-Manhattan, at times added to the distress of the older generation who wanted greater loyalty to the old culture. (*Courtesy UNHCR, Gloaguen*)

marry, have children, I will work hard to support my wife and my children, then when they grow up they know what I do for them and they want to go the way I want. If I do nothing for them, then they not go the way I want. They do a lot of bad and I can't stop them. The family is the foundation. If everything good with family, children grow up good.

"Young man like me learn a lot in New York. I learn more problems than anywhere. The condition is very difficult and if you do well here you will succeed anywhere. I advise young people: 'Stay in New York. It is tough. It make you smarter and stronger.' People here work harder than anywhere. It is exciting. Rush hour, hard work, opportunity to have a tough test. Competition make you stronger and you deal with all kind of people. New York is hard to live, but hard to quit.

"Most of New York Vietnamese live in Queens. We celebrate some Vietnamese customs like on New Year's Day we celebrate together. I like it very much. The sentiment is very important. We live not with food, not with home. We live with something inside, with the way we feel. We become close. Even we are not friends from Vietnam. We say, 'When your eye hurts easy to love a blind person.'

"I was sad here. I left my parents. I received my father's order to take my sister and brother to United States. I do that. Now my sister marry and my brother go to school. Myself, I am twenty-eight years old. I know a lot of Vietnamese girls. Not a lot of good Vietnamese girls. But I don't want to get married now. The reason: my parents in Vietnam. I don't want anybody involved in my difficulty. If I get bad news from my parents. If they die or I lose contact with them or they came here to live with me maybe my problems be over. Some people think I have mental health problem. I get homesick everyday. I get high emotion when I talk about my parents. I say, 'I have a good job—for what? To get money? No!'

"You know even if I want to marry it is a problem. People think you're twenty-eight. Probably were married in Vietnam and leave wife and children there behind. So I have problem with the Vietnamese who come in 1975. And American girls less close to family. Less respect for father and mother. It would not be good with me.

"Now there are new people coming from Vietnam, but they are ethnic Chinese. My feeling: I have parents in Vietnam. I waiting to get letter from them saying they will come here to live with me. Okay, I see a lot of people running to escape the country, mostly ethnic Chinese. I would like for my parents to get out. But the Chinese they are human beings too and they need food. Save them, save the human beings.

"Some Vietnamese refugees do not like the Chinese. They say after a year or two when people will ask them where you are from they will say Taiwan or Hong Kong. Nobody will say from Vietnam. It's a country everybody now wants to forget. Only Vietnamese are proud to be Vietnamese."

Perhaps a television reporter interviewing a boat person in Malaysia did not mean precisely what he said. He had asked a haggard refugee why he felt Americans should help. "Because we lost everything," replied the Vietnamese, missing the point while making another. But the reporter brought him firmly down to reality: "America is not in Vietnam anymore. America is finished with Vietnam." To many of the boat people escaping in increasing numbers, it seemed by 1978 that the whole world was finished with Vietnam.

But Vietnam would not fade. Doggedly it drew the world's attention by producing a new refugee crisis, one that would finally cause the United States to move toward a comprehensive refugee policy.

Many factors contributed to the 1978–79 situation. Unusually heavy typhoon rains generated the worst flooding in Vietnam in decades, and the waters claimed thousands of lives and millions of crop acres. Coming after years of drought and the effects of a decade-long war with its bombs and herbicides, it left the agricultural economy devastated. Moreover, in March 1978, the government finally implemented its Communist economic apparatus, expropriating thirty thousand private businesses. A month later it introduced a new currency, wiping out the hoarded fortunes of the middle class. And after decades of war a new conscription called up young men to fight a war against Cambodia.

An additional, far more complex, issue revolved about the large ethnic Chinese population, which the new regime set out to uproot. For all its inhumaneness, this did not seem to offend most Vietnamese, even those who opposed the new government on other grounds. Said a 1975 refugee:

> Chinese took over my country over 1,000 years. So many misunderstandings. So many bad ideas in Vietnam about the Chinese. During war the relationship between ethnic Chinese and Vietnamese was not normal in South Vietnam. They have an area like Chinatown here. They control everything. They have money and businesses in Saigon. They have a lot of experience about commerce. Year by year they control everything. I predicted very well, correct. When I left my country I said, when Communist take over they will kick out Chinese. Reason is for national pride and because they are the property owners and Communist party wants to control economy.

The roots of this attitude go back to ancient times. Southeast Asian history was often a story of people on the move, at war, or under the domination of others. Shifting military fortunes and geographic instability left the people with few touchstones. This tended to inflate the importance of ethnicity. Ethnic identity served as a means for national survival amidst the wars and the migratory life style.

Over two thousand years ago China extended her domain into Southeast Asia. Campaigns to spread Chinese culture left their mark on much of the region; Vietnam became virtually a Chinese colony. Chinese hegemony bred a lasting resentment. Some years ago a Vietnamese historian Nguyen Van Huyen characterized Chinese control:

> The Chinese Governors . . . were more concerned with their own well-being than with the happiness of the people. Wicked, ambitious and avaricious, they only sought to further their own interests on the road to power and to enrich themselves at the expense of the people. History has preserved the memory of their exactions, their injustice and their cruelty.

Even after political separation the Chinese shadow remained—in language, art, and, most explicitly, in trade. Concentrating in urban enclaves, ethnic Chinese dominated key sectors of the economy as traders and investors. In good times these middlemen were considered essential, even positive, forces; at other times they stood as a hated and vulnerable minority, holding in their hands what all sought. In the Vietnam War they supplied the armies and the black market for a handsome profit. Moreover, the Hoa (ethnic Chinese) constituted the most visible bourgeois group of the old order.

Thus ethnic, historical, and ideological forces placed the ethnic Chinese at the target center of the Communist regime. The new economic plan destroyed private enterprise, the backbone of the ethnic Chinese economic superiority. Non-Hoa craftsmen and artisans were often left at their own trades, but not the ethnic Chinese; they were sent out of the cities to New Economic Zones to clear jungles and forests in forced-labor cadres. Communist officials cut their rations, curtailed their activities with special curfews, and closed down their schools. So determined was the new government to destroy this people that it willingly scattered a much-needed middle class of scientists, technicians, clerks, and professionals.

After a border war with China in February 1979, over two hundred thousand ethnic Chinese were pushed across the Chinese border; an even larger number chanced the sea. From one hundred fifty a month in early 1977 the number escaping by boat had risen to fifteen hundred. But after the China War as many as three thousand persons a day fled Vietnam. Vietnamese who had tried unsuccessfully to get out in the 1975 evacuation, those seeking to avoid the new draft, those disappointed in the new regime, those disaffected with the strapped economy, those who resented the forced expropriations, and those fishermen who still had boats joined the fleeing Chinese to form a floating population in the hundreds of thousands. To observers it seemed that Vietnam was hemorrhaging its people into the South China Sea in "floating coffins," while filling its treasury with millions in gold extracted as an emigration fee from these panicked masses.

Boat 0105 is an example of a fairly successful trip. It did not capsize and many of its passengers did in the end reach safety, but the experience was

Refugees converting the boat that took them safely out of Vietnam into a
temporary shelter. (*Courtesy UNHCR, Van Dongen*)

typically harrowing. By journey's end 0105 had an escort of sharks enticed
by the expired human cargo so regularly dumped overboard.

When it set out on April 4, 1979, 0105 bore sixty-six families, three
hundred eighty people, ethnic Chinese and a handful of Vietnamese, who
had paid off the local security agent to allow them to pass as Hoa and pay
the regular tariff to leave (only Chinese could emigrate legally). On April 6
the engine died and the ship bobbed its way frighteningly across the sea,

Nearly 75,000 Vietnamese came to Hong Kong as the place of first asylum in 1979. Hong Kong continued to allow the "boat people" to land even after her shores were overflowing with new arrivals. (*Courtesy Hong Kong Christian Service*)

signaling for help. Thai fisherman sighted the crippled junk and quickly lashed alongside. Bearing axes, knives, and pistols they clambered aboard. They took the men on their own boat and stripped them of all valuables. The women too were forced to give over necklaces, rings, and religious statues. While some pirates guarded the men on the Thai vessel, the marauders selected a group of young women aboard 0105 and in front of the old women and children, raped them. They then switched places with those on the other boat and the horror was repeated.

Twenty-three more times 0105 was boarded by Thais as it floated helplessly across the sea. Gold teeth, clothing, combs and blankets, almost anything of value, was removed. The last group of pirates, apparently touched by the pathetic sight, gave them some food and water. Passing freighters either did not see them or simply ignored them. Not until April 27, did a nearby ship take notice and tow them to the Malaysian coast. There they were confined to a holding camp and provided with essentials paid for by United Nations funds. They remained in this camp until June 17 when the overburdened Malaysians towed them out to sea and cut them loose. Six

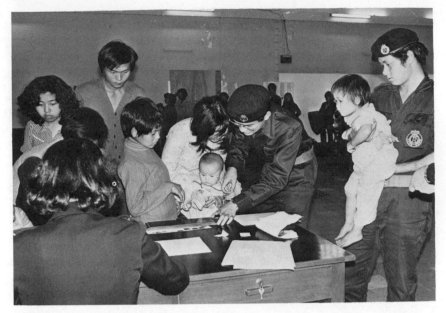

Authorities in Hong Kong joined with representatives of other cooperating
nations, volunteer agencies and the United Nations High Commissioner for
Refugees to help process the refugees into the temporary camps and to provide
their basic needs. (*Courtesy Hong Kong Christian Service*)

days later a friendly fishing boat pulled them into an Indonesian refugee
camp.

By mid-1979 an estimated 380,000 refugees were encamped in ram-
shackle centers in Malaysia, Thailand, Hong Kong, Indonesia, and Singapore. But these nations reached a breaking point. "We have no choice,"
said a spokesman for Singapore, "but to turn away hundreds of thousands
into the open sea to face certain death. Let's not humbug ourselves. We are
sending them to death. . . . The Vietnamese are compelling us to be as
barbaric as they are. . . ." So many suffered. So many died, so many were
violated in so many ways that the twentieth century's sharpest image of genocide came to mind. Sinnathamby Rajaratnam, Singapore's foreign minister, called the entire situation "the poor man's alternative to the gas cham-
bers." Wrote the editors of *The New Republic*:

> One would think that the experience of Hitler and the Holocaust would
> have innoculated the world against genocide, at least for the rest of this
> century. One would think that no national leader or regime, for as long as
> the memory of Nazi Germany remains vivid, would want to repeat its acts

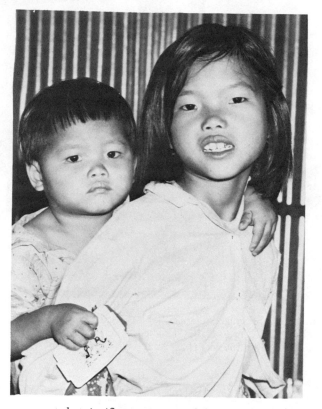

Children represented a significant segment of the Vietnamese migration. In the camps special classes and activities were set up for the youngsters. (*Courtesy Hong Kong Christian Service*)

and share its odious place in history. . . . But of course one would be wrong.

Malaysia sheltered the largest number of homeless Vietnamese. After 1975 it provided over 120,000 with temporary asylum on previously uninhabited islands. But with more than 75,000 still in the camps in mid-1979, the Malaysian government feared that the continuing stream of refugees would drain the economy and exacerbate ethnic tensions between Moslem Malays and the ethnic Chinese and Indians who made up half of the population. Then on June 15, Malaysia threatened to force all of its refugees back out to sea and to shoot any "invaders" on sight. Malaysia demanded that the rest of the world share the responsibility.

The plight of the encamped refugees and the boat people could not be

While in the camps refugees destined for America received training in "survival English" and went to classes designed to orient them to American culture. (*Courtesy Hong Kong Christian Service*)

ignored. In summer 1977 the United States opened 15,000 parole slots for an additional Indochinese influx, and several months later Congress approved a presidential request for 7,000 more. But, withal, America could not quit Vietnam, as the number of homeless continued to climb. Americans were bothered by the fact that other industrial nations seemed unwilling to shoulder some of the effort. As late as 1979, Japan, a nation that responded with generosity when it came to funding, underwriting 50 percent of the United Nations High Commissioner's costs for the Asian camps, accepted only three Vietnamese for permanent resettlement. Like most nations, Japan had little experience with multi-racial situations and feared the consequences of admitting new ethnic groups. Despite many imperfections in the relations between its various groups, the fact that the United States developed as an immigrant society, built by succeeding immigrant increments of widely varying nationalities, has made it less narrowly race and ethnicity conscious than most other nations. Sweeping around the globe one is struck by the regularity of national composition; most countries reflect one or two primary cultures and one dominant ethnic group. It is this group that identifies the national character. The notion of a multi-racial, multi-ethnic society, a country of many cultural nuclei, is not a global norm. Thus it might be difficult for a German or a Japanese to believe that Indochinese actually belong in his nation.

Of course, American generosity was praiseworthy only in relative terms. Opinion polls consistently showed more Americans opposed than supporting a liberal refugee program. Senator Strom Thurmond, given to much concern over such matters, counseled that "our nation . . . must weigh the cultural and demographic impact. . . ." A weekly newsmagazine published the following letter from a reader.

> I am sick, sick, sick of Vietnam, the boat people and Southeast Asia. How many Americans who are poor, elderly or disabled and living in our ghettos can buy their way out with gold? Instead of bringing in 14,000 Indochinese and spending half a billion dollars on them in a year, we should spend the money on our own refugees.

Others argued that the United States had a historical duty to heed the call of a stricken humanity. Writing on "The Moral Problem of Refugees," Michael Walzer pegged his demand for hospitality to a more specific point. "About one group of refugees, there can be no question. The boat people of Vietnam are our responsibility . . . They should be taken in quickly and ungrudgingly. . . . These people . . . are *our* Vietnamese, they are men and women who worked with us. . . . Or, . . . they are men and women who shaped their lives to the contours of the American presence—as merchants, journalists, doctors, miners, smugglers, prostitutes and so on. . . .

If they flee with images of California dancing in their heads . . . who put those images there? . . . [A] few hundred thousand more Vietnamese, easily absorbed, strong immigrants and . . . good citizens. . . . They will pay us back in lives for the lives we took, and the lives we lost, in their country. It is a moral bargain."

The worsening situation in Southeast Asia and in the South China Sea challenged a president who had made human rights a basis of his policy. On the anniversary of the United Nations Declaration of Human Rights, President Jimmy Carter said:

> Refugees are the living homeless casualties of our world's failure to live by the principles of peace and human rights. To help them is a simple human duty. As Americans, as a people made up largely of the descendants of refugees we feel that duty with a special keenness.
>   Our country will do its utmost. . . . I hope that we will always stand ready to welcome more than our fair share. . . .

Responding to the crisis, the United States pledged to double its quota admissions in June from 7,000 to 14,000 Indochinese a month and dispatched rescue craft to save those stranded on the high seas. In this way it sought to dramatize its own commitment and to encourage other countries to make similar moves.

The refugee situation made clear again that the United States had never systematically considered the complexities of refugee policy. Even on the definition of the term "refugee," itself, there has been no unanimity of opinion. At the height of the boat-people crisis, when Malaysia threatened to expel all refugees and shoot any new ones who tried to land, that nation labeled the hapless Vietnamese "invading illegal aliens." Moreover, Southeast Asians represented only a fraction of the world's homeless in this "century of refugees."

For the first time in history in 1979 the President appointed a special ambassador-at-large for refugees and Congress began holding hearings on a refugee act. Existing law defined refugees in narrowly political terms. Individuals fleeing Communist regimes or the Middle East qualified, while émigrés from right-wing governments, even dictatorships, did not. Moreover, those who fled poverty—"economic refugees"—were not recognized as a special class.

Chairman of the Senate Judiciary Committee Edward M. Kennedy took a strong position: "There are few greater tests of the democratic and humanitarian ideals for which we stand than how we respond to the needs of the world's displaced people."

On March 17, President Jimmy Carter signed into law the Refugee Act of 1980. Recognizing the impossibility of single-handed solutions to a steadily expanding global refugee crisis, the United States strove for reasonable generosity, to assume a fair share of the world's burden. In this effort Congress, for the first time, set a uniform policy for refugee admissions, putting an end to the erratic *ad hoc* approach of previous years. Congress defined "refugee" in basic conformity with the United Nations Convention and Protocol: "Any person outside his country, victimized by persecution on racial, religious, political or social grounds."

Critics argued that this definition made unfair distinctions, keeping out "economic refugees" from Haiti for example, although their distress was no less real for the fact that it was not overtly political.

Still, with many native Americans unemployed or making only marginal salaries, the United States was not prepared to throw open its portals to the world's underprivileged. If a line had to be drawn (Americans were certain that their nation could not accept all who wished to come), then offer asylum only to those who were aliens in their own countries. Economic distress was neither government induced nor sufficiently rare to make it a reasonable criterion for refugee status. Americans judged political, religious, and even racial (despite their own difficulties) persecution as critical violations of national rights. Life, liberty, and the pursuit of happiness were offered as man's inalienable rights when Thomas Jefferson penned the Declaration of Independence. It was to secure these rights that "Governments are instituted among men." Americans made no such claims for economic equality.

Beyond defining the term, the 1980 Refugee law set in place a flexible annual quota of 50,000, which could be increased for "grave humanitarian" reasons. The office of United States Coordinator of Refugee Affairs was made permanent, to serve as an advocate, coordinator, and representative before world bodies on the refugee issue. The law also established a list of basic entitlements, guaranteeing refugees help with settlement, transportation, language instruction, job training, and child care as well as medical, educational, vocational, and social services.

Although the new law grew out of a crisis half-a-world away, its immediate benefit went to boat people fleeing Cuba, scarcely ninety miles from the American mainland. Again Americans learned that a world ever-changing would create new and unpredictable refugee crises with unwelcome regularity.

In April of 1980, a group of disenchanted Cubans seeking asylum crashed into the Peruvian embassy with a truck, killing a Cuban guard in the process. This unlikely opening phase set off the Cuban refugee crisis of 1980 because Fidel Castro surprised all by announcing that Cubans wishing to emigrate were free to join this first group on the embassy grounds and leave from there. Thousands flocked to the compound and emigration fever soared.

At first the United States hesitated as it had done so often before. Then it moved almost grudgingly to deal with the crisis. Warming to the task, President Carter at one point promised to welcome all, only to cry "enough" as the numbers continued to grow.

Manipulating the movement to his own purposes, the Cuban premier, eager to filter off various elements of his island population, then declared that any citizen might leave if an American relative came to claim him. Florida's large Cuban-exile community jumped at the chance to bring out relatives and friends. Chartering anything resembling a seaworthy craft they rushed to Cuba's Mariel Port sinking their savings into this chance of a lifetime to bring out parents and relatives. By mid-May, 56,000 Cubans (among them a number of criminals whom, ship captains contended, Castro's officials forced them to take on board) had arrived. This crisis ended within fifty days but not before more than 114,000 new Cubans had come to the United States. Again the reception centers opened. Again sponsors came forth to initiate the newcomers and assist them into American society. And again Americans learned the burden and pride that came from hearing a recently arrived refugee say what so many voiced in similar words: "I come here and be free."

This idea of the American haven was as potent half-a-world away, in the miserable holding camps of Asia where, by 1980, fewer than 13,000 Indochinese still occupied Malaysia's Pulau Bidong island. Those that remained continued to talk of going west, of political freedom, of Cadillacs, of wanting "to go to America like everyone else," and their hopes appeared attainable. The United States, with 500,000 Indochinese already here, nonetheless, reserved a generous 160,000 slots for 1981. Only a few years earlier such numbers would have evinced a strong negative reaction among Americans but old fears about Asians and displaced persons had faded. The Vietnamese saying seemed appropriate: "The road is difficult not because it is blocked by a mountain or a river, it is difficult because people are afraid of the mountain or the river."

2

Don't Have My Papers Yet

Undocumented Aliens

Each year of the 1970s about 75,000 immigrants, their documents perfectly in order, arrived to live in New York City. They possessed most of the rights of citizens—the right to buy property, to open bank accounts, to enroll in schools, and to travel freely. Although they would not be allowed to vote or to serve on juries until they became citizens, in their other privileges and obligations they resembled native-born Americans.

Each year, a number of immigrants equal to or even greater than this 75,000 settled in New York under very different circumstances. They lacked immigrant status and were generally called "illegal aliens." Many American writers reject the term illegal alien to describe this special group of immigrants. Except, the writers argue, for the single act of either entering the United States without inspection or violating their visas by overstaying the time allotted, these people are among the most law-abiding residents of the country. Instead, writers refer to these people as "undocumented aliens." The term undocumented has not caught on, at least not with the people being referred to. They usually describe themselves as illegal or "don't have my papers yet," implying that their temporary illegal status will soon be righted. Journalists, government officials, and others also persist in applying "illegal alien" to a broad group of people living in the United States who have not obtained completely legal immigrant status.

No one knows for sure how many persons without legal immigrant status currently reside in the United States. In the late 1970s estimates ran no lower than 3 million and as high as 30 million, with 7 million being the most frequently cited figure. Estimates came from a variety of sources: from Immigration Service agents, who based their estimates on the number of apprehensions they had made during the past decade; from New York City

71

Department workers, who investigated the high use of water in low-come apartment buildings and found that these buildings housed many illegal aliens in addition to listed residents; and from teachers, social workers, and employers who were most likely to come into contact with the illegal-alien community. In New York, the currently accepted number is 750,000, or 1 in every 10 people. Whatever the total, there is no doubt that the number of illegal aliens in the country has increased gradually but remarkably and for a variety of reasons.

When the United States moved in the 1920s to limit immigration, it did not succeed in stopping the flow, only in putting off the more timid. Many people facing delays of a dozen years or more, along with those given very little hope of ever entering the United States legally, refused to be stopped. They simply found other means. Some jumped ship or sneaked across borders at night. Others forged documents. Many simply failed to fill out the necessary forms although they qualified for admission. No one knew the total number of people who circumvented the laws.

By the time the national-origins quotas were dropped in 1965, the magnetism of the United States no longer worked as it once had to draw immigrants from across the Atlantic. The Lady of Liberty in New York's harbor still faced east, toward Europe, but for many of the country's new arrivals their first sight of America was the Golden Gate Bridge. For others, the trip was neither east nor west but north. Again in the 1970s, the pattern repeated itself so that by 1976 almost 40 percent of the immigrants to the United States came from Latin America, another 38 percent from Asia.

The contracting of the world's distances and the increased power of individuals to shape their own lives, at least as far as their country of residence was concerned, had immense repercussions on American immigration. Half a century earlier, a *contadino* leaving Italy relied on a network of runners and contractors to provide him with the papers, services, and job necessary for his emigration. For a woman, arrangements were made even more cautiously. By the 1960s a high school graduate in any of a dozen Latin American countries could walk into a travel agency and lay down cash. Her information about America as well as her funds had come, most likely, from friends, family, and newspapers. Although she could have qualified for an immigrant visa, she did not bother. A tourist visa would get her into the United States and, because the price of international travel had fallen relative to a day's wages, even this young woman of modest means could pass herself off as a tourist though her real intention was to acquaint herself with a series of American paychecks. A few hours later she might step off a plane at John F. Kennedy Airport, walk to a telephone, and report that she had arrived. Within hours she could settle into a New York apartment with relatives, without having given much thought to the shrinking of the world's distances or to the revolution in education and communication that had eased her move, one that her grandmother could not even have considered.

With such easy travel, men and women who could not qualify for legal entry or who did not wish to take the time to comply with bureaucratic requirements considered other ways. Some continued to use old strategies of stowing away or crossing borders without inspection, but many others entered with legitimate tourist or student visas, fully intending at the time to overstay their allotted time or deciding to do so later on. Immigration officials distinguished between the two groups: "EWI" (Entry Without Inspection) and Overstays.

Easy travel and fast communications have complicated the assignment of the Immigration and Naturalization Service border officials; nonetheless these officials report having made more than 200 million inspections each year in the 1970s. Of the 10 million people who were not returning crewmen, military personnel, or people crossing land borders, two-thirds were citizens returning from business or pleasure trips, some making several such journeys each year. The other third were aliens, most of whom had a legal right to enter—as tourists, businessmen, students, or as legally established residents of the United States. Only about 400,000 declared themselves immigrants, leaving INS officials with the hard job of deciding who of the others had that intention. Even when suspicions were aroused, action was difficult to take. New York City's Planning Commission reported an amazingly thriving tourism from Barbados—about 8 percent of the island's population had visited New York within a six-year period. Nobody knew how many had returned. Nor did anyone know how to find out.

New York's illegal alien population came predominantly from overstays—people who entered with tourist or student permits that provided for a few weeks stay, usually with relatives or friends who accepted financial responsibility. Lacking such sponsors, a visa holder could show a return ticket and a significant sum of money as evidence that he planned to go back to his home country. In the case of a student, he demonstrated proof of acceptance and enrollment at a college and promised to leave at the end of his studies.

In the Southwestern United States, the problem was different—that of, entries without inspection. Each year hundreds of thousands of Mexican men crossed the border to pick grapes, harvest grain, and do seasonal gardening. Mexican women worked as nursemaids, domestics, and seamstresses in Texas, Arizona, and southern California. Those apprehended and deported returned within days. "I know a little clothing factory," one Los Angeles garment cutter said, "where they rounded up 21 illegals one night and sent them back to Mexico. The next week 19 of them were back working in the same place." The result: Los Angeles, the city whose history and name

The U.S.-Mexican border is one of the most often crossed boundaries in the world. Of the millions who cross it annually many do so without legal sanction. (*Courtesy Center for Migration Studies, Mark Day*)

suggested a mission to the homeless, has the highest number of illegal aliens of any city in the country. Almost all (97 percent in 1970) of the deportable aliens apprehended and sent out of the country were Mexicans, some of them making many trips back and forth and being counted and recounted each time. "Of course they're going to keep coming," the Los Angeles clothing cutter explained. "Without the Mexicans, our factory would have to shut down. If they don't find a way to get across, we'll help them."

In the East, entry without inspection occurred less frequently but the Vermont border attracted people who saw it as relatively unguarded, providing easy access to several large cities, especially New York. Smugglers were tempted by Route 91, running from Canada's super highway down through Vermont to Hartford, Connecticut. From Route 91, other roads spiraled out to major industrial centers. From Hartford, New York was a short ride

Raids against undocumented workers aim to round up and deport those who are found without proper papers. These raids have become a sensitive issue with Mexicans, both in the United States and south of the border. Here young Mexican Americans demonstrate against raids. (*Courtesy Center for Migration Studies, Mark Day*)

away. Success in crossing undetected, however, was not assured. Hidden devices could touch off alarms and alert officers to suspicious vehicles, thwarting many attempts.

New York City's hundreds of thousands of illegal aliens cited a variety of reasons for remaining beyond the expiration of their permits. Lorna Mor-

gan, for example, worked as a nursemaid for a family on Manhattan's West
End Avenue. Five years earlier in Montego Bay she had met a vacationing
Jamaican journalist, a permanent American resident. Thinking they had an
agreement to marry, she applied for a tourist visa to follow him to New
York. They shared an apartment on the Upper West Side although marriage
had to wait, she learned, until his divorce became final. Before the granting
of that decree, he died in an automobile accident. Lorna Morgan stayed on
in New York, an illegal alien, reluctant to return to Jamaica and face family
and friends who believed she had come north to marry a successful man.

Felipe Gonzalez represented another kind of case. Although he entered
as a tourist in 1969 his real reason for leaving his native Honduras was more
political. As a broadcast journalist he had so loudly criticized the government that wisdom dictated his going. Though not exactly a refugee, he did
not want to consider returning to Honduras. In New York he married a
Puerto Rican woman. Because she was a U.S. citizen, he qualified to apply
for permanent residence as her husband. Years passed, however, and Felipe
Gonzalez failed to file the necessary papers. When the marriage ended several years later, he became an undocumented alien.

The case of Mrs. Sus McCready reached the city's newspapers when her
husband, an American citizen and actor, was killed on a Greenwich Village
street while struggling with a mugger. His widow, who was waiting for permission to stay in the United States after coming here from her native Denmark, was told she had to leave since her reason for staying (to be with her
husband, an American citizen) no longer existed. A few months later the
decision was reversed (due perhaps largely to press coverage of her story) and
she was allowed to remain in New York.

The document that legitimized residence in the United States for non-
citizens was a small blue and white laminated card, officially designated the
alien registration receipt card but generally referred to as the green card. On
one side appeared the holder's name, registration number, date of birth,
place and date of entry into the country. The other side exhibited a photograph of the individual and gave the recipient instructions for registering
each year with immigration authorities. At the bottom, a clear warning: "If
18 years of age or older, you are required by law to have this card with you
at all times." Legally, 4.5 million of these cards were in use. Nobody knew
the number of fraudulent copies produced for sale. In April 1979, a Dominican was arrested in New York for printing and selling green cards for one
thousand dollars each. Officials estimated that he had trafficked one
hundred of them each month.

Such operations were not new. At the 1972 hearings of the House Subcommittee on Immigration, Congressman Peter Rodino examined examples
of counterfeit green cards and pronounced them "pretty sophisticated . . .

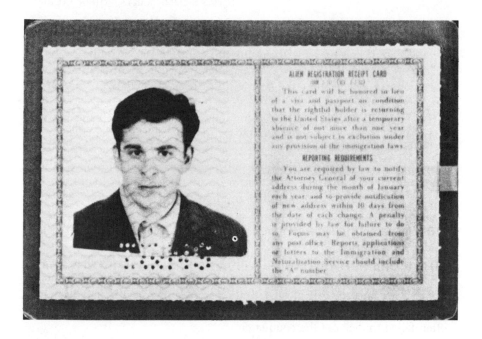

A Green Card

not being produced by real amateurs." Maurice F. Kiley, then deputy district director of Immigration, testified that the alien registration receipt cards were selling at that time for up to one thousand dollars. Printing could be accomplished on simple presses, Kiley noted, but the sophistication of the operation depended on the duplication of a special "safety paper" imported from outside the country.

As Kiley compared samples of authentic and fraudulent cards for the committee's inspection, he noted how difficult detection of the fakes could be—a wrong shadow here, a jagged edge there. Except to the very careful observer, such differences remained imperceptible. For employers who saw the cards only occasionally, detection was extremely unlikely. In at least one case, a major New York bank hired an alien in a responsible position after he had shown a green card as proof of residence. Later, bank officials were surprised when immigration officials pointed out features that marked the card as fraudulent.

Because inspectors at ports of entry were fooled less easily than people who saw the cards infrequently, men and women carrying false documents mixed with large crowds at busy times in order to pass through with less scrutiny. In the hurry and confusion, even a highly trained investigator often failed to pick out the counterfeit.

Although some forgeries were obvious fakes, purchasers were duped into buying them anyway. One illegal alien, contacted by a "runner" to look at samples of green cards before buying one, was satisfied with the cards he examined (they were authentic documents). He handed over seven hundred dollars and got photographed. A few days later, he received his own card in the mail, his picture carefully attached to a transparent fake, so poor even his untrained eyes detected irregularities. He and others duped in such schemes were obviously reluctant to testify against forgers, even where they possessed hard evidence. In addition, most often they knew neither names nor addresses.

Instead of purchasing green cards, some illegal aliens obtained them through marriage to an American citizen or legal resident. A bona fide marriage carried the promise of permanent residence, but lacking such a prospect an illegal alien might enter into a green card marriage, performed precisely for the purpose of gaining legal residence. A Chicago notary public was convicted of arranging 11 sham marriages for one thousand dollars each (he admitted responsibility for 673 others); a New York attorney charged less—six hundred dollars for arranging matrimony between Africans and American citizens. In the latter operation, the legal spouse collected four hundred dollars from the illegal alien but increased his or her profits by going through several ceremonies, each under a different alias. The New York immigration office reported investigating 469 marriages as suspicious and finding two-thirds of them having been performed for the sole purpose of circumventing the law.

Such marriages often complicated the life of an alien rather than solving his problem. The spouse might disappear, even before exchanging the necessary papers (but not before collecting a few hundred dollars). The remaining spouse was left to prove to inquiring officials that the marriage had actually occurred and, more important, that it was sincerely motivated rather than simply for the purpose of obtaining residency. One young woman paid five hundred dollars to marry a Dominican whom she had never seen before the ceremony (and would never see after). She complained: "Really he just took my money and that was all. I don't even think he had a green card himself but the people who set it up told me he did. That was five years ago. I was young and scared. I didn't know what to do so I married him. He immediately disappeared. If I'm really married to him, I want a divorce because I've met somebody else. But maybe I'm not even married. And I can't find him to find out."

Often the citizenship documentation was legitimate but not for the person who held it. An intricate scheme to produce such papers involved going through obituaries in old newspapers to find the name of an individual who was born in the United States at about the same time as the alien but who had died in infancy. Since American birth records were available to very nearly anyone (if required, the mother's and father's name appeared in the obituary), the alien could acquire the birth certificate of the deceased simply by writing to the home county. The issuing office often had no way of knowing that the child died (even with that information, it still issued the document since relatives might need it to complete a family history or for some other legitimate reason). Once the illegal had the birth certificate, he could apply for a social security card and other documents, taking on the name of the deceased person. Most illegal aliens lacked the sophistication in dealing with American bureaucracies to carry out this complicated and potentially risky scheme but entrepreneurs set up profitable businesses in false documents, particularly in Southwestern United States, where a Spanish accent was not remarkable in a native-born American.

Only the truly desperate or the audacious made such arrangements for bogus documents. Most of New York's illegals played a waiting game, hoping something or someone would come along to legitimize their stay before they got caught. Many avoided detection for years. If the dreaded moment came, they planned to appeal for help and mercy while they devised ways to delay their departure.

Fear of deportation did not preoccupy many undocumented aliens. The backlog of persons involved, the number of apprehensions, and the cost of legal action in any one case rendered chances of deportation very low, especially in New York. During 1972 congressional subcommittee hearings, officials from the New York INS office admitted receiving about 175 leads a day. Because of a small staff (only about eighty field agents), a backlog of 44,000 cases had built up. From this large reserve, the Immigration and Naturalization Service had deported only a few thousand each year.

An attorney who handled immigration cases, explained: "I don't always tell this to the people who come in but it's true. You're not going to get deported unless you've gotten into a whole lot of trouble. You ask for a delay, a stay. Argue the case. Put it off." He did not bother to list the people who profited from prolonging the process but they included the employer, who got cheap labor, the landlord, who gouged on rent, and even the lawyer himself, whose bill in most cases ran into thousands of dollars even though he never promised success. "Can't promise anything," he said "except time. Buy me—you're buying time."

High legal fees remained a common complaint of illegals. One young Irish woman, her legal residency still in the gray area, objected: "I've been in New York nine years. You know where my money has gone—to dentists and lawyers. The dental work I got done at New York University, so it was cheaper than it might have been, but lawyers! I don't even know how much it's been. I'm afraid to add it up. Seven hundred dollars once, a thousand another. And once you've talked to one of them you've got to keep paying. They've got everything on you—can call the INS anytime. You pay them first."

A Latin American journalist emerged from a tangled immigration history with large bills: "Now I'm married to a legal U.S. citizen and I'm pretty safe but you can't imagine the things that pile up on you when you're in a country illegally for seven years. All sorts of violations—taxes, forged documents, those things. Once you've opened your life to a lawyer, you're over the barrel, as you Americans say. My bill is thousands of dollars and I'm paying it a little bit at a time. Along with a big hospital bill. Four years ago I needed surgery. No hospitalization insurance. You can imagine the bill. Of course I wasn't filing income tax returns (although taxes were being withheld from my pay) so I didn't get any break there. I keep paying. Maybe one day I'll have them both paid off—the hospital and the lawyer."

The daily life of an undocumented alien included difficulties not easily imagined by an American citizen or legal resident. One young South American told the following story: "I was sharing an apartment with a girl—somebody I met in evening class. We hadn't talked much about marriage. She was an American citizen—legal—but we didn't even talk about a green card marriage. Neither of us wanted to feel forced into anything. One day her handbag was stolen with her keys, wallet, credit cards, everything while she was eating lunch in a midtown restaurant. She had left it on the chair beside her or something and somebody just walked off with it. So the first thing she did was call the landlady—who lived downstairs below our apartment—to say what had happened and to tell her to look out for burglars. Then she called me at work to see if I could go over and change the lock before they got there to clean us out. I went right then, bought a new lock and straight to the apartment to install it. The landlady heard me and called the police. When they found me messing around with the lock, they thought they had the burglar and the landlady was no help at all. Since I wasn't legally living there—Lisa had taken the apartment in her name alone—the landlady didn't know me. Well, I thought to myself, I've got to get out of this before they take me down to the police station and start asking for my papers. So I said, 'Let me call Lisa. She'll tell you I'm okay.' I dial her office number and right there in front of the police I have to talk English, right? We always spoke Spanish between us but I didn't want to make them suspicious. So I said in my best English, 'Lisa, tell this man who I am.' I must have been scared too, my voice was very low pitched, and that plus the English—Lisa didn't recognize me! But I didn't know that so I passed the phone to the policeman and you can imagine the rest. She started asking him what I looked like! I guess she was upset and confused about the bag being stolen. Well finally we straightened it out and the police left without asking for my papers, but you know how I sweated."

Round-ups of undocumented aliens at subway stations occurred infrequently in the late 1970s but rumors of large numbers of illegals working in the city's restaurants and small factories encouraged raids. Although employers could protect themselves by hiring carefully, asking for documents and reporting all income as taxed, many avoided such legalities for their own gain and convenience. Forgetting to file social security reports came easily. Job applicants were often quite open about working "off the books." Such arrangements benefited others besides aliens, including housewives and college students who planned to work for a short time and did not wish to bother with filing for tax refunds due them at the end of the year. Cleaning women, nannies, and live-in companions for the elderly frequently preferred to take less rather than assume the responsibilities of working "on the books." In small businesses, it was the rare employer who refused. One housewares merchant, operating a shop in Queens near the city's largest center of illegal aliens, recalled: "I advertised for an assistant. Somebody to help with the stock and do general work. Got this call from some guy who openly admitted on the telephone that he didn't have papers. Sounded surprised when I told him I wasn't interested. Acted like everybody did it."

Newspapers frequently carried details of raids on establishments that hired illegals or were suspected of doing so. Some accounts offered scenes for situation comedies. During inspection of a fashionable East Side restau-

rant, everything appeared in order and satisfied immigration officers prepared to leave. Suddenly a ceiling over the bar collapsed, yielding nine men
in kitchen aprons—all illegal aliens.

Another restaurant across town employed a manager at five hundred
dollars a week. As immigration officials arrived, he passed a word around
that sent the entire kitchen crew scurrying down a concealed back stairway.
Only a slow-moving kitchen boy was caught. As he was led away in handcuffs no one lingered to check the manager's papers—he too lacked legal
documents.

Although restaurants and factories proved the most common targets for
raids, other catches made news: inspections of the kitchen crew at West
Point's Military Academy and of men painting the Statue of Liberty yielded
illegals. On the West coast, an undocumented alien tended former President Nixon's garden while others manufactured toys in a plant owned by a
former cabinet member.

Common methods of avoiding apprehension were passed on from one
person to another. One Ecuadoran said that a priest advised him to carry an
English newspaper, preferably the *Daily News*, each day when he went to
his job at a clothing factory near Broadway and 14th Street. In case of a
raid, he and his co-workers were instructed to dive into piles of clothes or to
go hide in the toilets. One man had hidden in a freezer for twenty minutes
during a search.

The Ecuadoran, who carried the *Daily News* he could not read, and his
wife had left their native country with visas citing her need to get medical
attention for a lung condition; when their visas expired, the couple stayed
on. At their backbreaking jobs in a dusty factory, they gave little hint of the
lives they left behind: he had worked for the government and she, a graduate
of a private school, had been a laboratory technician. "The price of tickets
to New York makes immigration a luxury of the middle class," he explained, "but once we're here, we'll do anything to stay."

"Do anything to stay," was a frequently uttered phrase among New
York's illegals. A young Colombian woman appeared at her job in a city
hospital after a week's absence with this story: "I've been sitting home waiting for my cousin to come back. He came here on a tourist visa—my husband and I signed for him. But I felt responsible for him. We had told his
parents we'd look out for him—he's only 17. When his time was up, he
wanted an extension so we got him one. Then he immediately disappeared.
Has our housekeys and everything. I think he's gone to live with someone
up in Harlem but I don't even know the man's last name. Now I don't
know what to do—write to the boy's parents or give him some more time to
come back. He'd do anything to stay."

Many illegal aliens believed that large rewards awaited informers, an impression nourished by rather ominous sounding recordings that New York's immigration office played to callers. The same office designed a poster, headed "The Immigration Service needs your Help," which aimed to enlist the help of police officers. It read: "If an alien comes to your attention who appears to be in an illegal status, or if you wish further information, you are requested to telephone or wire collect to the following address. . . ." The size of the awards was greatly exaggerated since the INS spent only forty thousand dollars or so on rewards in any one year, and individual payments exceeding one hundred dollars required authorization from Washington. The average payment in the Southwestern United States was only about fifty dollars, but some informants earned parole status rather than money.

To undocumented New Yorkers even casual threats nourished real fear. One young woman living in Queens illegally for two years told about breaking up with a boyfriend: "You know what he said to me? His last words when I told him we were finished? He said, 'Just wait till I tell Immigration.' I didn't think he'd really do it but I didn't know how angry he was or how mad he might get the next day. One of my friends got a call from a friend who accused her of borrowing a couple of records and not giving them back. My friend said she had never had the records but that didn't help. Then the other woman said, 'See that I get them back or I'll tell you know who.' My friend knew exactly who she meant so she went out and bought the records and took them over. Figured it was easier that way than running the risk of getting turned in. It's used like that a lot—blackmail in little things. I don't suppose one-in-a-hundred really goes through with the threat but you never know so you're careful."

Large immigration and easy amnesty for violators found a variety of supporters in the 1970s. Employers praised illegals' docility and their acceptance of low wages; humanitarians and patriots pointed to the country's long history as a place of opportunity and refuge. When native workers objected to the job competition that illegal aliens posed, defenders pointed out that the illegal entered at the bottom, took the worst jobs and pushed others, who got here earlier, up into better jobs. Some observers explained the persistence of underground immigration, even in times of high unemployment, by the dual market theory that saw two supplies of laborers. One market carried much lower status and pay, too low to attract a native population that had access to various income transfer programs. In this view, illegals did not take jobs from the native work force; they filled slots that no one else would consider—as porters, dishwashers, live-in maids, pieceworkers in factories. Without illegals, this view held, the jobs would remain unfilled.

The opposition countered that only a limited number of jobs and services were available. When these went to people without legal immigrant status, fewer opportunities remained for citizens and legal residents. To add to the strain they put on the American economy, many men and women working without documents in the United States maintained families in their home countries. Each month the remittances they sent out contributed to the country's dollar drain. Congressman Peter Rodino estimated in the early 1970s that one billion dollars left the country each year in the form of remittances from illegal aliens, an excessive drain he felt, when added to the sums sent out by legal resident aliens.

The most serious objection to illegal aliens was raised by those who saw the illegal in competition with a specially needy segment of American society—those workers with few skills or little education. Edwin T. Redding, U.S. Labor Department, testified in 1972 that aliens took jobs for which qualified applicants were available in the local labor force and that this hiring cut across job lines from the largest factories to the neighborhood barber shop. Redding pinpointed the greatest damage:

> Such employment [of illegal aliens] is concentrated primarily in the service, trade and other low wage industries and at the lower end of the occupational scale. Here they provide serious competition to American citizens who are unskilled and uneducated. It is this same group of citizens that the government is addressing itself to with its billion dollar manpower programs. Thus, these aliens are seriously affecting the Department's efforts to upgrade the skills of the United States labor force and to improve and protect the working conditions of the American worker. Our experience in operating a wide range of manpower programs leads us to conclude that these aliens take jobs which would normally be filled by American citizens or resident aliens, depress wages and impair working conditions, increase the burden on American taxpayers through added welfare costs—not only by getting on welfare rolls but also by taking jobs which could be filled by U.S. citizens already on welfare. . . . [They] constitute for employers an unskilled group, ripe for exploitation—aggressive, enterprising workers with low wage demands and with few if any complaints about working conditions.

Redding suggested that legislation be passed to penalize employers who knowingly hired aliens in violation of their visa status as well as recruiters who transported such workers.

Sanctions against employers had been suggested earlier in the Nixon Administration but at that time businessmen objected that such a law would place unreasonable demands on them by holding them responsible for upholding a law so easily violated. One employer explained: "If a Spanish-speaking applicant comes in, how do I know if he is a legal U.S. citizen from Puerto Rico, or an immigrant who has naturalized, or an illegal? I can't unless I ask for some proof. A card. If a resident alien has to show it, so does the Puerto Rican and so does the naturalized. I won't hire without it. Not with the risk of a fine for every illegal I hire. You see the outcome—everybody would have to carry a card—the citizen as well as the resident alien. Who wants that kind of police state?"

Other objections toward illegal aliens arose from their use of services. In 1974 a Human Resources administrator in New York reported on the results of an examination of 370 illegal aliens who had been apprehended. While holding more than 1.4 million dollars in assets, they had collected half a million dollars in welfare benefits. If this small sample was typical, the city's outlay for welfare to illegals reached 100 million dollars annually. Additional monies went for educating their children, although school funds came largely from outside the city. One New York newspaper blamed illegals for breaking the city's hospitals by ignoring their bills. The director of Elmhurst Hospital in Queens County, where many illegals lived, reported in 1979 a deficit of 5 million dollars caused by unpaid medical bills, the bulk of which he attributed to accounts of illegal aliens. City officials estimated a total cost to New York of between 3 and 30 million dollars annually for unpaid medical bills.

Observers listed the other ways illegals cost the city. Because they were not counted and their earnings were omitted from those of New York's population, income and tax reports (which formed the basis for allocations from Washington) were distorted. Mrs. Evelyn Mann of the City Planning Commission estimated in 1979 that the inclusion of 750,000 illegals in the city's population would entitle the city to 20 million dollars a year in revenue sharing, another 9 million in countercyclical aid, 3 million in community development block grants, and an unspecified amount in Title 20 aid.

Into the 1980s, debate continued over undocumented aliens. Their backers (church groups, unions, and ethnic organizations) testified before congressional committees, appeared on national television, and wrote articles in support of their views. Many of those defending undocumented aliens urged sympathetic treatment for them, particularly those who had lived in the country for several years, raised families here, and led productive lives.

Opposing voices came through as less organized but very angry. One letter to *The New York Times* vented a father's resentment that his son could not find a job because of the competition from illegal aliens. Headlines in the same newspaper in 1979 read: "Woodside Rages Over Influx of Illegal Aliens." One man from Woodside volunteered his own opinion about the newcomers: "Send them back where they came from. . . . This is a law-abiding country. We just don't like the illegals."

Into the debate over illegal aliens, many people threw possible solutions. Early in his presidency, Jimmy Carter admitted that the country's immigration policy needed overhauling and he suggested a three-part approach. The first would legalize the status of anyone who had resided in the United

States for several years if during that time he had acted in a responsible, law-abiding way. The second part provided for putting more recent immigrants (those entering illegally after January 1, 1970) into a special category that permitted them to remain in the country while their numbers and impact on the economy were assessed. They would live in a kind of gray area, a limbo, no longer outside the law once they had registered but still without a legal right to remain in the country indefinitely. Because their role in the economy could not be evaluated, Carter noted, until more information was available, getting them to register seemed the first step to responsible action. The third part of Carter's plan entailed economic sanctions for anyone employing an illegal alien—a one-thousand-dollar fine for every one hired.

Three young women sit around a coffee table in a Greenwich Village apartment. They range in age from twenty-two to thirty and all three work as nursemaids for young children. Bertha, the youngest, wears jeans and running shoes, the uniform of her New York age group. Mary and Ann are older, both dressed in skirts and cardigans similar to those worn by the Upper East Side women for whom they work. Although they grew up within thirty miles of each other, near Cork, Ireland, they met in New York. They see each other infrequently for a drink or dinner but they share a great deal: they are all illegal aliens.

Bertha, who lives with a doctor's family in Queens, arrived in New York in 1976. After graduating in 1973 from a Cork school she left her family and went to London where she worked in a restaurant. Four years later, having returned to Cork for two more years, she came to America. Bertha explains her many moves casually, as though they were to be expected: "I stayed in Ireland nearly two years. Just to show I could do it. I was a taxi base operator—dispatched taxis to people who called in. Funny thing I didn't know much about driving around Cork—always had to get out my old map to tell them where to go. But I got along all right. I had a job. I think I decided to come to America more because of my dad than anyone else. He always talked about wanting to go to America. He never did. But I got a tourist visa and came over. That was two years ago. Nobody ever checked to see if I left when I was supposed to. Got a job. They treat me okay. Will I stay? That depends. Should I be so lucky as to meet somebody in the next year or so that I want to spend my life with—fine. I'll stay here. I'm not one of those people who suffer from homesickness. If I don't meet somebody, I'll fly my wings and take off for someplace else. Doesn't need to be Irish I marry. I've been told, 'Stick with your own kind,' but I don't know. I'm friendly now with an Eastern Orthodox. If he could offer me a good life, I might marry. I've got plenty of time. I guess that's the way I feel about life—I've got plenty of time to do whatever I want."

Mary, seated beside Bertha, speaks more quietly and less enthusiastically. Part of an informal network that finds work for newly arrived Irish immigrant women, she passed her old job on to Bertha when she decided to find her own apartment. After four years in New York, with only one trip back to Ireland, Mary knows the city well. Her accent is almost American.

"I came on a two-month vacation in 1975. Met this doctor and he offered me a job with his family. I wasn't really looking, at least not very hard. He was never very concerned that I was illegal. Said if it bothered me, I should go down to the Bowery, get some guy, pay him a thousand dollars to marry me. People from Mexico might go for that but not us. Our religion's a bit stronger. There are implications later. If you decide to marry, your husband might not believe that nothing happened between the two of you.

"I can't complain about how I've been treated. Nobody ever refused to pay me what they owed me or anything like that. I was threatened once by somebody. I was working for this family—taking care of their children—and we went to the country for a weekend. Well, I didn't care for it and then they told me I would have to spend the summer there. I told them I wouldn't go and the man threatened to turn me in to Immigration. I guess he thought I was threatening him—to leave his children—so he threatened me.

"Of course the people who hire you—they're outside the law too—but they cover their tracks. The threat for us depends on how much we have to lose. If you just say, 'It doesn't matter, I've had my time here, and there are plenty of countries to go to,' then there's no threat. But if you feel strongly about staying, it means more.

"When I came in with a tourist visa four years ago, they asked me how long I wanted to stay. I said, 'Make it a couple of weeks because I have to get back to my teaching job in Cork.' Of course it wasn't true but I knew they wouldn't check. Really they're not very diligent.

"A funny thing happened when my parents came to visit. I told them to give the name of a friend. I didn't think they should say they were visiting their daughter. Somebody might start asking questions or something. By that time I had overstayed my visa by about two years and I was working. My parents were tourists, of course, and were planning to take one of those Greyhound bus tours of New England after they visited me. Well, when the immigration officer asked who they were visiting, my parents forgot my friend's last name. They had never met her. So they said, 'Oh it's Teresa somebody on 85th Street.' Can you imagine? But the immigration officer just said, 'Well, be sure you have enough money,' and he let them go. It all depends on keeping cool—you have to keep cool."

Ann, the oldest of the three, nods agreement and begins to tell of a friend whose lack of composure doomed her: "She was coming in from Ireland to work for a family. Everything had been arranged through friends—she even carried a letter in her bag from the family who was hiring her, giving all the details of the job. She must have felt guilty and showed it or maybe Immigration questions thoroughly every tenth person or something. Anyway, they started in on her and she broke down and cried. Even showed the letter. Well, she was on the next plane back to Ireland. It was too bad—for her and for the family because they were counting on her.

"When I went back to Ireland for a visit, I really was afraid I wouldn't get back in to the States, so I made sure I had my return ticket and plenty of money for a two-week stay. That's all I asked for—just two weeks. That way, they don't get suspicious.

"What makes all this possible is the passport system. They stamp when you enter but not when you leave. So all my passport showed was that I came to New York once in 1972. Didn't say I left in 1976. If they asked, I was prepared to say I stayed only two weeks in 1972 but they never even asked.

"The secret really is in acting like what you're doing is all right. I remember I went right into a bank and opened an account. Nobody told me I couldn't and I had a little money with me. Opened a savings account. When they asked me for my social security number, I just said, 'Oh I don't have that yet,' and they didn't blink an eye. Just said to bring it in when I got it. Same thing when I went to get a driver's license. Took the test like everybody else and got a license. Nobody asked me to prove where I was born. Course if you didn't speak English, you might have a bit more trouble. Or if you're black, that's probably very different."

The three Irish women seemed very comfortable, not frightened or even furtive as they discussed openly offers made them of green cards and jobs, even though they were speaking in front of people they had never seen before. They appeared not to have considered carefully the disadvantages of their status, or if they had, they remained unconcerned.

While some blacks talked freely with white interviewers about illegals, others were reluctant. A Haitian student, questioned about illegals from her country, drew back quickly and answered that she knew none at all. A Trinidadian schoolteacher, employed "off the books" as a domestic in Brooklyn, volunteered to talk about her situation then failed to show up for the appointment. "You never know," a young Jamaican explained, "You're probably honest and I would like to help, but I better not."

Few of the illegal aliens who talked about their own problems went beyond their individual cases to consider the larger problem of American policy. They saw their own needs, valued their own contributions to the country, and argued that they should be admitted—as an exception, if necessary. Of those who saw their plight as part of a larger picture, many were Haitians, and their story aroused particular sympathy and controversy.

After 1959, more than 200,000 people fled Haiti and perhaps half settled illegally in the United States. The poverty and the political repression they escaped threatened their lives so that they felt they qualified for admission as political refugees. After risking their lives in small boats to reach the Florida coast, they faced American immigration officials who, they said, treated them like criminals. "It's unfair," one of them argued. "While hundreds of thousands of Cubans are granted asylum from a Communist regime, no one listens to us about a rightist dictatorship."

Others who criticized American policy on immigration included the more articulate from all countries. José Lopez Rivera, thirty-five years old, lived in a brownstone on Manhattan's Upper West Side. Spanish was the principal language of the household, which included three other men, each of whom spoke excellent English also. The others aspired to acting careers; during José's interview, one of these three who shared the house reported that he had just gotten an assignment to do a commercial in Spanish and another left to audition for a play. José had no such ambitions—he indulged his interest in photography in a darkroom he had converted from an attic on the top floor. He spent his days taking pictures of New York, hoping to market them as postcards. Thoughtful and articulate, he told his story:

"I came to the United States July 31, 1978. From France. New York was later, at the end of October. The idea is this: I was born in Spain—Seville. I left there in 1967 and moved to France. I was very unhappy in Spain. Life was very unpleasant. No joys. All kinds of restrictions. Moral restrictions. Political restrictions. No time for fun. I thought about going to Australia but I was never convinced that life was very attractive there.

"First I went to France (Strasbourg) and I was a student for about a year. Then I married and started to work. Because I married a French woman I had no problems—this is one of the big differences between France and the United States. A totally different approach they have. In France, every two years you have to get approval to stay. They give it automatically if you are married to a French citizen, but still you have to get constant approval. In the United States, it's only once. Then that's it.

"I worked for the same company for eight years and then it started to go. They were laying off people. The situation in France was very bad. Very, very depressing. My wife and I got a divorce. I had nothing in France but my family—we had a son—and my job. After my divorce I realized with no

In Haiti extreme poverty and political repression have encouraged people to leave. This scene helps document Haiti's claim to the title of the "poorest country in the western hemisphere." (*Courtesy Center for Migration Studies, Michelle Bogre*)

job and no family, I had no reason to stay. I had always wanted to come to America but my wife never wanted to.

"I was sure about America because I could see what America could do. In electronics, for example. My field. I was trained in France to be an electronics engineer. I could see what tremendous progress America has made. Or in photography—because I'm an amateur photographer. You can see the pull America had for me. I don't know whether the average middle-class European person realizes what America really is. They hear so much political rubbish about how America controls everything. It scares people. But I never took it very seriously. Freedom was most important in why I came here. Freedom, that's the word. Freedom in everything. It doesn't look like I made a mistake. I don't think I will ever go back to any other place.

"I came into the United States on a visitor's permit. Good for one month. You can get an extension. How do you do this? Well, people say you go to INS and show a return ticket to prove your intentions are good and you say you want to stay another month or six weeks. They almost always give it to you. But I didn't do this. I was very confused, even about what I wanted to do here. I had signed up before I came here to attend New Mex-

Haitians demonstrate at the United Nations in New York to emphasize that they flee political repression and should be admitted to the United States as refugees. (*Courtesy Center for Migration Studies, Rocco Galatioto*)

ico State University but somehow things got delayed there and I had to come in with a visitor's visa instead of a student's visa. It was valid until May 1979. I thought that meant I had nearly a year. I didn't realize that a visa and a visitor's permit are different—two different things. The permit to stay—the I–94—is what you get when you arrive in this country and it tells the date you are supposed to leave. The visa is given by the State Department in your home country before you leave. It gives you the right to come to America anytime in the duration. Then when you arrive in the United States, immigration officers (they're from the Justice Department), they give you a permit to stay. I had a visa for one year—I got that in France but when I arrived in New York, immigration officers asked how long I planned to stay. I knew it was a sensitive question and I lied. There is no way not to lie because for every specific thing you may want to do they have a specific time limit. If you say one thing and then change your mind, you find yourself going in the wrong direction.

"I said I wanted to be a visitor for four weeks so they gave me four weeks. That's what they put on the I–94 but it does not show on the passport. There is a stamp that says, 'Permitted to stay until ____' but if they don't fill it in, who's supposed to do it? So I say, until when? Until the date of my visa, May 1979. That's how I became illegal.

"I never gave it much thought, to tell the truth. No problem developed. In New Mexico, the very first day I went to the bank with some money I'd brought. They said, 'Well, in order to put money here, you have to have a social security number.' So I said, 'Okay, how do I get a social security number?' They said, 'Call the social security people,' and when I did they told me to come along and they'd give me a number for people who don't work. Here it is. Looks like anybody else's. Maybe its number means something special, I don't know. Maybe if you fed it into a computer, it would come out that I am an alien who's not supposed to work. But there is no problem getting a number. I told this to my lawyer later and he said, 'Oh yes, whenever we have a new client, we tell him to apply immediately for a social security number.'

"In New Mexico I talked with students. Looked around and I didn't like the picture at all. I realized that the school was going to cost me a fortune and I wouldn't get anything in return. I had planned to switch from engineering to journalism but I saw that schools were out to get students. They'd do anything. Then they gave me no guarantee of a job later. Journalism here is very badly paid. Competition is rough. After four years at the university to get a degree in journalism, I would be nearly forty. So I say, 'Forget it.' On the other hand, I saw that electronics was booming over here. So I decided to take my time to make up my mind—to take a rest. A year off. Try to arrange to stay legally and work as an electronics engineer. A friend of mine in Boston offered me a job. I mean his boss did and he said he would take care of getting my papers."

José explained that he changed his mind several times in his first months in the United States. With no way to evaluate American universities or journalism employment possibilities while he lived in France, he waited until he arrived in the United States to decide. An engineer in his thirties, he was simply changing careers. Yet the crossing of international borders complicated that change, leading him to conclude, "There's almost no way not to lie about what you want to do. You don't even know yourself. The immigration law was written for people who know exactly what they want."

The law was also written to provide relatively great liberty to people living in the United States legally, most of whom did not have to carry an identification card. Although legal aliens were required to have a card, citizens were not. Employers could hardly insist on the identification document as a requirement for work—that would have barred the citizens. José questions the wisdom of this freedom: "Really it is wonderful to be on the street and not have to show any official document to prove that you are who you are. You Americans are very flexible. There's only one country in Europe that doesn't make you carry an identification card, to my knowledge. That's Great Britain. In Spain, you have to. Terrible bureaucracy. I like the idea over here, but it would simplify things if you Americans had an identity card.

"The other thing that would help you control immigration is if you put it in the same office as the police. In other countries the police have responsibility for aliens. If you are an alien, you report to the police. In France, my immigration file was at the police office. Not somewhere else the way it is here. Here the police have nothing to do with immigrants. No concern. Maybe they cooperate sometimes with immigration officers. If a policeman suspected you were an illegal alien, he might check but many don't care. Police reflect the attitudes of the rest of the population. There are two: one says, 'If you are an illegal alien I am going to bust you.' The other says, 'Well, you may be here illegally but I haven't seen anything.' These are the two sides and I think there is an equal number on each one.

"The whole question of being illegal became a problem for me when I took a trip to Puerto Rico about seven months after I came to this country. Now Puerto Rico is very sensitive because it is not part of the mainland. It's there in the Caribbean near a lot of other islands, many of them very poor. Economically depressed. Many people sneak in. Come over by row boat. Some stow away in bigger boats or come in small planes.

"Apparently you can get a Puerto Rican birth certificate very easily. Once you have that, you can come into the United States without problems. There are hundreds of possibilities to get some kind of papers there. I'm not interested—this is considered a criminal offense. Immigration people say that of fifteen people they catch trying to come in illegally to the mainland, maybe one is carrying fake papers. Some of them obviously fake—I hear about visas with United States misspelled. But most people don't bother."

Leaving mainland United States presented no problem for José. Nobody checked his Spanish passport with the I–94 permit that had expired. After

five days of relaxing and enjoying himself with a friend, he tried to return
to New York. Then his troubles began.

"I was arrested. It was Monday, the end of a busy holiday weekend and
a woman was checking everybody who came through the airport in San
Juan. At first I didn't notice anything but later I realized the set-up. There's
a long corridor before you get to the gate where they check for weapons.
High walls. No escape. As bad as any international airport.

"Everybody going to New York was directed to this woman. I never
figured out who was this woman. She didn't look like an airport employee
but everybody going to New York went through her. She asked where we
were from. My friend said, 'the United States.' That's okay. Then she asked
me. I say, 'Spain.' She asked for my passport and immediately checked the
I–94. There it was—I only had permission to stay until August 1978 and
here it was—February 1979. The woman had a shock. Started saying, 'Step
over here. You are going to be deported.' I tried to convince her to let me
come to New York. No way. She got very excited. Lot of people around.

"I started to get nervous so I decided the best thing was to get away from
there and talk to somebody else. They took me to the immigration office
there in the airport but the responsible man—the one in charge—wasn't
there so we had to call him. That took about an hour.

"My friend had to leave because she had to work the next day in New
York. I waited alone at first. Then another man came in—he was from the
Dominican Republic. How he got there I don't know. Still the officers there
kept saying, 'You are going to be deported. You are here illegally and we
caught you so you have to go.' They talk like there's a plane waiting to take
you to wherever your passport says. I say I don't want to go to Spain. My
things are in New York. I have a ticket for New York. Anyway if I have to
go to Spain, they don't have to deport me. I will buy my own ticket and
leave.

"The man in charge said he couldn't do anything but arrest me. I knew
that the prison in San Juan had a very bad reputation, and that's where he
said he would detain me. I filled out some papers—some forms—and they
gave me the option of going to see a judge or leaving right away. But to be
practical, I couldn't leave so I had to go and see the judge. By that time it
was about eight in the evening.

"When I said I wanted to see a judge, the whole atmosphere changed.
The whole attitude. I don't exactly know why but I guess they give you that
option. Suppose you have a ticket to go back to your country and you decide
to leave right away—it's good for them. They accompany you to the plane
and see you leave. Saves them a lot of paper work.

"When we got ready to go to jail, they told me not to take my things
because there was no safe place to leave them. They would be stolen. I

Those Latin Americans who find great difficulty entering the United States under the regular quotas are sometimes forced to turn to other methods, often illegal, of entry. (*Courtesy UNHCR*)

must say the jails there are really bad—not that the jail is bad but that it is badly run. They don't have any idea about how to run a jail. They don't know how to count prisoners. Don't know how many they have. We were awakened three times in the middle of the night for counting—by different officers and they found different figures. They had these fantastic gates that they lock and all but. . . . Each time somebody asked them how many prisoners they had, they went to count.

"I was with the Dominican when the police drove us to the jail in a beautiful van. The police said to leave our things in the van, to trust them. We had no other choice. The jail doesn't have any place to store things or any system to make a description of the things you have. Next day when I came out of the jail, my things were still there in the van. I was surprised.

"We were thirteen illegal aliens there. Other people were charged with crimes or waiting to be released. It was a jail but I don't think people stayed there for years or anything like that.

"Some of the other illegals were Dominicans. One of them explained the situation in the Dominican Republic—how people were forced to go somewhere else because they were fighting hunger there. Young people have to be supported by their families. There are no jobs. No openings really. Corruption is high. Repression. People get shot but it's not reported in the papers. If you are poor, there is little you can do. So they leave. Young men in their twenties. These came from Dominican Republic in an open boat. Rowed for two or three days. Paid somebody to show them the way, food, water, a place to land. Puerto Rico has plenty of beaches. Some of these people had been in New York before, had married American citizens or permanent residents. They had worthy reasons to stay but they never took care of things because they were afraid of lawyers. You need a lawyer.

"There are lots of people like this who have a good reason for staying in America but they have no legal aid at all. They are afraid of being found guilty. I have a friend with a worthy case. He could have had a legal green card years ago. He was married to an American citizen but he didn't do anything about changing his status. Then they split up. He just didn't have a clear picture in his mind of the whole thing. The same is true of a lot of people."

José insisted (and here he had the support of others in his situation and of academicians studying immigration) that the most recent immigration law (the 1965 law) had been written to be broken. Like the law it replaced it was out of touch with reality. With legal advice expensive and frequently unavailable, with consulates appearing uninterested, immigrants fended for themselves as best they could—the way José did that night in the San Juan jail.

"When I got there, men stood outside with weapons. Spotlights. Double fences. I say, 'This is Alcatraz.' I was very scared. I thought, 'You're getting in there, no charge against you. You can become a number and they'll forget all about you.' I was very glad my friend in New York knew where I was.

"The forms we filled out were like Spain in colonial times—you have to give your religion, your father's name, mother's name. Crazy.

"Somebody decided we could stay there in the office for the night since we were going to appear before the judge the next day. No need to take us into the jail. But the officer who decided that went off duty and the new one was a real fascist, a sadist. Wanted to show his authority. Made everybody undress and he commented on everything about them. Everything. Threatened people. But he let me sleep there on the bench.

"Just when I was getting settled, a third officer came and he turned out to be worse than the one before. He sent me into the jail. Made me change into some jeans and a shirt, then sent me into this communal room where everybody was sleeping on the floor. No beds. There were some kind of foam pads but not enough for everybody. Filthy. No sheets or anything. Two huge latrines. Most people had some kind of dysentery. I don't know how many people there were—they didn't know themselves—around one hundred. Organized in some sort of way. They sent me in one direction—to sleep on a cement floor. No pad even.

"I was thinking before I went to sleep what I was going to face the next day, what kind of questions and what kind of answers I could give. The big point was I did not want to stay in that jail another night. I knew I could get a lawyer but it would have delayed things. Probably would not have been able to see a judge the next day. I say to myself. 'Get out of jail first.' I thought very deeply. It drains you out. I mean it was worse this all happened in Puerto Rico. I feel at home in New York, but believe me I didn't feel at home in Puerto Rico. No way. Even though I am Spanish.

"All night they kept on with their counting. Three times they turned on the lights. Came with big sticks in their hands. The prisoners were all very submissive. Didn't want to complain or anything. Many of them knew each other; they'd been there several days and were used to it.

"Next morning early we had breakfast. Everybody got ready about forty-five minutes before breakfast was really available. I noticed everybody was carrying a glass container of some sort—an empty Coke or 7–Up bottle. Something like that. And I was wondering why. Well, the reason is that if you don't have a container, you don't get coffee. You have to provide your own container. So I have no coffee. They give you a kind of porridge, on a platter, and a spoon. A huge metallic thing. When you finish, you have to wash your spoon and give it back to them and they give it immediately to somebody else. No wonder the prisoners get sick in there.

"Then they wash the floor and that means everybody has to go somewhere else. The only place you can go is the toilets. Then when they wash the toilets, you have to go to the showers. The showers don't work. The whole thing is a mess.

"After about an hour, they took us out by groups. We were counted several times and the people didn't match with the names on the list. When we got to the waiting room, I saw the immigration officers from the night before and I felt very, very good to see them there. I thought at least they knew we were there. They had to take us from the jail to the immigration office again. Took a good half hour—with the same incredible counting. I mean only thirteen of us! Incredible!

"It was still early morning. That beautiful Puerto Rican sun was rising. It seemed like freedom again. And off we went to Uncle Sam's federal building.

"The guards tried to be nice, to explain what would happen at the hearing. They said we could get a lawyer, even if we didn't have any money. Or we could buy a ticket, depart voluntarily, and no charge would be held against us. If we didn't depart on our own we would be deported and if we were deported, we could never come back to America again. Now at the very end, when we got to the parking lot, they said, 'We're not supposed to tell you these things but we're trying to be nice and in exchange we want you to be nice to us. We are supposed to escort you in handcuffs but we don't want to do that' (Maybe they didn't have thirteen pairs of handcuffs). So they said, 'We ask you to march in two rows and go straight there and don't mess around.'

"I was one of the first in the line. The Dominican was with me and the rest behind. Not all Spanish speaking. Some from St. Kitts. Spoke English. We got into the building and into the elevator. After the big door closed on the elevator with us inside, somebody said, 'Do you notice we are one less?' If you could have seen the guards' faces! I don't know how he managed to escape. I saw something funny outside. We all did, but nobody said anything. Everybody saw except the two guards. Thirteen is not so many people to watch and the man got away from them in the distance of half a block. In daylight.

"The guards were stuck. They couldn't leave all of us with one man so they both took us to the office where they had to turn us over. Now there were only twelve of us but there were thirteen names on the list, and their problem was to find out which one was missing. It took them half an hour. They'd call a name. Somebody answered. Next name. And so on. It didn't occur to them to move the people who answered to the other side of the room so no one could answer twice. Finally a real gringo—a very tall person from the Midwest—came in. He said, 'You don't know how to do that. I will do it.' So he found the missing person's name. By then, when the guards went to look for him, it was too late. He was gone.

"The twelve of us were in these two rooms. Doors could be opened only from outside—really like cells. A metallic toilet and water tap. I realized people could be held there for some time. Days even. Then we were split up and I was left in one room and the others were taken to the other room. It got very hot where I was. No air conditioning. No windows. Very small room.

"While I waited I got a call from my friend in New York. She said she was trying to reach the governor's aide, a friend of somebody she knew. I said she should have him call me, but I didn't want to say too much. I suspected the call was being taped but I knew if she could get in touch with him, it would be some benefit.

"He called back about noon. He didn't know anything about me, except what my friend in New York had told him. He advised me to get a lawyer right away. Said that's what he would do in a foreign country. I thanked him for calling but said that I was being given legal advice, that the people holding me were very nice. The whole conversation was being listened to, so I really put on a show. Said the people there were wonderful. No reason to get a lawyer. I told him if I had any problems at all I'd get a lawyer. I said I was just interested in getting a hearing in front of a judge, and of course I didn't want to go back to that filthy jail. Well, as soon as I said those words, somebody came on to the line and started apologizing to the governor's aide, saying how terribly sorry they were that the jail was not better kept, that they were trying to get the Salvation Army involved in improving it. That sort of thing. I thanked the aide for calling and hung up.

"Immediately the man who had interrupted my call came into my room and said, 'Thank you very much.'

" 'For what?' I said.

" 'Well, you said you were being well treated and you were getting the right advice.'

" 'Well, isn't that true?' I said.

" 'Yes, yes. Of course,' he said and at that point the whole attitude changed.

"At one o'clock I went down to the hearing room with a Peruvian stowaway. Very clean, charming place. The U.S. Department of Justice. The judge was a fat man, serious, in a big black coat. The stowaway went first. The hearing was in English but they offered an interpreter. I was lucky to have his hearing before mine because it gave me a wonderful chance to see what mine was going to be like.

"The stowaway didn't speak a word of English. He had gotten off a boat illegally and was to be sent back. The judge asked him if he could leave on his own. And the Peruvian said, 'No, I want to be deported.'

"The judge asked, 'To where?' and the Peruvian said, 'To Venezuela.'

" 'Well,' the judge said, 'is there any particular reason why you don't want to go back to Peru?'

" 'If I go back to Peru, it's a poor country—no jobs there. I don't want to go back there.'

" 'But if we send you to Peru, is there any kind of danger for you?'

" 'Yes,' the Peruvian said, 'I would be put in jail.'

" 'All right,' the judge said, 'We will try to fix you up with Venezuela but we can only request entry for you three times in three months. If they don't accept you in those three months, we will have to send you back to Peru. Those three months you will have to remain in jail.'

" 'I don't care,' he said, 'I will wait in jail until I can go to Venezuela.'

"It occurred to me that the judge was trying to work out the best possible solution for this man. He was young, in his early twenties. I'm sure he would have been thrown in jail. He might have been a criminal or it could have been a political offense. Anything can happen in South America.

"I came next. I had to swear I would tell the truth. They asked me if I wanted an interpreter but I said, 'No!' After he asked me some questions, my name, birthplace and so on, the judge said, 'How's come you speak such wonderful English?'

"That shook me up and I started explaining what I had been doing, what had happened to me. When we got to the part about my immigrant status, I said I pleaded guilty but that I thought the date I had to leave was the date on the visa. That was still four months away.

"The judge said that was a very common mistake and he gave me voluntary departure. But first I had to post a bond promising that once I got back to New York I would leave within seven days. Now how could I get the money for the bond? It was in New York. So they offered me a telephone but I knew that it would take some time for the money to arrive and in the meantime I would have to wait in that filthy jail.

"I said, 'I don't want to go back to that jail. I want to be let free to go back to New York to do the things I have to do and then leave.'

" 'Why do you think we will let you go?' they said.

" 'Because I am not a criminal. I have never been in jail before and really I don't see why I should be treated this way.'

"Well, they talked about it 'off the record,' they said, and the judge cancelled what he had said before. Gave me six weeks to leave New York and didn't make me post a bond.

"I left there to get my things. They discharged me, gave me my passport and a new I–94 saying that I was under deportation procedure. Also put my new date of departure on the I–94. Very nice. They even gave me a letter just in case any of the immigration officers stopped me.

"This time when I got to the airport there was nobody there from immigration. Nobody asked me anything. The night before had been a holiday and lots of people were going through. But when I left, there were very few passengers and nobody paid any attention to me.

"In New York I went to the Immigration office and asked for an extension but they became very tough when they looked at my file. Didn't want to give me any extension. Said I'd have to leave.

"So on the first of April I left and went to Ecuador for nineteen days and then I came back. Just to get that stamp on my passport—to show I had left. This time they asked me the same silly questions that they asked the first time—how much money I had, how long I intended to stay. I said, 'One month,' and they gave me one month.

"In a few days I got a certified letter from Immigration saying I was going to be deported. If I signed, that meant I was still here. They didn't know I had gone to Ecuador and come back. I called a lawyer—somebody gave me an address. I think he was a fake. He didn't show any interest at all. I called another one. He said, 'Okay first you go to Immigration and

show them your passport so they know that you went out of the country.
They will lift the charges and you can leave.'

"But I really wanted an extension so I could try to get a green card.
There is no way to wait legally. You have to go. What you can do is ignore
the departure date and stay. But if they catch you working, then they will
deport you.

"I didn't want to go back to Immigration by myself because I knew they
were going to intimidate me. Make me get things mixed up. So I say, 'Let's
get a lawyer' and I got a lawyer—a good one with a good firm.

"This lawyer said, 'Well there is really no problem. We're going to go
there and we're going to get rid of this charge. Then we will apply for an
H-1 type visa. We can buy time. While you apply for a different type visa
you have the right to stay. That's the way to do it.'

"The lawyer is asking me one thousand dollars. I think it's outrageous.
He is not doing anything that I couldn't do but Immigration doesn't tell you
what you have to do. A lawyer knows. Lawyers drive Immigration a bit and
Immigration drives the lawyers. We are out. We are the ball in the game.

"For me, the result will be the green card which will come along one
day. Somebody will say, 'Why was this guy here so long?' Somebody else
will say, 'He was waiting for something else.' It's a very awkward position to
be in. Believe me. Everything depends on the information and advice you
can get."

José paid the one thousand dollars, realizing that it might be just the
first installment of his total bill for legal immigrant status. Others made
additional arrangements, besides the large payments. One woman, tired of
paying thousands of dollars to a lawyer working on her husband's immigration case, finally got help from a congressman. "We had been waiting pa-
tiently for more than a year," she complained, "doing everything the lawyer
told us to do. We appeared more than once in front of immigration officials
and tried to convince them that our marriage was real—not just to get him
a green card. They didn't believe us because I had taken a job temporarily
in another city. I'm a journalist and I go where the wire service sends me.
But my husband's job was in New York—he stayed, and we saw each other
when we could. Well, the immigration people made us show airline tickets,
phone bills, wedding invitations—everything to prove it was a real marriage.
Even asked us very personal questions that only people who had lived together would know about each other. Finally I had had it! Too much! I
know the sister of a congressman pretty well. We roomed together in college. I got an appointment with her brother. Saw him about noon one day.
When I got home about four our phone was ringing. It was the immigration
lawyer saying everything was okay. Do you think that was a coincidence?

You might—but I don't. In this country, with immigration as with every-thing else, it's who you know that counts."

People who lack the money or the contacts to apply special pressure in favor of their cases become illegal aliens, a term José Lopez Rivera uses but finds inappropriate: "There's nothing illegal about us—we are just people who want to move around. We have no attachment to one country. I went back to Seville last year for a few days—to see my parents. Couldn't take staying there—it's not my style. I'm used to another type life. There are people everywhere like me. Patriotism—the idea of nations and of people behind a border, behind a line, behind a political identity—that no longer has value. Patriotism is dead because it leads to war. What has patriotism to do with, except war? Your country makes you patriotic so you will defend your homeland. People just don't accept that anymore.

"So people like me come here. I could have gotten a visa in France—I applied for one in 1974. I had visited America for four months, as a tourist, and I thought I would like to come here to live. The consulate said to get a job in America, then have the employer fill out a form. A lot of red tape. They put you on a list or something with other prospective immigrants. It takes a long time. I didn't bother but I would have qualified.

"Most people do it legally. I don't know very many illegals. But the country is gaining from the illegals. They are often single people, young, able to work, more ambitious, no kids to send to school. They are easy-going people and they don't belong to anybody. They will never use most government services.

"But they have a really bad reputation. I am outraged by what people think about illegals. In France they have a terrible problem with the Al-gerians who work for the benefit of the French, of course, but they are still mistreated all the time. People say they don't pay taxes and they abuse the national medical insurance. It's not true. The statistics are there for the asking. To prove the contrary. Those Algerians contribute to many financial programs and they are not getting anything back.

"If you asked me what to do about illegals, I would say first you have to figure out what this country wants. Right now there is not a commission working on it or anything. Then you have to see what is going on, see what the immigrants mean for the economy, for industry. See it from the Amer-ican side. Then you have to stop talking about these big numbers of illegals. You see 6, 7, sometimes 40 million as the estimate of how many are here. It scares people, telling them that illegals are everywhere, draining the econ-omy. If you subtract the Mexicans and the people who've been living here for years, then the others are a very small number. Relatively easy problem.

"But Americans have never faced up to the problem. They want to stop with an old law. Don't want to hear about anything. The only people they really want are the elite of the world. If you are famous in any field, you don't have any problem."

José Lopez Rivera was wrong in at least one respect: an interagency commission charged with reviewing immigration and refugee policy was preparing, while he spoke, to recommend changes. While the country waited for the report of the Select Commission on Immigration and Refugee Policy, other suggestions were considered.

Leonel J. Castillo, while director of the Immigration and Naturalization Service, advocated temporary measures. First, he wanted to legalize the status of people who had resided in the country for years, built up equity, and obeyed the laws. While the literacy requirement stopped some of the older ones from legalizing their status, others were afraid they might face large penalties. Castillo thought community groups in other countries could be trained to assist applicants with forms and correspondence. He urged setting up offices in countries of treatest emigration interest. While the INS maintained three offices in Italy, it had none in Latin America outside Mexico. Other volunteers could assist immigrants once they had arrived in the United States. The *Silva* decision of the U.S. Supreme Court had ruled that many people who applied for visas to come from South America to the United States between 1968 and 1976 were wrongly refused because the large number of Cubans admitted as refugees exhausted much of the Western Hemisphere allotment. Although the *Silva* decision provided that people who applied for visas during those years and then came without them should be entitled to remain, most of those who might have benefitted from the ruling remained unaware of its existence.

Leonel Castillo also advocated increasing penalties for smugglers and for employers who habitually hired illegals and then exploited them. He had already directed the establishment of a laboratory to develop detection devices for fraudulent documents and to work on an alien-registration card that could not be easily copied.

Some aspects of a more efficient immigration process seemed easily implemented, especially the computerization of the records of departing aliens. Lax controls at many of the country's airports made it possible for aliens to leave without filing the required I–94 form. Until the record keeping improved, there was no way to know for sure which of those who did not file had remained in the United States beyond their allotted time.

Most of the problems involved in regulating immigration appeared considerably more complex, further complicated by the reduction of the world's size that jet planes, satellite beams, and international exposure to movies and magazines had accomplished. To people around the globe who searched for adventure or looked for a better life, the United States held a special interest. For many of them, that meant New York City. For the determined ones who failed to meet legal requirements or became impatient waiting for a visa, other ways existed. Information about how to circumvent the law circulated through travel agencies in South America, pubs in Ireland, and medical schools in Bombay.

The Immigration and Naturalization Service, charged with enforcing a law obviously lacking in popular support and easily circumvented, retreated from its responsibility. No clear mandate emerged either for administering the old law diligently or for enacting a new one. The debate continued, old as the country itself, over the value of immigrants and the relative merits of different kinds. José Lopez Rivera's words rang true: "The first thing you have to do is figure out what Americans want."

3

Ten Years Is a Long Time:

A Woman from Rural Peru

Peru

"My mother is a *Quechua* Indian. I am a *chola* [half-breed] but my sons are American and we live in the Bronx. In 1968 we were still in Lima, Peru— my mother worked as a domestic and I had just graduated from high school. Neither of us could speak a word of English and we had never heard of the Bronx. I tell you everything has changed— Lima, New York, and us. Ten years is a long time."

Five hundred years ago, the Inca civilization spread over thousands of miles of South America. An intricate tangle of communications and government, the Inca society was considerably advanced for its times. But further development was abruptly cut short when Pizarro and the invading Spaniards brought the cross and the flag of Catholic Spain to South America. They also brought the cannon and centuries of Spanish domination. Its power now a memory, its buildings now ruins, the Inca empire today endures only as an unravelled maze, a dynamic of contradictions.

Machu Picchu, in the Cuzco Zone of Peru, is a famous tourist site as well as a symbol of the engineering skills of its builders. (*Courtesy United Nations, Rothstein*)

By one set of standards the Inca civilization never attained more than a modest level of development. It does not appear, for example, to have evolved a written alphabet. Yet attesting at least to its engineering genius was the Machu Picchu, that magnificent fortress city on a high mountain ridge, which stood firm for half a millennium. The Incas appear not to have known about the wheel. Nonetheless, their political system formed a perfect wheel, with lines of power and authority radiating out from the capital city, Cuzco, along amazingly distant spokes. From the Inca king at the center out to an inner ring of chieftains, out again to a series of wider command rings, the Incas demonstrated themselves to be highly advanced in their political organization. Facilitating this political network was an equally extensive road network stretching thousands of miles and including suspension bridges and tunnels. Even at the peak of their influence, the Incas lacked fast animals for communication and transport. Ingeniously, however, even here they developed a reasonably successful substitute system, one relying on a system of human relay runners, called *chasquis* who operated at more than eight miles per hour. Each man marked off a mile and a half in the oxygen-poor air of Peru's high altitudes before he passed his load on to a

or. The system worked so well, it is reported, that fish from the coast
d at the emperor's table within hours, and messages moved along at
st two hundred miles a day.

The Incas' use of fertilizer, especially the nitrogen-rich guana manure,
and their knowledge of terracing to prevent soil erosion remain impressive
even to twentieth-century agronomists. They were able to construct sixty-
foot-high walls of locked stone that withstood earthquakes. But ultimately it
was the crucial process of making iron that escaped them, leaving them
vulnerable to European conquest. The mixture of the two worlds, one advanced and the other less so, is the locked enigma of Inca history.

Pizarro claimed Peru in 1533 and the outmatched Incas saw the end of
their empire. But the people and their rich culture lived on. Rosa Marcos
Guerro, living in the Bronx with her *Quechua* mother and her American
sons, testifies to that. But Rosa's story stretches back, far before her birth,
into the intricacies of Spanish colonial policy in the New World.

Sixteenth-century Spanish law attempted to keep families together and
races apart by requiring that Spanish men sailing for the Americas secure
special permission to leave their households behind. Husbands could begin
their journeys only with the approval of their wives and then the separation
might not exceed three years. But the sexual imbalance in the overwhelm-
ingly male immigration (ten men to one woman) and the distances that
stretched stays of years into decades led to frequent cohabitation between
Spanish men and Indian women. Before bed went baptism, at least a ritual
conversion to Catholicism, and this particular step was carefully noted in
the records of the time. As a result of frequent intermarriages between the
races, half the population of twentieth-century Peru is mixed Spanish and
Indian. Peruvians call these mixed-blooded people *cholos* to distinguish
them from the Spanish *criollos* and the Indian *indigenas*. Today almost
everybody is Catholic.

Rosa Marcos Guerro tells how intermarriage affected her life: "I don't
really know much about my father. He was Spanish. I know that, but my
mother never talks about him. A miner, I think. First, he lost his eyesight
in a work accident and then, when I was only a year old, he died. His
family, who didn't like the idea of an Indian daughter-in-law, just forgot
about us. My mother had to raise us alone—two sisters, two brothers, and
me. Really only four because one brother died from pneumonia when he
was only two. I am the youngest.

"My mother had many different jobs. First selling fruits and vegetables
and then later she worked as a domestic. Without any education—she cannot even write her name—she had to take the worst jobs. She is not stupid.
She can do accounts in her head faster than anybody I ever saw. The *Que-*
chuas have a system of knots, called *quipu*, a way to communicate numbers

An Indian woman spins yarn near Lake Yarinacocha in Peru. (*Courtesy United Nations, A. Jongen*)

and messages without writing anything down, but my mother says she doesn't use that. She is just smart.

"We never had much money. I remember when I was a child, I had no toys and so I played with dirt. Made little castles and people—like my sons play in the sand at Coney Island. But dirt is different from sand. You cannot do the same things with it. My dolls were just pieces of cloth I rolled up. Their arms and legs, even their faces, I had to see in my mind.

"One of my mother's jobs for a while was taking care of the rooms where people came to do their laundry and bathing. In La Oroya, where I was born, people didn't have their own bathrooms. That was how it was then— it's probably different now. A dirty job. My mother wanted something better so she went to work for a rich family. As their domestic. When they moved to Lima, they took us all.

"I must have been about ten when we left La Oroya. I know I had already started school. I remember that because boys and girls went to school together there. In Lima we had separate classes. Very proper. When you have money, you can be proper but in La Oroya where everybody seemed so poor, nobody thought so much about things like that.

"In Lima we lived with our godparents—it's a different system in Peru. Godparents aren't just chosen for babies. They are picked for children on many occasions—first haircutting or ear-piercing. Not so much anymore and not in the capital, but in the country it was like that. The richest, most successful are godparents even if they aren't such good friends. That way the children maybe will take on some of the good luck of the godparents. Besides, if anything happens to the real father and mother, the godparents can take over the children.

"It was lucky we went to live with them in Lima. Some of the people I knew had to live in those 'new towns' just outside the city. Circles of huts where country people live. In the last about thirty years—my mother remembers when it began—lots of people have been moving to Lima from the country. Better jobs, they think. Or modern houses. They say they just want to make money to take back to the country. But most of them end up staying. There are lots of clubs—each one has people from a different town—and these are supposed to help people get used to the city. But it's awful living in these 'new towns.' No sewers or telephones or buses. The lucky ones have radios running on batteries, but they don't have electricity. Maybe it's different now. My sister—she still lives in Lima—she says everything's changed. She even has a telephone, but it cost a lot of money. About a hundred dollars. The other things I have—mixer, blender, toaster—she doesn't dream to have.

"In the center city where my godparents lived, everything was much nicer. They were Spanish, you see, and in Peru the best you can be is Spanish. Then *chola* like me. The bottom is like my mother—Indian.

"My godparents treated us pretty well but some of their relatives used to complain that we were spoiled. 'What's that *chola* doing sitting on the sofa?' they used to say. Oh I hated to be called *chola*. It's a bad name—means a person from the country. How do you say? Hick? I tried so hard not to look *chola*. I remember my cheeks were very red and cracked when I first got to Lima. La Oroya is so high in the mountains that it's cold and dry. Of course we didn't have lotions or creams. I hated my red cheeks—like a big sign, they said, *chola*. There are other ways to tell who is *cholo*. The people in the capital can tell by how you speak—your accent and how you dress. Everybody tries very hard to look *criollo*.

"For my mother that change was hard. She stopped wearing the *pujeros* [pajamas] and the *panyalon* [shawl] that Indian women wear on the streets. Even tried to talk like the city people. *Quechua* is her language but she never taught it to us. Said she wanted something better for us. That's why she made us go to school and study Spanish. I took commercial subjects—

Indians in Peru work mostly in agriculture, living as they have for centuries outside the mainstream of the nation's economic and social life. (*Courtesy United Nations*)

bookkeeping and accounting—but I never liked them. Somehow my mother thought I would. Maybe that's what she wanted to do herself.

"I went to public school but my sisters went to Catholic school with the nuns. They were always getting in trouble. I was a good girl, so I stayed in public school. When I graduated in 1968, I couldn't find a job. A friend of ours, a Japanese girl my sister knew, started talking about New York. Her family had a restaurant in Lima so they weren't poor. But she had gotten into some kind of trouble—wanted to marry a man that her parents didn't like or something like that. I never knew the whole story. In the travel agency where she worked she found out a lot about New York and how to get here.

"You know what I heard about New York? Two things. First: you got paid by the week instead of the month and that sounded so big. In Lima my mother was making fifty dollars a month. Of course she got food and a place to live but I heard that in New York you could make fifty dollars a week. The other thing I heard was that education was free. You could go to school at night and it didn't cost anything. That sounded so good.

"My friend, Kumi, said for me to get money for the ticket and she would take care of the tourist visas. In the travel agency she had learned how to do it. I asked everybody for money—my sister, my mother, my aunt, my god-mother. They all gave a little and it was just enough for the ticket.

"But I wasn't worried. We knew a man in Brooklyn. He used to live across the street from Kumi's family in Lima and he said he would help us. We went right to him and he got us an apartment for ninety dollars a month. Jobs were easy to get, too. I remember he took us out the first day and we found two jobs—two jobs for each of us! From 8 A.M. until 4 P.M. I worked in a plastic factory making bottles. Then at 5, I went to another job in a factory making clothes—stayed there until midnight. For each job I got seventy dollars a week. A week! More than I could make in a month in Lima! And I had two jobs! That was really a lot of money and I still don't know what I did with it. A little bit I sent back to my mother, but not much. Ten dollars a few times. I just can't think where it went. Even today I say, 'Where is my money?' I guess I was making so much that it didn't matter.

"In a few months I met my husband and we went to live in the Bronx. It is funny. When I first came to New York I said I would never live in the Bronx. It was the worst. Queens, Brooklyn, Manhattan. They were all right. Not the Bronx. But my husband's family lived there so that's where we went.

"My husband was Puerto Rican. Maybe somebody who wasn't Spanish would think we were the same but it's not true. We both spoke Spanish but his was a very funny kind, not like in Peru. In every way we were different. He was more than six feet tall and I am only five. He was very skinny with almost no chest at all. We Peruvians have big chests, I think because we lived where there was not much air.

"After we were married he went to Vietnam and was killed there just two months after our sons were born. They're twins. We named them Foster—that was my husband's name—and Emanuele—that's for my side. Because my husband was Puerto Rican, my sons are American citizens and I want something special for them. When I came to the United States I was not thinking about my family. It wasn't for them that I left—but for me. I wanted something better for myself and I found it. But life will be much better for my sons. Here they can go to college. They can do anything they want. I won't push them, but I know their lives will be very good.

"I have never become an American citizen. Most of the rights are mine anyway because my husband was American, but I cannot pass these on to my mother and sister. Now this is a problem. When my husband died, I had to bring my mother here to help. I had already paid for my sister and my brother to come to New York and I found them jobs when they got here. But my mother was still in Peru, and I needed her here to take care of my sons so I could work, too. I didn't have anybody else to help me. Well, it wasn't so hard to bring my mother then, but now everything is much stricter and I don't know what to do. She wants to go back to Lima to visit. My oldest sister still lives there. But I am afraid that if she goes, she won't get back in. So we hired a lawyer. I paid him $700. He said, 'Rosa, it would be so easy if you would become an American citizen.' He doesn't understand what it means to change citizenship. I feel Peruvian.

"Maybe you are thinking that I want to go back to Peru one day to live but that is not true. When I left, I knew I would never go back and it did not make me sad at all. I would like to see my sister, yes, but only for that I would go back. I like to see things change, and my life here is really changed. Besides, I can't return because of *soroche*. That's a sickness people get in the mountains when they are not used to being up high. Me—I never get it because I grew up in the mountains—but my sons will get it, I know. And it's terrible. Causes vomiting and headaches. So you see, my sons really are American and we can't go back.

"Not all parts of our lives have changed here in New York. We have a mixture—like in religion. My mother is Catholic, a really strong Catholic. She goes to mass every week but she still believes things that the Catholic Church doesn't like. Sort of magic and part of this carries over into medicine.

"My mother always says not to eat hot foods when you are sick. If you have an operation or an infection, you shouldn't eat fish. I think it's true because when I was little I was very sick. Somebody gave me fish and I got much worse. Then last year my friend had an operation and when she was

Like generations of farmers before him, this peasant works the land in primitive fashion depending heavily on the versatile llama. (*Courtesy United Nations*)

just ready to come home from the hospital they gave her tuna fish. Yes, and it almost killed her. Things doctors do not know about, my mother teaches me. When I have indigestion, she tells me to drink tea made from oregano or celery leaves. It works much better than any medicine the doctor gave me.

"In Peru only the rich go to doctors. Most people take care of things at home—we have many cures. I use them here. If my sons are really sick, I take them to the best doctor I can find. Not a clinic, but a private doctor. Last year I paid forty dollars for the best eye doctor to look at Foster. But simple things I take care of at home. For colds, I still use my mother's remedy—I make a syrup out of grated onion with sugar dissolved in it.

"Some of the *Quechua* ideas are primitive and we don't use them anymore. Maybe they don't even use them anymore in Peru—at least not in the capital. A long time ago—well, not so long ago because my mother remembers hearing about it—they took the urine of the llama and used it for special baths, like washing your hair. Said it made your hair shiny and healthy. For babies, too. Gave their children baths in llama urine to make them healthy. Of course the llama has many uses—for meat and wool. They even burned the manure for fuel. Maybe they had to find some purpose for the urine and that's how it started. I don't know.

"Another habit they had in the country, but not anymore I think, is the way they made *chicha*. That's a special beer made from corn. Women used to chew the kernels a while and then spit them out into a big pot. Their saliva and the corn would ferment and that made *chicha*. I never drank it made that way but my mother remembers people saying it was good.

"Of course everybody has heard about the cocoa leaves they chew. In the country, but not in the capital, they get three or four ounces—whatever you want. Some people start chewing in the morning and they keep a big ball in their mouths all day. Say it helps them feel better, especially if they are sick or have a toothache. Instead of going to a dentist, they just let the teeth come out when they are ready. Well, I want something better for my sons and I take them to the best dentist every year for a checkup. Whether they have a toothache or not. I don't have much money, but I have enough for that. It is always more than in Peru.

"After my husband died, I had to work and since I didn't know English very well, I got a job as a domestic. Made good money and worked only for people I liked. I kept my apartment—nobody even suggested I should live in.

"Sometimes people ask me if I wasn't tempted to steal things when I worked in those nice apartments but they don't understand my people. For the *Quechuas*, the worst thing you can do is take something that doesn't belong to you. I remember once I was in a supermarket here in New York and I said the wrong word for corn-on-the-cob. I got it mixed up, and a woman corrected me. Then she said, 'Don't be ashamed. Everybody makes mistakes.' I said, 'I'm not ashamed. My mother taught me the only time I need to be ashamed is if I take something that doesn't belong to me.' I don't think the woman understood.

"I made good money as a domestic but I worried about insurance and what would happen to my sons if I got sick and couldn't work. So I changed to a job in an office—a bank cafeteria. I clean up and help with the salads. They pay me well and I get insurance too. They even pay for my English classes at New York University. When I first came here, the high schools gave free English lessons but now it costs money. So it's good my company helps. It's really funny in my class. There's an architect from Belgium and an Italian lady—I think they are very rich because they talk about all the places they travel to. But the teacher treats us just the same. That's the way Americans are.

"Another thing I like about Americans is their attitude toward sex. You know when I came to New York, I was almost twenty years old but I did not know where babies came from. I remember when my sister was married, I was about fifteen. She started talking to my godmother about sex and they told me to leave the room.

"I don't want that for my sons. When they ask me something, I tell them. Undress in front of them. At first they paid attention. Now they don't even notice. I still don't undress in front of my mother because I have respect for her, but I want my sons to be more open. I hear people talk about going to bed on their first date. I think that is too much. I like change but for me that is too fast change.

"Change is something you have to go along with. You know many Puerto Ricans decide they don't like New York after a while and they want to go back. Well, that's not easy. I hear about it from my husband's family. If you go back to Puerto Rico, they call you *Americano*. If you stay here they call you Puerto Rican. I always say, stay here. Things changed after you went away. You can't stop it. That's just the way it is. A few years means a long time."

Rosa Guerro's immigration to New York City is not unlike that of hundreds of thousands of other women who have abandoned the islands of the Caribbean and the lands of Central and South America to earn more money. Fifty years ago it might have been Rosa's older brother, Miguel, who made the journey first, but now it is more often the women in the family who come. This pattern, more and more pronounced since 1950, reverses a much older tradition, one in which men were the ones to leave their families to enter America's unskilled work force. For some nationalities the disproportionate male ratio occasionally reached 80 or even 90 percent. Further, these men often came to work, not to live—to save up American dollars and return to their native countries to buy land or start small businesses back home.

This large immigration of men depended on an abundance of unskilled jobs, and when New York's employment scene changed, immigration did, too. Jobs that had earlier been wide open to immigrant men became highly unionized and in some cases, skilled. An applicant needed a recommendation, an acquaintance, and sometimes, even a diploma. Those fortunate enough to follow countrymen already here reaped benefits. Italian construction companies looked out for *paesani*, Jewish manufacturers hired Russian Jews as tailors, and Irish camaraderie softened entry for new men from Dublin.

Latin men who came north in the 1960s and 1970s encountered a scene very different from that which European men found in the early part of the twentieth century. Because routes north—from the Caribbean and South

America—became well traveled only after the United States cut off the flow across the Atlantic, there were few Colombians and Peruvians in important places in the 1960s and 1970s to smooth the way for others. The American economy had changed too. While the old industrial boom had welcomed brawn and the willingness to lift a shovel, more sophisticated labor requirements were now common. Opportunities still exist at the bottom—for doormen, porters, day laborers—and some Latin men with little education, such as Rosa's brother, Miguel, put on the uniforms and go to work. But earning with one's hands has, in the meanwhile, become less acceptable and South American men get that message.

Those who take manual or service jobs can save enough for a car, perhaps even a house, especially if several members of the family earn. Or if they are like Rosa's brother, who spends reluctantly if at all, they may do even better. "Miguel's going to buy a house," Rosa says with some pride. "He never spends his money. Just saves. Works and saves. For him that is enough. Much better than he would have had in Peru. I know another man from Peru who just bought part of a delicatessen—he saved his money and had all his children working too."

But today for many other Latin men, the climb seems too slow. Taxes, inflation, and higher expectations claim a larger chunk of family income today than they did fifty years ago. The old promise, "Save and you can get ahead quickly," appears more hollow to Latin men (Miguel and a few others, obvious exceptions) than it did to Europeans and Asians in their mass immigration periods.

But for Latin women, the promise still holds. Immigration today draws them out of their native countries as it drew European males fifty years earlier. Some have argued that the difference lies partly in the fact that unionization has not taken so total a hold on "female" occupations, making entry into such occupations far more informal. Others point to changes in mechanization that have put work that once required great muscle power within women's reach. And the definition of women's work has altered too, with American-born women moving into jobs higher on the ladder, leaving a gap at the bottom to be filled by new arrivals.

Wives and sisters of European immigrants can refuse the worst jobs. Their families have already served apprenticeships and these women wait for something better. Irish young women turn down cleaning jobs to take work as governesses while second- and third-generation Italian women claim secretarial and teaching jobs. An old plot replays itself with different characters. The last to arrive on stage get the least desirable parts and, after 1965, the wings have been full of Latin women. In dark Manhattan lofts, they paste feathers on designer pillows; in Chinatown clothing factories or toy plants in Queens, they work "off the books," if they are illegal or undocumented.

Sometimes their employment occurs with the tacit cooperation of law officers, even when their earnings fall below the minimum wage and social security and income taxes, whose benefits will never be claimed, are collected. One priest, familiar with the employment of women in factories, explained: "Of course it happens all the time. Women work. Pay taxes and social security, but most of them don't know how to file for refunds or how to apply for social security benefits. Many of them know little English. A lot of them don't want to call attention to themselves because they're here illegally or somebody in their family is. They're just happy they have a job."

New and broader job opportunities for women make up only half the changed picture. Social conditions have altered, too. Today, women living alone or in groups draw no special attention to themselves as they would have had they come half-a-century ago. Landlords and neighbors accept female tenants. Protective agencies intrude less on their lives, and families do not insist on placing their single daughters with "good" families as live-in help.

Some women take jobs as domestics, but when they do, it is by choice, and if they live in, they maintain their own network of information about such rights as weekends off, bonuses at Christmas, "Don't do windows," and are thereby able to protect themselves better than any law or army of investigators could do. Their negotiating power lies, very plainly, in their scarcity. They do the work that others shun.

No one knows how many Latin women arrive in New York each year because, like their brothers, they have learned about nonlegal entry. Rosa's case is typical—not illegal, but not entirely honest either. In her tourist visa application she promised to visit relatives, and even gave names and addresses. Then she agreed to go back to Lima after a period in the United States not to exceed six months. But her return ticket, offered as proof of her intentions, was cashed in within a week, its proceeds put down as deposit on a Queens apartment. Other women come as students, take jobs, and melt into the city's neighborhoods.

When Rosa packed her bag to leave Lima, she had few national statistics of how much people earned in Peru but she knew how much her mother made and that her friends, just out of high school, were accepting jobs paying less than three dollars a day. Then she heard of New York's very different scale and her mind was made up. Wages, for Rosa, pointed the way to a better life than her mother had had, and work opportunities in Peru for women appeared limited. Single women, in their early twenties were most likely to work while they considered marriage and prepared for their first child. But even among this age group, more than half did not work. America seemed much better to Rosa. At fifty dollars a week, who wouldn't work? The contrast appeared striking. In agricultural Peru, unskilled women with little education earned so little that all except the poorest did not bother. And those who took employment the first years of marriage looked forward to the time when they could stop.

In the United States, working had become more and more acceptable for women, both for middle class and blue collar women. The wives of senators and the widows of former presidents of the country saw that their job histories were included in publicity releases. Not only had work lost the stigma for American women that it still carried in Peru, it had become a badge of competence. The contrast in attitudes presented Latin American women with new alternatives, and many of them decided to break out of their restrictive molds and compete for better paying jobs in the north.

When Rosa's plane landed in New York in 1969, she joined these thousands of other women seeking to change their lives; but immigration officials checking arrivals had little to go on in trying to ascertain her real intentions. At large airports, signs above passport control divide international arrivals into categories and the lines behind them are of unequal length. Peruvians at the immigrant gates numbered only about twelve hundred in 1969, a low year for the decade; but almost two-thirds of them were female. Another gate, for "non-immigrant aliens," is usually much busier. Ten times the number of immigrant Peruvians line up here, Rosa among them. Most in this category claim to be on a pleasure trip, generally to one of two places— either Miami, Flordia or New York City. No one checks the progress of their visits, but if someone were to do so, he or she would see how little time is passed at the tourist sites of Manhattan and how much at the factories of Queens and Brooklyn. Permanent "temporary visitors" escape detection because they are so many and inspectors assigned to question them so few. Adding to the difficulty is their diversity; among the "non-immigrant" Peruvians who came to the United States in 1969 were businessmen, students, wealthy tourists, and Rosa.

Officially, the Peruvian population in New York at the time Rosa arrived was still very small. Only 3,400 Peruvians registered that year as aliens, but many thousands of others lost themselves in the Spanish sectors of the city. This "melting in" is easy in a metropolitan area such as New York City, where 25 percent of the city speaks Spanish, even easier in some parts of the Bronx that are solidly Spanish speaking.

Ironically, it was this northernmost New York borough that Rosa, who has made the Bronx her home for most of her American sojourn, perceived as the worst when she first arrived. Walking down its streets one is painfully aware of how many are unschooled here and how little each family lives on. There are pockets of wealth in such elite areas as the Riverdale section, where such arriviste as former Deputy Mayor Herman Badillo live. But the South Bronx is ravaged by crime and arson, the pocked streets so much turf to competing gangs and drug pushers. One large slum.

New York's South Bronx, known internationlly as an area of extreme poverty, nonetheless is often the first environment for many newly arrived Latins who try to retain their familiar customs among fellow Hispanics. Below, young girls tend pigeons on their apartment rooftop. (*Courtesy Neighborhood Documentation Project of Community Studies Incorporated*)

But the Spanish flavor extends throughout the city and Rosa could have settled down in any one of its other boroughs, raising her family without learning a word of English. While to the outsider, they are all Spanish, for those inside, there are immense differences between the many Spanish-speaking residents of the barrios of New York. More than two-thirds are Puerto Rican. Another 6 percent are Cuban, and about 300,000 come from other areas of Central and South America, with just a sprinkling from Mexico and the Iberian peninsula. Distinctions often blur between them, except to those most familiar with accents and vocabulary variations.

Julio Rodriguez, a real estate agent in Corona, Queens, tells why he is never fooled: "When I have them fill out forms, many tell me they are Puerto Rican but they are not. I am Puerto Rican and I know our dialect. These people are really Dominicans or other Hispanics trying to pass as Puerto Rican since Puerto Ricans have full rights as American citizens. But people who don't speak Spanish would believe them. They think anyone who speaks Spanish is Puerto Rican. But we are all so different."

Within Spanish-speaking communities in Brooklyn—in the Williamsburg and Crown Heights sections—and in the Inwood section of Manhattan, enclaves of separate Hispanic nationalities have grown. Parts of the old stronghold of the European immigrants on the Lower East Side of Manhattan have turned increasingly Hispanic, along with Washington Heights on the Upper West Side. These Spanish-speaking enclaves do not stop at the city limits but reach out on Long Island to Freeport and Hempstead, up the Hudson to Mount Vernon.

While the total picture remains fluid, one element appears distinct and clear: Spanish women have helped make New York increasingly female. While 51 percent of the nation is female, New York's figure is 53 percent, with every borough except Richmond reporting this percentage or higher. In Rosa's age group, the female preponderance is most marked.

Immigration only partially explains the imbalance. Women also hold an advantage in longevity, outliving their male contemporaries by seven years or so. Among people over fifty-five, women hold a large edge, especially among blacks. (Puerto Ricans offer the one exception, their elderly women evidently preferring the sunshine of their native island.) Only among children under fifteen does New York report more males than females. In every other age group, women hold the edge.

Whatever the current numbers imply, some observers say Latin women will not stay in New York. As soon as their savings books reach a certain goal, they will leave for warmer, more familiar towns, where they grew up, just as European men did in the early twentieth century.

Rosa's observation and objectives refute this view. "I know there are lots of women in New York," she says. "My mother and I noticed how our building is mostly women. I guess I won't find another husband here. Probably makes it harder for me to get a job, too. But I'm not worried. I've done okay. Why do I need a husband if I have a job? You know I always got paid in cash when I cleaned for people. Sometimes they gave me food or a dress or something. At Christmas I got a bonus from everybody. If they didn't give me a bonus, I quit. I saved that for the summer—to rent a house in New Jersey on the shore. I even started checking on charter flights to Lima."

As Rosa's sons grew up, they acquired toys unlike those their mother remembers from her childhood. Trains, fire engines, and cowboy hats—an American arsenal. When they were four, she enrolled them in a daycare center with an American teacher who did her job so well that within months the boys began to ridicule their mother's English. Rosa tried to improve her grasp of English by reading the newspaper when she had time and by making a list of unfamiliar words, but she had little opportunity to speak English. Her mother, who came to live with Rosa, did not want to try a new language, and Rosa could not keep up with her sons.

Rosa's feelings about her lack of progress with her new language led her to change jobs, but the position yielded other benefits besides free English classes. Employees in the bank were generous with tips on where to shop and gifts of surplus from the kitchen. They even insisted that she take a cab when she went on errands around the city for them. Rosa observed the clothes and hairstyles of those around her. She imitated them.

She learned fast. Like other immigrants, Hispanic women enroll in language courses, sign up for classes at the community colleges, and join the banks' Christmas clubs. They learn about discount stores but they prefer carrying cast-off shopping bags from Saks or Bergdorf's. These paper status symbols are reused day after day until the corners open up. The women can distinguish one designer signature wallet from another and the fake from the real. They buy the imitation, but they covet the real. Women's liberation and feminist causes hardly touch them. They have little or no interest in the Equal Rights Amendment and Title VII. For them equality is simply the chance to work and collect a check at the end of the week. As long as they have that, New York seems attractive.

Some do not work, preferring the city's welfare system, but Rosa claims that the women from Central and South America who take this route are few. Her old argument still stands strong—at this wage, who wouldn't work? She collects insurance because of her husband's death in Vietnam but welfare is another matter. She angrily defends her Hispanic sisters from the charge that their decision to immigrate was predicated on the availability of welfare payments. She believes most want to work.

"I didn't mind the work. It was kind of an adventure. Even when we went to the Bronx, I kept my job—one job. I bought lots of things. Everybody had lots. A TV set. Some people had two. A lot of women even had washing machines so they could do their clothes at home. I thought laundromats were wonderful—not like those rooms my mother kept in La Oroya so people could wash their things by hand. But my own washing machine in my own kitchen! That was really America!"

Rosa emerges from the mid-Manhattan office building where she works and, raising one index finger, she summons a taxi. In careful English, she gives her destination and then settles back, a used Bergdorf shopping bag beside her, to enjoy the ride. Her hair is cut in a fashionable flip and her makeup reflects the latest style. Occasionally she looks left or right but mostly she keeps her eyes straight ahead. She never looks back.

4

I Don't Know Where They Came From:

Greengrocers, Doctors, and Other Koreans

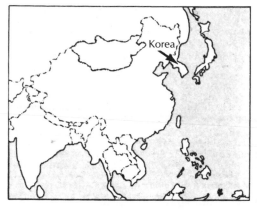

"I don't know where they came from, but I swear they weren't there last week," the history professor is telling her colleagues, "but now they've opened up one of those fruit stands on my block. You know Koreans are taking that business over." The editor of trade books for a successful New York publishing house proposes that Koreans in New York are working their way into the produce industry in hopes of capturing it and that the Korean Central Intelligence Agency is coordinating the effort. "Where else could they get all that money?" Another theory comes from the executive vice-president of a major camera distributor: Koreans are coming in large numbers to extend the teachings and influence of self-styled preacher-Messiah Sun Myung Moon and his Unification Church. "He takes these idealistic kids looking for answers, programs them to worship him and take his instructions. But he is not a religious leader—he is a politician. He wants to control American politics." Others note that the legend "made in Korea" is now found on consumer goods ranging from pots to men's suits. And a letter to the editor of *The New York Times* by an American physician warns that New York City hospitals are being increasingly staffed by foreigners, often Koreans. Plainly there is a new family on the block and New Yorkers are wondering why the Koreans are coming.

National-origins quotas (which were in effect until 1965) had severely limited Asian immigration into the United States. Under this policy, such favored countries as Great Britain and Germany were annually assigned 65,000 and 26,000 visa slots respectively, while Japan could send only 185 persons and the Philippines, 100. Those Asians who did come to the United States in these years generally entered under special categories. Thus, of approximately 13,000 Koreans settling in the United States between 1961 and 1964, 12,000 were the wives and children of American servicemen—a type of immigration not limited by the quota. By 1970, with the new law in effect five years, Asians were immigrating to the United States in ever-increasing numbers. In 1970 alone, 25,000 Filipinos entered and the new wave of Asians included 10,000 Koreans. A decade later close to 300,000 Koreans lived in the United States, 90 percent having arrived after 1965.

New York has dramatically reflected these changes. In the span of a decade Asian colonies have mushroomed, filling interstices between the older ethnic neighborhoods and often spilling over into these once-solid Italian, Jewish, Irish, Puerto Rican, and black "turfs."

In 1950 the census reported 27,909 residents "other than black or white" in New York City. The numbers doubled by 1960 and reached 177,906 a decade later. In the trend-setting sixties, the Chinese, Japanese, and Filipinos more than doubled their numbers in New York City, but the Korean migration was even more striking. The New York State Advisory Commission on Civil Rights forecast in 1976 that Koreans would "demonstrate the highest growth rate of all by 1980."

Estimates by the late 1970s placed New York's Korean population between 60,000 and 80,000 and spiraling. Despite this huge increase and the concurrent takeover of a significant portion of New York's fresh produce market, little was known about these immigrants except for sporadic headlines over the years about influence peddling in the U.S. Congress by Korean businessman Tong Sun Park and the controversy swirling around Sun Myung Moon's Church. That the picture drawn from such headlines is distorted was not doubted, yet a general suspicion of Koreans lingered. Rumors about the Reverend Moon and the Korean Central Intelligence Agency touched sensitive points. "Don't tell me about those things," says the Korean owner of an Oriental food store in Hunt's Point, Queens. "I get headaches." And to answer the unspoken charges, Lin Y. Chung hangs a sign in the window of his Aloha fruit and vegetable stand, one suspects more for native New Yorkers than for anyone else, "Moonies not welcome." Shouts another Korean at the mention of Moon's name: "You know what this Moon is? A very shrewd businessman who calls himself reverend so he have no taxes to pay and have all the Moonies work for him for free."

Though the Reverend Moon's church may divide Koreans living in America, as a nation the Korean people have shared a rich culture stretch-

Summer boathouses outside Seoul by the Han River. In the background
stands Kwan Ak, the Menacing Mountain. (*Courtesy United Nations*)

ing back over 4,000 years; modern forbears are believed to have included
invaders from the Manchurian Plain, Mongolia, and Central Asia. In response to these repeated invasions, ancient Korea tried so hard to seal itself
off that it earned the sobriquet "hermit nation." But Chinese force prevailed
and by the time of the Western medieval period Korea was nominally a
tributary state with a Buddhist religion and a Chinese system of government.

The land of Korea is generally mountainous in terrain with numerous
rich valleys, major rivers, and well-stocked forests but these natural gifts
have shaped Korea's history to a far lesser extent than has her geographic
location in the shadow of the Soviet Union, China, and Japan. Here is a
case where the map has been the message. An anomalous tongue of land
pulling the Asian perimeter into irregular shape, Korea licks at Japan from
the neighborhood of China. And because of its strategic location, it has
been subject to the will of larger powers. Japan, for instance, used the argument that "Korea [was] a dagger pointed at the heart of Japan," as if
geography alone were a threat and warranted preemptive retaliation.

In the late sixteenth century, Japanese Emperor Hideyoshi tried to use
the Korean corridor as a route to China. The Chinese sent their own troops
to stop the Japanese and both armies clashed in Korea. For these battles
staged on her soil, Korea paid a price. The "Land of the Morning Calm"

was despoiled by friend and enemy alike. Fields were torn up, treasures plundered, and skilled artisans kidnapped to be carried off to teach the secrets of their craft. The lessons of history were taken to heart and Koreans cultivated a spirited xenophobia. Late into the 1880s, signposts on Korean roads are said to have warned: "If you meet a foreigner, kill him."

By this time Japan, as well as several western powers, offered their blandishments in the hope of piercing Korea's hard shell of medieval isolationism. These repeated attempts at securing trade rights and security arrangements were rejected with protestations of fealty to China. By 1876, however, Japan refused to be put off and thrust herself into Korean affairs. The initial battleground this time was the Korean court, where intrigue and counter-intrigue twisted around the ruling power. By 1894 Japan was at war with China, a contest Japan won easily. Within the decade Japan had to prove that she could keep the spoils she had claimed and did so by thrashing the Russians in the 1905 Russo-Japanese War. These wars had one major goal: to assert, as Japanese documents phrased it, "paramount political, military and economic interests in Korea."

The Japanese insinuated themselves into Korean life with a vigor and insensitivity that left many bad feelings and fractured many Korean traditions. The Confucian system was undercut. Shortly thereafter Japan forced Korea to sign over all diplomatic freedom; by 1910 half measures were abandoned and Japan annexed the land entirely, renaming it "Chosen."

Today, more than thirty years after the end of World War II, which marked the end of Japanese control over Korea, Koreans in America still carry the anger and bear a grudge against their former rulers. "They messed up our society. Korea was a tranquil nation," Il Soo Chung, a young Korean business executive, says. He is too young to have actually seen Japanese rule in Korea. Still he knows it is their fault: "Koreans argue all the time, they don't trust each other. It's all because of them. The Japanese realized they could control more easily by setting us against each other." Koreans still speak with the passion of the wronged; not until 1965 could Japan and Korea tolerate each other enough to sign a commercial and diplomatic agreement.

The young Korean executive considers the question of ethnic identity. "No. If I were in a room full of people and there was one or two Koreans I would not feel closer to the Koreans." And it bothers Il Soo Chung that he lacks the proud brotherhood that other ethnic groups seem to have. Or it bothers him just enough at any rate to lay the blame on the Japanese. "That is what the Japanese did to us. They made us strangers to each other."

Japanese meddling, together with indigenous poverty and wretched conditions, helped set off emigration early in 1900. Some Koreans went to Cuba and Mexico, securing entree to the New World on the promise of back-breaking work as agricultural laborers; several thousand traveled to Hawaii, taking jobs on American-owned sugar and pineapple plantations; a handful came to America. In short order, however, the Korean government placed limitations on emigration, and this, together with reports of mistreatment and unfavorable working conditions, caused Korean emigration to dwindle.

Not until the end of World War II and the agonized death of Japanese imperial control did Korean immigration rise again. At first the increase was virtually imperceptible. In 1948, forty-six Koreans were admitted to the United States and in the following year only forty, hardly enough to strain the limits of America's national-origins quota. But the postwar division of Korea, the hard-fought Korean War that followed, and the consequent instability prepared many more Koreans to leave.

Fear of foreigners, one of the most formidable obstacles to emigration, gradually abated. Seoul and other cities grew into commercial centers, outposts for the world business community. Europeans, Asians, Arabs, and Americans plied their wares and produced a more cosmopolitan élan. Television, perhaps unwittingly but no less effectively, served as a perfect vehicle for cultural change, spreading western styles and attitudes far more ably than Japan had been able to do in many decades by force. Aliens and their ways became less strange, less fearsome than they had been before.

The fears that daunted emigration in the past, especially the fear that children would grow up alienated from the old traditions, were placed in modern perspective. Noted Kwong Sung Hee on the eve of his emigration in 1979: "Customs are changing in Korea too, too quickly." Even foreign diets were no longer strange to Asian palates. One Korean preparing to leave told a reporter for *The New York Times*, "I am familiar with Western food, I have eaten hamburgers."

The old style of life had strapped Koreans to one particular pattern of living. Gradually, however, this style faded from view in cities such as Seoul. Such wisps of Confucianism as persisted were sustained more by a respectful nostalgia than by a vigorous devotion. The young viewed these loyalties with curiosity, but from a respectful distance. It was as foreign to them as it was to Western teenagers to read of homes constructed as a complex of inner and outer rooms reserved for the different sexes. A Seoul youth asked about Confucianism creased his face quizzically. "Today? No way. That was in the old, old days."

Cultural tone, however, generally remains long after intellectual commitment to the past has been abandoned. A residuum persists. In 1980 modern Korean families continue to make arranged marriages; adolescence is still comparatively short and teenagers are expected to be young adults; respect naturally gravitates to the eldest male in the household; a bride is

Women cleaning mackerel unloaded at the Pusan fishmarket. (*Courtesy United Nations*)

still expected to bring her husband a dowry. The same men who wear the latest cut in men's Western clothing and follow the newest trends in business continue to believe that a wife should serve her mother-in-law. Housework in Korean is *nolda*, literally, "playing." Custom and its imperfect handmaiden, law, still provide that only a father has total control over the children, including automatic custody after divorce. Moreover, while a woman may legally have been forced to accept as her own the child of her husband's mistress, when the husband dies she receives only a small part of his estate, the greatest share being reserved for the eldest son. Not incidentally many of those emigrating from Korea have been women.

A farmer cutting rice straws in the village of Kae Bong Dong near Seoul. These straws will be mixed with soy beans to produce animal feed. (*Courtesy United Nations*)

But men are leaving too, and in ever-growing numbers. Indeed following a 1979 survey, *Dong-a-Ilbo*, a leading Korean newspaper, reported that, given the opportunity, 50 percent of South Korea's population expressed an interest in emigrating. Visitors to Korea found this unsurprising. The need to work hard and long was especially striking. "People under 60 there look like a 70-year-old American," reported one observer. "You see old-looking men and women pushing and hauling and heaving these huge bundles, the physical exertion is very heavy." Coupled with a disheartening inflation and an average per capita income of $1,500 these conditions provide sufficient cause for disillusion.

Others have bridled at the government's authoritarianism. "My father," says graduate student Jae Won Lee, "was a military officer, but he was so controlled. He was educated and he knew that the government's repressive authority was not necessary. He also knew that each one of his sons would have to serve in the army for at least three years. He thought this was a waste of years that could be used to get an education or to gain business experience."

Instability has been a many faceted curse. It has made more frightening the possibility of a North Korean attack, threatening businessmen and other members of the middle class with the possibility of a Communist takeover. And it has simultaneously provided successive South Korean regimes with the excuse to limit freedoms, to build a huge military apparatus, and to operate a dreaded secret-police system. Bourgeois Koreans, not well-enough connected to make profits from the military or from government contracts, joined those less well-off to consider emigration to America.

Only America. Reverend Song Sun Lin, pastor of a Los Angeles Church, explained: "Jews go to Jerusalem, Koreans go to the United States. America stands for freedom, liberty and security." And economic opportunity. "It is," said Ty Sok Hee who settled in New York in 1978, "a country of more and more and more." For many Koreans this impression was formed early. They remembered the war years of 1950–53 and the cornucopia of goods that always seemed to follow the American GIs—the chewing gum, the cameras, the canned foods.

Many Koreans had also invested heavily in education but could find no outlet for their knowledge in Korea. "No country the size of Korea," pointed out a college professor from Seoul, "needs as many college graduates as South Korea has." (In 1970 over 50 percent of all adult Koreans in New York had four or more years of higher education.) And such training brought far more attractive dividends in the United States than in Korea.

In the decade after 1965, more than one-quarter of all Asian immigrants were professional workers. In New York City, in 1978, two of every five doctors were graduated from foreign medical schools and many were Korean. Indeed, far more Korean doctors practiced in American cities than in Korea's rural districts. But Hyung Lum Kin, an internal management consultant for the Nestlè Company, who helped his brother and sister, both doctors, leave Korea considers the criticism leveled at emigrating physicians unjust: "In the sixties and early seventies America's medical establishment limited the number of doctors trained in the United States and when the country found itself short of doctors, foreign-trained ones were let in. These doctors had to pass very tough exams before they were allowed to practice here. For these fellows of course it was a big break. In Korea, being a doctor is no big deal. He is no higher in status than a successful businessman or attorney. In fact, medical school is easier to get into at times than business school. So the schools in Korea produce many qualified doctors. The truth is they have more doctors in Korea than they can support—not more than they need, but then American cities can use more too. So the Korean government encouraged doctors to leave. People in medicine who want to do research here can do advanced work that they just could not do in Korea."

The liberalization of Asian quotas—26,300 Koreans received visas in 1978—also brought a considerable number of Korean immigrants seeking Horatio Alger's America. The testimony of many who know the community is that a surprising number do combine ambition, thrift, and a powerful drive for education into economic success. "We can make more money here," says Byong Wook Yoon who came to the United States as a student in 1966 and built his own shoe chain. "I'm doing better than my father and I want my children to have better than me."

"Listen," exclaims another Korean, "you ask me why they come. One fellow I know was so poor in Korea that he went to join the Korean army and fought in Vietnam for the few dollars it gained him. He made friends with some American GIs and came to the United States. South Koreans who imported wigs gave him a box-full to sell. He went up to Harlem—this was in the early seventies—and stood on the streets selling, hawking, really. On some days he cleared three hundred to five hundred dollars. A day. No taxes. He took the money and opened a fruit stand in the Stuyvesant Town area. It did well. Rich Koreans bought him out and he used the money to invest in real estate. You can't buy this guy today. That could never have happened in Korea.

"My wife's distant cousin," he recalls, "was a very poor girl. Some American Koreans helped bring her here. She came in through California. There she met and married a Korean doctor and they settled in a small western town. They make an excellent living, and the money together with his status have gained her social acceptance. This could only happen in America. Now she is bringing her parents, brothers and sisters."

Bo Wey Han, who works for an American importing firm, tells a more typical story: "A friend of mine came over with his family. He invested a few dollars in a vegetable stand in downtown Manhattan. He and his sons got up early, went to the market early, and tried to pick out the best fruit. He worked hard, very long hours—one thing you have to say, for people who are willing to work hard, New York is a good place to come to—and he built it up. He took some of his earnings and invested in a candy store. Then he bought two more vegetable and fruit stands. They are still trying to establish legal residency here (they came as visitors). Their kids work hard too and they make a lot of money."

Over the five years from 1976 to 1980, hundreds of Korean-run fruit and vegetable stands sprang up all over the New York metropolitan area. "You don't need much money," explained one immigrant greengrocer, "maybe $5,000 to open a store, and this business is easy to learn." All family members, in a throwback to a previous immigrant era, pitched in, working long hours and ploughing profits back into the business. Days, sixteen- to eighteen-hours long, were not uncommon, starting with a pre-dawn trip to the wholesale produce market at Hunt's Point and not ending until the last of the rush-hour crowd settled down for their suppers. "Americans think we set up or something, think we are set up by Reverend Moon

Recently arrived Koreans operating a Sunnyside, Queens fruit market. Koreans have flocked to this business, opening about six hundred such businesses in the New York area since 1970. (*Courtesy Korea News, Hankook Ilbo*)

or somebody because so many Koreans are in this business. Not true. It's just that we put in sometimes twenty hours a day. In Korea we always work long hours."

For many, the fruit and vegetable business represented the first step toward larger enterprise, and these plans often seemed to work out quite well. One newspaper, in 1979, counted more than twenty-five Korean wholesalers, mostly in textiles and electronic equipment, along a twelve-block area in midtown Manhattan. And other observers reported Korean-operated businesses scattered over the outer boroughs as well. Except for a few, all these businesses were opened by recently settled immigrants.

Koreans in America have formed two large communities, one on each coast. Los Angeles holds the single largest Korean community in the United States, and New York the second. In Los Angeles the tightly concentrated immigrant community, "Koreatown," was established along busy Olympic Boulevard, supplanting what used to be Mexican, Japanese, and Jewish businesses. The community was heavy with professionally trained Koreans, but even those who came credentialed often encountered their difficulties at first. Kim Mook Lee, a pharmacist by training, could not get into that field so he sank what money he had into a risky garment factory. "The only

Koreatown in Los Angeles, California which contains the largest concentration of Koreans in the United States. (*Courtesy Korea News, Hankook Ilbo*)

thing my wife knows is sewing. The only thing I know is pharmacy. Pharmacy is impossible so sewing is the only way."

They were sustained by examples. Hi Duc Lee came to Los Angeles with fifty dollars in his pocket. He took a menial job as a dishwasher and today operates his own restaurant. The examples are riveting. More than 2,000 Angelino Koreans have invested in such businesses as gas stations, insurance agencies, nightclubs, dance schools, martial-arts parlors and, of course, greengroceries.

No identifiable Koreatown developed in New York. Smaller, less distinct Korean neighborhoods sprouted in such Queens neighborhoods as Jackson Heights, Flushing and Woodside, and along the Grand Concourse in the Bronx. The largest, the Flushing community, grew to about 20,000 Koreans by 1980 and on almost every block in this polyglot community, which also held a sizeable number of newcomers from Japan, India, China, Colombia, and Cuba, stood a Korean-owned business. When Queens builder Richard Fiorenze opened a seven-story, forty-one unit apartment building in this neighborhood in 1979 he was so overwhelmed by applications from Koreans, who paid $50,000 and more for the two-bedroom condominiums, that he named the complex "Seoul Plaza I." Although the Korean community in New York produced four foreign-language newspapers and a variety of

A conference of local leaders in the Queens Koream community studying
the results of a recent neighborhood election. (*Courtesy Korea News, Hankook Ilbo*)

business, community and professional associations, little overt "Koreanness"
marks their neighborhoods. Driving down their streets one cannot discern a
special Asian flavor. Churches often meet in the basements of nondescript
buildings and no street festivals or other visible cultural activities draw attention to these neighborhoods. The community appears happy with its hard
work, low profile, and good name.

Articles in *The New York Times* in the 1970s used such adjectives as
"studious," "industrious," "driven," "resourceful," "intelligent," "hard-
working," to describe the Korean communities and *Newsweek* wrote of Koreans' "thrift," "cleanliness" and "patriotism." Even in the sensitive seventies, when stereotypes often upset editors, these Horatio Alger heroes seemed
to be understood only in broad terms, as a group, and from a respectable
distance.

At first glance Il Soo Kim seems to fit all the stereotypes as he steps
confidently into his office at a major airline and waves his visitor in. The
office is neatly furnished, orderly, and utilitarian. Indeed, the single most
striking aspect of the office is its sparse orderliness. Even the collection of
interminably folded computer printouts stands neatly piled in the corner.

The walls are clear of any ornaments except for a lean sketch of an airport hangar.

Mr. Kim dresses well and carefully. He earns a good salary and he spends it all so that he can live well. Part of living well is dressing tastefully. Another part—according to office gossip—had been his reputation with women, particularly pretty stewardesses who found him attractive and interesting. That part, however, ended abruptly several years ago when he walked into the office one day and told his shocked friends that a marriage had been arranged with a girl from Korea and he was going to settle down to his obligations. Arranged? A Korean girl who spoke no English? Did he think that was what he wanted? They did not understand. He was twenty-eight, time to settle down, and therefore he was certain this was the right thing. The only way.

The phone rings and he excuses himself. At first he speaks English although the caller is clearly Korean, but then he breaks into Korean. It would not do, he later explains, to speak English to a compatriot. It would be taken as putting on airs.

Kim has been in the United States for twelve years, and many Koreans who have come more recently turn to him for advice or help. He is ambivalent about this role. It is nice to be needed, he explains, but sometimes it is even nicer to be left alone. Yet he would never say this to any of his callers, who are invariably older than he and would likely speak badly of him in the Korean community if he did not respond to their needs with proper respect.

The Kim family came to America in 1965. Il Soo, his brother Il Won, two sisters, Susie and Nancy, and his parents. His father, a military man since 1945, had achieved the rank of colonel in the Korean armed forces but the continued instability and political intrigue in Korea convinced him to leave for the United States.

Il Soo settled with his parents in Princeton, New Jersey, where the elder Kim worked as a research physicist. The children took the change of countries in stride. Members of a generation that knew the American world from television and movies, they were neither surprised by nor interested in New York (where they entered the country); Princeton was even less remarkable.

"I expected all Americans to be blond and blue-eyed like, like Robert Redford. I also thought the buildings would be higher. The Lincoln Tunnel, though, was really impressive. But my father was happy. We could develop freer. You can't study with a clear head if you're always on guard. Afraid of North Korea, of war, of Communism, of all sorts of restrictions.

"Harlem was real scary. I had never seen anything like that in my life. The movies and TV never showed that part of America. I was really shocked. By the conditions *and* by the people who lived there.

"Korea is a society of one race. Coming here I felt very uncomfortable with black people. The American Negro soldiers in Korea are really considered inferior and even dangerous. On the other hand I was surprised when we visited an army buddy of my father in Georgia and he could not eat with us in the restaurant because he was black.

"We settled down in Princeton. I did not feel much discrimination or hatred. Ignorant people might make faces or some kids would pull their eyes into a slant, but it did not bother me. It didn't scare me. I grew up American. Let me put it this way. If I had Caucasian features I would have been a 100 percent American.

"I remember mostly that I was bored. It was so rural. I was used to Seoul, a big modern city. And in Princeton there wasn't much to do. There weren't any baseball parks, no sports teams, nothing. So I was excited at the idea of going to Columbia University in New York.

"I felt good at Columbia. Some Koreans feel discrimination if they go out with a Caucasian girl and fall in love and then are rejected by the parents. I never got serious with Caucasian girls. My father taught me to anticipate racial problems and to expect some prejudice. That way you are prepared.

"Look I have some handicaps. I can't speak or write like a native American. I don't feel it's necessarily wrong if therefore a company doesn't make me president or public relations man. That's not racial injustice, it's just my own shortcomings.

"Columbia had a lot of Asian students and it was okay. We hung out together. We were not political at all. I did not give Vietnam or civil rights much thought. But I did well on my grades. Koreans do well in school. Most of those who go to college here are from upper-class families. Koreans are a small minority and we know it is tough to get a good position. If I were an American I would choose a native over an immigrant. So I have to do better in school. You have to be better than the American to compete with him. Just like Jews who borrow money or sell property to send their children to school, Koreans know the value of education. Koreans study harder and, just like blacks are better athletes because they play more ball, we are better students because we know education is so important.

"When the radical students took over the buildings at Columbia in 1968 I really hated what SDS [Students for a Democratic Society] did. I was a jock on the baseball team, but my roommate was in SDS and we argued all the time. I felt it was wrong to be so disrespectful toward government, school, and professors. I look back and I still feel they were wrong, but they were effective—you see I'm more of a New Yorker now, I measure things pragmatically—they got what they wanted. Anyway I thought college was classes, parties, and sports, not political confrontation over things like building a gymnasium in Morningside Heights. So when SDS took over the college buildings and the cops smashed them, I was off at the beach having a vacation."

Kim does not live in a Korean neighborhood. He considers these communities crutches for people who do not know their way around the language and customs of New York. He knows both and so he rejects the "ghetto" for the full challenge of living "American" in New York. His bond with other Koreans is not through proximity but through the telephone. It is his duty to talk with them but not to live with them.

"I don't want too many Korean friends. There are problems and social demands. It was okay when I was single. It's part of the Korean culture to go to bars and drink into the night. I remember once drinking with my friends, talking about, you know, sex. Suddenly they are all talking about circumcision. It's common for Korean teenagers to have this done; it's supposed to increase sexual pleasure. My friends all had it done in Korea and were surprised to hear I didn't. So they taunted me and dared me, and one offered me five dollars, betting that I was too afraid to go through with it. So I got it done. It was painful.

"That kind of thing was fine before I got married. But I have a wife. I am supposed to be with her and not running around. I don't even like to see these fellows too often because if they come by and call for me I have to go with them. You don't refuse. That's the way the culture is. If an American friend came over and wanted to stay at my apartment for a night or two I could refuse, but a Korean would be insulted. We don't even go to Korean cultural events; it only means meeting more people and doing more favors, checking this or that or making telephone calls. It would take them five hours to get an answer and it takes me one hour, but it's one of *my* hours. If I refuse I get a bad name in the community.

"Most Koreans I know and keep friendly with are professionals, scattered around the city. They avoid the Korean neighborhoods. The people living together in the neighborhoods are from lower-class backgrounds. Back home my family would not mix with such people. Even if they do get lucky and make money they are still essentially lower class. No education, no sophistication. There are no facets on their personality. They can't carry on a conversation. Some people can only make money.

"I have much more in common with a native New Yorker than with a Korean greengrocer. The world is so much smaller that people from cities like Seoul, Paris, Rome, and New York have a cosmopolitan culture in common. Except for language I had less adjustment problems than someone coming to New York from Mississippi. The same would go for someone coming from Milan or Rome; a Sicilian would have big problems adjusting but he would have problems in Rome too.

Assimilation American style. A Korean beauty pageant held at Town Hall, New York in 1980. (*Courtesy Korea News, Hankook Ilbo*)

"I like the big city. It would bother me if my neighbors came around and welcomed me to the neighborhood. I want to be left alone. I want no obligations, and New York gives me that. My neighborhood is not at all a community. It's a place to live, a base from which to go to work, live with my wife and go out for entertainment. Older people from Korea might need a community life, I don't.

"Don't get me wrong. I am a Korean. I still speak and think Korean. When I was ready to get married I knew it must be a Korean girl. For national and racial reasons it was important, but also because my Korean past would have no outlet if I married an American.

"My wife's family is in business in Korea. If my grandfather were alive he probably would have opposed the marriage for that reason. I am from a family of scholars, government officials and military men—we are higher status. And I now realize that these things do make a difference. Her family is very materialistic and money conscious. It took me a while to show her my way of thinking—that money is not everything.

"Yes, it was an arranged marriage. I had been going back to Korea once or twice a year—working for an airline, that's not unusual—and I had been going with a girl. But her family name was identical with mine and Korean law prohibits such marriages. The situation is changing and sometimes such couples just settle down together and after they have a child the marriage is recognized. Her family thought it was a terrible thing for a Kim to marry a Kim so her family used its connections to kidnap her and stop her from seeing me. And that ended it.

"Then I did it the right way. My relatives back home knew when I would be coming to Korea and arranged meetings with four or five girls who

The annual Korean Parade passing by Macy's on Broadway. (*Courtesy Korea News, Hankook Ilbo*)

came from good backgrounds. I chose one, we went out four or five times and then got married.

"My friends here at the office could not understand how I could marry without knowing the girl. The truth is you can make a terrible marriage with someone you know three years. The chances are probably just as good for a bad marriage after three years of going together as after three months. It's after marriage that you work together to build it, not before. I knew that my wife was Korean, that she came from a good family and that she was very pretty. Of course I didn't love her when we got married—I hardly knew her. But we were ready to work at it and falling in love could come later.

"We were of different religions, but that was not a problem. Religion is just not that important in Korea. I was baptized a Protestant and my wife's family is Buddhist, but we got married in a Catholic Church. My wife's brother married a Catholic, and my wife thought the church was beautiful, so when we were ready she asked the priest if we could be married there. It didn't bother him that neither of us was Catholic.

"I brought my wife to the United States a month later, and it was pretty rough. She missed her friends and family, but her own parents wanted her to live here. It's a move up to come to America—you escape the fears and the narrowness of Korea. But she couldn't get used to it. After about six

Students playing the Kaya-Ko, a long zither with twelve strings, at the National Classical Music Institute in Seoul. (*Courtesy United Nations*)

months we went back to see Seoul and then she realized that she wasn't comfortable there anymore. In Korea she realized how American she had become.

"She has no job although she is a trained pianist. Her parents forced her to study piano eight to ten hours a day for twenty years and she obeyed. She hated every minute of it and now she refuses to touch a piano. She has no other skill. The only thing she could do is be a waitress and I don't want that. I wouldn't mind if she was more independent. If she wanted to go to a bar drinking with her friends it's okay. If she doesn't want to wear a bra it's okay with me. Others think it's improper, but if she is comfortable it's okay with me. But, well I'm 60 percent Korean and 40 percent American and sometimes I am close to 100 percent Korean. I worry how it would look if she took a job as a waitress. People would think she had to work because I don't make enough. In Korea appearances are very important. Here if I lost my job I could go out and drive a cab. In Korea I could never do that. I must save face. I would rather stay in my house—even starve, even die— to keep my honor and reputation.

"That's something I can't understand about some of these people living in New York. The Korean idea of honor may be too much, but look at these Puerto Ricans. They don't care about their name at all. They don't have any pride. I would never hire a Puerto Rican and I could never be friends with one. They are so irresponsible. Those F.A.L.N. [a group devoted to militantly working for an independent Puerto Rico] bombings serve no purpose. You go up to Spanish Harlem and it is filthy. If you park your car they steal your battery, your antenna, everything.

"I don't have black friends, but I can understand the black people. They were forced to come here and whites never gave them a chance, but Puerto Ricans could have stayed home, and if they do come here why do they have to ruin the city? They don't contribute to this society. It's not right. Let them go back.

"I can't really say they are all alike and maybe I just don't understand them and their problems. But I don't think I ever will.

"Korea is a society of one race and nationality. Prejudice comes easy. I remember how surprised I was about Jews. I heard so much about them being stingy and how they dressed in weird clothing that I asked a student next to me at Columbia to show me a Jew. It turned out the guy I asked was Sheldon Bernstein.

"Now one of my best friends is an orthodox Jew, but some Koreans do have bad feelings for Jews. Businessmen from Korea find that their competitors are often Jews and they resent the sharp business practices. They are also envious. Take Columbia, Jews got in because they had high grades; blacks got in because the school wanted to be liberal. Blacks were no threat, but the Jews were. They are so competitive that they are self-centered. But many Koreans are like that too. Education is always useful. A vegetable stand can burn down; education lasts. The situation in South Korea is uncertain. If North Korea comes down and Communism should take over, money means nothing, but education would still be valuable.

When the subject turns to politics Kim says: "The Korean political system is similar to the one here in the United States." His statement, comparing the two governments, is surprising. In 1978 when he made the comment, it did not fit with newspaper reports outlining an authoritarian political regime in stark detail. Kim, however, seemed quite aware of the contradictions, and of his listener's disbelief. He continued, "I can't speak freely. I have to be very careful. You know there is a Korean Central Intelligence Agency, I am afraid to tell you everying. . . ."

But Kim is too acclimated to New York, where people speak openly, almost defiantly, about what is on their minds. He looks out a window as if to remind himself that yes, he is in New York, and he steps out of his prudence.

"Yes, the Korean constitution guarantees all freedoms. People there can vote and speak out and write in the press, but the government stuffs ballot boxes and is very hard on critics. You can be arrested for criticizing the government. It's not spelled out anywhere what you can and what you cannot do—but you don't try too much.

"Growing up in Seoul the other kids and I just knew that it was not proper to say bad things about the government, just like you didn't say bad things about your elders. As you got older you knew it could cost you a college education or a good job to say something critical. Most of the teenagers consider it smart to keep quiet.

"I don't like that situation. Maybe it was necessary in the fifties when South Korea was at war, but there is no immediate danger today. It is not right for people to have to be so afraid.

"Even here in New York a Korean has to be very brave or very foolish to speak openly in criticizing the government of Korea. KCIA has agents all over. They take pictures and put people on blacklists. If these critics ever go home for a visit they can lose their passports and be locked in jail. Even if they don't go back, their relatives can be harassed and denounced as Communists. The grapevine tells about people who have even been kidnapped here in America and taken back to Korea. It's a scary situation and people generally keep quiet. In Los Angeles it is even worse. There the people live in a tight community and the KCIA has set enough examples to terrify them. They are like Mafias; they come at night and destroy everything you have."

Kim opens up, exploring his complex feelings toward his homeland. He speaks of his fears, and his hopes, but the depths of these fears become apparent when in mid-sentence he stops, looks around quizzically, and asks "Why am I telling you this?

"Until I am well known and can do something I must keep quiet. I can't afford to become an enemy; I want eventually to go back. I love Korea and I want to change it, through political action.

"Americans just don't understand. I once told an American that if I could save his life by cutting off my arm I wouldn't think twice, because to me life is very important, even if it is *your* life it is more important than *my* arm. Koreans understand this. Koreans are a philosophical people; they sit and talk about life." Kim pauses and reflects a moment. "I don't like to do that. It might be interesting, but there is no definite answer to these questions and talking about them just puts me behind my everyday work. I guess in that way I've become a real New Yorker."

5

Someplace Else If Not America:

Irish Women's Journey

Ann Gilvarry sits on a bar stool on Manhattan's East Side. Her hair is fashionably cut and she wears the latest velour top. She might as well be in a separate room for all the attention she shows the men who sit down next to her, try to strike up a conversation and then, finding themselves ignored, move on. Ann Gilvarry is very intent on what she is saying.

"I'm Irish. I came to New York in 1968. It was March, I remember, but very warm. I was just seventeen but I always thought I would come. Two things I always said I would do—grow taller than my father and go to America. I succeeded in only one—I am just five feet tall.

"I don't remember when I first started thinking about emigrating. Probably I was very young. My uncle had come over here. He and my aunt lived in the Bronx and when they came back to visit us they seemed to have a good life. They would rent a car—something that seemed very extravagant to us. They just seemed to have plenty of money for whatever they wanted to do. Not rich. I didn't think they were rich but I knew they were very comfortable.

Irish farms have always lost young men and women to Irish cities or to cities across the Atlantic. (*Courtesy United Nations, P. Slaughter*)

"I would have gone someplace else if not to America. Maybe Dublin or Galway. I knew I never wanted to stay on the farm. My father had seventy-five acres. Started out with only twelve but by the time he died he had seventy-five. The neighbors used to say, 'He had a nice bit of land.' But everybody knew my brother would get that. Nobody ever thought different or even questioned it. So the four of us (I have three sisters) we all came to America.

"What did my parents say? Well, they couldn't object. Mind you I told them I was leaving but I didn't ask their permission. My aunt sponsored me so my parents knew I was going to be looked after. One sister was already here so it seemed more like I was going to join family.

"As soon as I got off the plane at Kennedy Airport I got my green card. They made it out right then so I entered all legal and I went to live with my uncle and aunt in the Bronx. 170th Street and University to be exact. That area still had some Irish in 1968 but now there's nobody left. My aunt was one of the last to go. Blacks had already started moving in even when I came but I didn't pay that much attention at first because black or white—it was just America to me. So many new things to take in all at once. Now if you go to 170th Street and University, you won't find anything but black and Puerto Rican—that's how fast it's changed.

"In Ireland we had a few blacks but no prejudice at all. I even dated one. Met him where I worked. His name was Abdul or something exotic like that and he was really a hunk of man. Six feet tall and I thought going out with him was really something. Can't remember if my friends or parents objected—don't even know where he came from or how he got to that tiny town in Ireland, but I found him exciting—out of the ordinary.

"Do I date blacks in New York? Never! I mean—after riding on the number 4 train, how can you ask? They aren't anything like Abdul or any of the blacks I knew in Ireland. Most of those were West Indian, I guess, with a few from India and Pakistan. Maybe I shouldn't group them all together and call them black but we did there. All the same to us.

"My first job in New York was taking care of kids. Good job. Roof over your head and fifty dollars a week. All I thought about was saving up for the trip back to Ireland in the summer. And that's what I did: worked until June, quit my job and went back to Ireland for three months. Then back to New York to find a new family to work for. Same thing the next year. After about five years of that I decided I'd do something else. Get a different kind of job for one thing. The last woman whose children I watched was a little crazy and that's what made me decide to go to beauticians school. Now I work on 53rd Street here in Manhattan. Make a nice bit of money. Pretty much can do as I please. Quite a few Irish girls go to beauty school—not the illegal ones, they have to work for families off the books—but those of us who have green cards, yes.

"I'm not quite sure exactly why I chose this kind of work or even when it was I decided I would probably stay in America permanently. Those summers back in Ireland just stopped. I guess in 1975. One thing—I had become engaged to a boy there but then we broke off. So really the reason for going back just wasn't there. And I became an American citizen. My younger sister had come to New York and my life seemed more here than there.

"You think the Irish have assimilated? Melted in? Maybe we have. I think we want to. I do. People say I have hardly a trace of the Irish accent and that makes me very happy. I never wanted to live in an Irish section of Queens. If I had wanted to live with Irish people, I would have stayed in Ireland. Maybe fifty years ago the Irish in New York felt they had to stick together—for moral support and to help each other out. But I think we're past that now. We're accepted everyplace. You soon forget you're Irish.

"Two of my sisters married Italians here in New York and then they moved to New Jersey. The husbands wanted their little patch of land. That's the way Italians are. But I'm still very close to both my sisters even though they have moved out of the city—only one, the youngest, still lives near me. None of us will go back to live in Ireland. Why should we? What's for us there? I don't mean to say Ireland is all poor or anything like that. I know many Americans think it's all straw huts or something. Where they get their ideas! Then they go there and see a lot of two-car garages—full! People dressed pretty well. It's not that Ireland is so poor. It's better off than England now, I think, but it's just that opportunities are better in America. And that's why I came here—for the opportunities."

As Ann Gilvarry walks out of the East Side bar towards her apartment on 68th Street, there is nothing about her to distinguish her ethnicity. Very little in her conversation—except her own admission—had marked her as having arrived in the city little more than ten years earlier. Even to the careful observer, she is a young American woman—very much at home in New York.

Except on March 17, when the city runs green from all its pores, or along a few blocks in Jackson Heights where pubs offer Guinness on tap, New York's shamrock is now a pale version of its once brilliant green. Its owners wear it less often, if not less proudly. Although no one dares write the obituary for Irish power in the city, just as no serious political candidate risks missing the St. Patrick's Day march down Fifth Avenue, the obeisance is a tribute more to things past than to things to come—to a time when Irish presence was more strongly felt in New York. It is not that the city lacks an Irish presence so much as that the Irish have lost their sense of being one ethnic group united around important commonalities and continually revitalized by many new immigrants.

The tribes and clans of Eire land are among the people who have always been movers, one historian observed. Whether their destination is the nearest city or the next continent, a distance one hundred miles or two thousand, matters less to those with this strong desire for change than that some move be made. In earlier centuries, clansmen in Ireland journeyed from one place to another to find greener pastures; much later, of course, instead of better fishing streams or richer hunting grounds they sought out factory jobs or domestic employment, no matter where these new opportunities presented themselves. It was this wanderlust, as well as the proximity of Ireland to England, which sparked Irish interest in North America from the earliest days of the new continent's settlement. Ireland sent its sons and daughters in the early seventeenth century across the Atlantic as though that ocean were just a longer version of the Irish Sea. Some of the more adventuresome among the first Irish to come to America signed on as indentured servants. Others tried to avoid that commitment only to have it thrust upon them by English captors who kidnapped them and shipped them across the Atlantic as their prisoners. A heterogeneous contingent of Irish settlers came to America before the American Revolution, supplying the largest non-English group in the colonies.

In spite of their numbers or perhaps because of them, Irish settlers often encountered a cool welcome. Catholics came up against hostile Protestants;

even non-Catholics, who constituted a majority of the Irish immigrants in the years before 1776, met with prejudice. (Later these Protestant Irish took the name "Scotch-Irish" to emphasize that they worshipped at a different altar.) Although their Protestantism and their knowledge of English might have equipped these Scotch-Irish for easy adjustment in the North American colonies, their fierce independence and preference for settling in isolated, rural areas got them a reputation for being difficult and uncooperative with authorities.

The American Revolution gave transplanted Irishmen a chance to fight an older battle against the English, an opportunity not many wanted to miss. A few sided with the British loyalists but most did not. On the rebel side, Irishmen proved dedicated fighters, causing the British commander-in-chief, Sir Henry Clinton, to charge in 1778 that the Irish were the colonists' best soldiers, meaning they were Britain's worst enemies. More than a few observers agreed with the conclusion voiced in the Irish Parliament at the war's end that it was the Sons of Erin who had cost Britain its America.

Irish immigration rose sharply in the first half of the nineteenth century. Of those arriving in the United States between 1820 and 1840, one-third were Irish. Then the great potato famine of the 1840s resulted in the largest immigration to the United States that the country has ever experienced, relative, that is, to its native population. Sweeping across the country and rotting undug potatoes in a wide swath, the potato blight of the 1840s rocked Ireland. Disease, especially cholera, played mercilessly on a people already weakened from starvation. In just six years the population decreased by more than two million, half going to their graves and the others to emigrant ships.

Their decision to leave Ireland and try again in America was made in many cases not by choice but in desperation. It is true that subsidized fares, discounted ship tickets, and scandalously misleading propaganda announcing abundant opportunities in America all tilted the decision for many in favor of the move, but thousands of others left the land and boarded the crowded carriers, which took the name "coffin" or "fever" ships, simply because this route offered the only way out.

After the worst of the famine was over, Irish men and women continued to look west. Between 1820 and 1920 nearly 5 million Irish immigrants entered the United States. Outnumbered only by German arrivals, these nineteenth-century Irish immigrants differed from the earlier arrivals in that they were almost all Roman Catholic. These later waves showed a clear preference for city life, particularly along the Atlantic seaboard. The frontier, which had attracted the colonial Irish, exerted little pull on the later immigrants. No more potato famines would starve them out. They would stake their claims in the cities of the East where they could find jobs for wages, a Catholic parish, and the chance to socialize with men who spoke in familiar accents in neighborhood saloons away from Protestant temperance crusaders.

The nineteenth-century Irish immigration made New York the most Irish of all American cities. (Philadelphia relinquished its number one spot after 1800.) By 1860 one in four New Yorkers spoke with a brogue. Yet the situation of the Irish during the third quarter of the nineteenth century was still a particularly difficult one. The times were such that discrimination could be openly stated in the city's newspapers. The *New York Sun* in 1853 ran this advertisement: "Woman wanted to do general housework: English, Scotch, Welsh, German or any country or color except Irish."

By the end of the nineteenth century, however, these attitudes had all but disappeared. Irish women became the largest single ethnic group in New York's private kitchens during these years. For the young women who came to America with the intention of working as domestics, this appeared perfect employment. Though other groups may have objected to their women working in other people's houses, the Irish saw it differently: domestic work offered a clean place to live and a chance to be one's own boss much of the time.

Whether Irish women immigrated because of acceptable employment in America or because of dissatisfaction with Ireland is unclear, but by the late 1890s they outnumbered Irish men in the crowds arriving at Ellis Island. Some women commented that life on Irish farms was especially hard on women, and mortality figures for the nineteenth century support their observation. Women died at increasingly younger ages due to a lack of medical attention, especially at childbirth, and from hard work and inadequate diet. After the marriage age began a steady climb in the 1800s and more women stayed single longer (by 1881 about 40 percent of women between twenty-five and thirty-four were single), more women could consider the option of emigration. Ireland's authority structure demanded strict subjection of women within the family but recognized that Irish girls would leave the family, if the farm could no longer offer employment, and go out to work elsewhere, whether that meant the next farm house, the nearest city, or across the ocean.

While Irish women concentrated in domestic work in the nineteenth century, most Irish men entered the American labor force as blue-collar workers. (In 1880 only 13 percent of the Irish men in New York City held white-collar jobs.) While men who lacked skills had to work by the day at whatever jobs they could find, others with more training took work as bartenders, porters, carpenters, and blacksmiths.

Irish men soon learned that politics formed an available route out of poverty. In the 1820s, when New York City permitted men without property to vote and the Society of the Sons of Tammany altered its position on

The tradition of the annual St. Patrick's Day Parade down New York's Fifth Avenue goes back to before the United States was founded. (*Peter J. Harris*)

foreign-born members, the Irish benefited. These changes, combined with the growing number of Irish in New York, put them in line for a share of political rewards. Soon the Irish sought the jobs of passing out the favors, developing tight organizations to serve a rapidly growing city. Their political ability had little to do with conviviality, Daniel Patrick Moynihan would observe later. Some of the most successful among them had the least charm, but their healthy disrespect for both propriety and the legitimacy of formal government, traits acquired during centuries of fighting against English rule, served them well. Rural Ireland had also put emphasis on the kinds of personal relationships and respect for seniority that were fundamental in the political machines that the Irish developed in American cities. Long after the Irish percentage in the cities fell, overshadowed by immigration from Southern and Eastern Europe, Irish bosses continued to hold on to power.

Guyl O'Dell, harpist, performs at the Irish Arts Center in New York City on
St. Patrick's Day, 1981. (*Courtesy Irish Arts Center*)

Their disrespect for the legitimacy of formal government diminished as
Irish men found themselves more and more in control of government, first
on the city level, then on the state and national levels. In no case is this
more evident than in the changed reaction to the cause for Northern Ireland's independence from British rule. In the late 1960s the Irish Northern
Aid Committee and other groups publicizing the cause of independence
passed out pamphlets on New York's sidewalks charging "Torture in Ireland" and outlining examples of brutality in prisons. When the St. Patrick's
Day parade closed Fifth Avenue in 1969 (the 207th time the Saint's day had
been celebrated by a parade in New York, making the festivity older than
the United States), some marchers wore black armbands. "The loudest ap-
plause I heard that day," said one observer, "did not go to politicians John
Lindsay, Hugh Carey and the others who were there. It went to the large
banners, saying, 'England Get Out of Ireland.' "

By the mid-1970s that part of the parade was missing, a casualty of
American Irish reaction to the violence in Northern Ireland. When the
city's newspapers carried stories of women and children being killed, new
questions were asked about the organizations in the United States that
claimed to be collecting money for relief of victims but were suspected of

supplying weapons for further damage. On Christmas eve, 1975, one New York newspaper reported that "relief" organizations in the United States sent 85 percent of the weapons used by terrorists in the Irish Republican Army (I.R.A.). The newspaper did not claim as its source either the United States or the English government but cited Garret FitzGerald, Foreign Minister of the Irish Republic: "Hundreds of the deaths in Ireland have resulted from money being collected in the United States being used for the purchase of guns by the I.R.A. Every dollar bill contributed to agencies such as the Irish Northern Aid Committee (Noraid) contributes to the killing of the Irish people."

Four prominent Irish American politicians called for a ban on contributions. A look at the offices they held shows how far Irish Americans had moved away from what Moynihan termed a "healthy disrespect for the legitimacy of formal government." Moynihan, by 1977 senator from New York, joined New York's Governor Hugh Carey, Massachusetts Senator Edward Kennedy, and Speaker of the House of Representatives, Thomas P. O'Neill, Jr. to call on Americans to "renounce any action that promotes the current violence or provides support or encouragement for organizations engaged in violence." They did not refer to the I.R.A. by name but their implication was clear. A few weeks later, Governor Carey journeyed to Ireland where he was even more outspoken. In Dublin he called the I.R.A. "killers" and "Marxists" and said they should not receive a nickel from Irish Americans.

The move to discourage contributions to the Northern Ireland cause was by no means unanimous. Paul O'Dwyer, a perennial fighter for the underdog, called attention to the misgovernment and maltreatment that the English had inflicted on Northern Ireland. Unlike those who called for the ban, O'Dwyer was born in Ireland and emigrated to the United States in 1924. "I was more or less attuned to injustice and tyranny," O'Dwyer said, "because I have seen it first hand." He criticized *The New York Times* for "ranting" against the I.R.A. when it should rightfully concentrate on other issues such as protecting the rights of those unfairly arrested and tried in this country for supplying arms to Northern Ireland.

The decisive weight, however, lay with O'Dwyer's opponents. Fewer and fewer Irish Americans in New York attended rallies or contributed to the Northern Ireland cause. As the older Ireland-born men and women with bad memories of English rule die, and as their American-born children express less and less interest in the issue, it has simply lost its life. For the newest Irish immigrants to the United States, the Northern Ireland question does not provide a strong cause for unity.

If every ethnic group needs, in order to develop a thriving ethnic consciousness, a home-country issue around which to unite, the Irish Americans lost an important cause with the obscuring of the Northern Ireland situation. That so many Irish held high political office in America—in 1980 the two most populous states had governors with Irish names—signaled that Irish Americans had also moved far away from their old stance of outsiders questioning the establishment. Now they spoke from inside. (When President Ronald Reagan was shot on March 30, 1981, he and the other three men injured all had Irish names.)

The other matter around which Irish Americans had formerly united—their Catholicism—had also changed by 1980. New York's Catholic churches demonstrate the change. As Irish immigration started to grow in the early nineteenth century, St. Patrick's was started at the corner of Mott and Prince Streets. It served the needs of an Irish neighborhood and provided Catholic leaders for the city. By the 1850s, Irish immigration had so swelled the number of parishioners and success had so increased the fortunes of the earlier arrivals that Archbishop John Hughes convinced his flock that they deserved a grander place of worship. When the spiraling, Gothic St. Patrick's Cathedral at Fifth Avenue and 50th Street was ready for dedication in 1879, New York's Catholic hierarchy read like an Irish men's club: Loughlin, McQuaid, Ryan, McNeiry, Wadhams, Corrigan, and Conroy. By the time the Cathedral celebrated its centennial in May 1979, the list of members and the language of the masses had changed, reflecting changes in immigration. A substantial number of the new immigrants from Latin America, many of them devoted Catholics, have put more Spanish accents in today's parish pulpits and confessionals—even the list of prospective bishops and cardinals. Only one in five of the Catholics in the United States is Irish.

If Irish immigration to the United States were larger, a sense of ethnic consciousness might be revived, but conditions both in Ireland and the United States have kept the numbers low. On the home island, Irish men and women in more recent years have tended to prefer the United Kingdom, often London, especially after English legislation in the early 1960s turned West Indians away and opened job opportunities. In the United States, the 1965 immigration law appeared to the Irish as an attempt to keep them out. The old quotas of the 1920s assigned them higher numbers than they were able to reach, but the new law gave every country the same limit (20,000) and stressed reuniting families, a provision that did not do much for the Irish. Their immigration had tended to be of single individuals who formed families in the United States while Southern Europeans, especially Italians and Greeks, had not only come over in family groups, they had then called over parents, brothers, and sisters. In the 1960s Southern Europeans in New York were well situated under the 1965 law to call over additional family members. The Irish were not.

The provision of the 1965 law that encouraged the immigration of skilled men and women also hurt the Irish. Critics of the legislation noted that the Irish had never had a highly skilled immigration to the United States but that the unskilled workers had made an important contribution. William F. Ryan, Democrat from Manhattan's Upper West Side which included many people of Irish descent, said, "My concern is with the near eclipse of immigration from many nations whose sons have built America." Concern for the effect of the 1965 law on Irish immigration went beyond the Irish American community, extending to others who asked that traditional immigration source countries, with close ties to the United States in language, politics, and culture, should not now be discriminated against in favor of people from more alien cultures.

As the effect of the 1965 law was felt, Irish protests grew louder. The Irish American Immigration Committee charged that immigration from Ireland was being reduced to "virtually zero." When St. Patrick's Day came around in 1968 the Committee was on hand to pass out buttons with the legend "Immigration or Die" surrounding a shamrock. Marchers in the parade carried signs urging that more Irish be admitted. "Why Keep Out the Bartenders and Maids?" one sign read. "We Need Them Too."

One letter writer to *The New York Times* mused on the irony of the situation. A century earlier, Denis Kearney, Irish-born labor leader, had led the fight to keep unskilled workers out of the United States. The target at that time was the Chinese worker. Now it was the Irish unskilled workers, desiring to come to the United States, who found entry difficult.

Because the 1965 law favors skilled workers and individuals with immediate family in the United States, the Irish who do enter tend to be highly trained. Indeed, they bring more skills than do most other immigrants. Almost 33 percent of the Irish are professional or technical workers, compared with 11 percent for the total immigrant population. Of the remainder, 18 percent are either private household or service workers (against 11 percent for the total) doing the jobs their grandparents might have filled.

The newest Irish immigrants are more likely than their predecessors were to come from city backgrounds and once in America, they indicate a clear preference for urban living. In one-third of the cases, this means New York City, usually Queens or Brooklyn. In fact, Queens reported in 1970 more Irish than any county in the entire metropolitan area—70,000—and Brooklyn showed almost 43,000.

Recent Irish immigrants have not all sought out neighborhoods of their co-ethnics. Many of them echo Ann Gilvarry who said, when asked why she did not live in an Irish community, "If I had wanted that, I would have stayed in Ireland." Others, because they tend to be professionals and white collar workers shun the blue collar neighborhoods often identified as Irish.

Two Irish American street musicians perform for New Yorkers: one at the Uilleann pipes and the other on a bodhran (goatskin drum). (*Courtesy Irish Arts Center*)

Because so many of the new Irish immigrants are single, their housing requirements do not send them to family neighborhoods. They prefer, instead, the high-rise apartments of Manhattan.

Still others, such as Mary Curran, go where they can buy some property, regardless of the ethnicity of the neighborhood. Sitting in the basement kitchen of her partially renovated brownstone in Brooklyn's Prospect Park section, she laughs: "This was an Irish neighborhood thirty years ago, but it's 90 percent black now." For Mary Curran, a tall blond woman in her early forties, the change does not seem to matter. She speaks clearly and firmly, emphasizing her words so that she appears completely in control of her life. Although she talks of changed plans and new directions, her tone indicates that she has never been indecisive.

"I came to New York in 1967 to stay but I had come the year before to visit a friend. She was here on a music scholarship. It was while I was visiting her that I decided to come here to live. I was thirty years old. Un-

married. I wanted to come here for five years. I found out later that everybody says five years. I'm now on my third five years.

"When I was growing up in Cork, it was a city of a hundred thousand
or so, and when I came to the States I didn't want a similar place. I *would*
not. I couldn't see the sense of that. Cork is a good place to grow up but
one should get away from it. New York is more alive. More stimulating—
in every way. It forces you to be more independent, more aggressive. I
would have been a different person in Cork. No doubt about it. I'm far
more sharp-tongued now—take no nonsense. New York made me that way.
In a small city people don't come on as strong as they do here in New York
where, if you don't look out for yourself, nobody will.

"In all fairness, Cork offered a more pleasant life. Easier. When I came
here at first I missed very much getting out of the city. New York nearly
killed me that first summer. In Cork I could get out to the sea in maybe
twenty minutes. To a nice place—not like Rockaway or Coney Island. I
missed that tremendously that first summer. Besides that, Cork was more
sociable. People had more time mid-week. Not like here, where people have
time to get together only on weekends. It's more rushed here.

"When I came here I never felt that I was burning my bridges behind
me. Maybe those who have to leave a place feel differently. Those that leave
the rural areas and have to immigrate, they may feel more frightened, more
nervous. I remember a friend of mine used to go down to the boat that went
from Ireland to London—at Fishguard. These immigrants that were going
over to England were just kids from the country, carrying only their brown
paper bags. Completely ignorant kids from the mountains.

"But people who come to the States from Ireland now are very different.
The ones from the rural areas can't come anymore—only professionals, secretaries, people with skills. You have to have a sponsor. I know when I
came here I had to sponsor myself—deposit a thousand dollars in a bank in
the United States. That was so if I got sick here or had some trouble I had
money to take care of it. Since I didn't have family here, that was the way
I showed I could take care of myself.

"I came from a family of four girls and I was the eldest. Being the eldest
made a difference—made me more independent. I didn't go away to college
and that was a tremendous disappointment. Unfortunately, I came along in
a very bright year and because so many spaces were blocked off for Gaelic
speaking girls from the West, I didn't get in.

"Going to the university in Ireland didn't have the same social distinction that it seems to have here. When I came to New York people thought
if you hadn't gone to college you just had no education. It was a shock to
me—to find that I was a second-class citizen. The whole university system
in Ireland is different. A lot of pressure. They don't have credits so everything depends on the exam you take at the end of the year.

"I would say I had a good education in Ireland. A lot of exposure to culture in Cork because it was a university town. A lot of people who worked at the university were involved in music and theater. Also the people who worked in the banks—in Ireland working in a bank is a very high status job. I was shocked when I came here and found how different it was. To work in a bank in Ireland, your family has to have money and recommendations.

"In Cork I worked for an insurance company. It was a Scottish company and they treated me very well. If I had stayed, I would probably have become the office manager. Things were just beginning to open up for women when I left. What happened in my office was this: the office manager died. While he was very sick I had been left in charge of the office. I was young at the time—about 24. After his death they brought this guy down from Dublin who was not very competent and the manager in Dublin said that the new man and I were 'jointly in charge.' I decided to leave and I hadn't been gone more than three months when they made him office manager. It didn't dawn on me until later but they couldn't give him the job over me because I had been there longer and knew the office but they wouldn't give me the job over him because I was a woman! But that would have happened in the States at that time too. We are talking about the early 1960s.

"When I first got to the States I went to work in Philadelphia but I left it because it was too much like Cork. Too small, too closed. I came to New York, and I had a chance to work for the Irish Tourist Board but I didn't take it. I couldn't see the sense of leaving Ireland to come here to work for a company that was 99 percent Irish. I took a job at IBM as a secretary but I couldn't stand it! Making the coffee and bringing in the mail! Forget it. I thought I would never get my two legs out of there. But I waited a year— see that's my Irish heritage. I waited the year so I could take my vacation and then when I came back, I went to work at Pan Am. Been there ten years now. Sales work. First at the ticket counter but now I do rates.

"I go to Hunter College at night—doing a bachelor's degree in European history. Something I could not have done in Ireland. Work and do a degree. The paper I'm doing now is on James Connolly—he was a leader in the 1916 rebellion. I remember hearing a lot of talk about him in the house when I was growing up. We always talked a lot about politics, especially during the depression, when nobody had too much to eat. I was small then and I remember doing without some of the things I wanted and I remember both my mother and my father talking about how bad things were.

"My mother always spoke her mind. I wouldn't say we were a matriarchal household but she ran the house. Without her, we would have been on champagne and caviar one day and bread and water the next. She was the stabilizing force. My father was more of a dreamer.

"When I was preparing to come to the States, my mother told me some-

thing that I had never known about her. When she was young, she had
wanted to come to America, too. By the time I left, I think America seemed
much nearer to her. By plane, it was just a few hours. After I started working at Pan Am, I went back twice a year, even more often—even for the
Irish wakes.

"My grandfather had come to the States. So you see moving is in our
blood. He came as a young man, went out to Sacramento and worked for
McCormick's machinery company. Then he went back to Ireland, started a
family and lived there the rest of his life. But he had a brother who was
training to be a priest and then quit—a spoiled priest. A disaster for the
family. He came to the States and started a school. Had Latin, Greek, the
works. When his brother back in Ireland died, he should have gone back
but he wouldn't. Then came the big fire in San Francisco and he lost his
mind. Lost contact with the family. Acted like a beggar. The family traced
him down later and had him sent home but all they could get him to say
was 'the fire—the fire.' My aunt says leaving the priesthood was a big
trauma so she feels that he was never 100 percent normal after that. Just
wandered around.

"Most Irish people like to settle down—feel they own something. When
my mother married a man from the city her family thought it terrible that
she married someone without land. The person from the country, if he
owns land, is more respected in Ireland than the person from the city. One
night I was visiting my mother's family. I realized that I was related to both
the husbands and the wives that were there. I'm talking about third and
fourth cousins who had literally intermarried to keep the land. It dawned on
me in the middle of the night—I was the only one there without land.

"I think owning something is important to most Irish Americans, too,
but for the most part I feel very removed from Irish Americans—people who
have been here for a generation or two. They are far more closed. I'm more
open racially. Just yesterday somebody called me. She's Irish American. Her
family lives down closer to Prospect Park. She was objecting to so many
West Indians moving in and she said, 'I don't mind sharing the park but I
hate it being taken over. But you seem to enjoy it,' She knows that I rent
the top floor here, the upstairs apartment, to a West Indian. She is very,
very afraid. She sees everything around her changing. I have to say that
since I didn't grow up here I have no resentment that it's my city that's
changing. Maybe if it were Cork changing, I would resent it too."

Mary Curran's kitchen is lined with crates of kitchen utensils and dishes
although she has lived here for more than a year. After putting on a teakettle
for a pot of tea, she takes out the only two cups on the shelf. Motioning to
the living room, not yet furnished, she explains: "I feel very temporary here.
Haven't become a citizen so I can't vote. Will I go back to Ireland? I don't

know. People say New York is a terrible place to get old in so I've left a certain loophole, like a safety valve. Moving on—that idea doesn't frighten me. We Irish have always been movers. I read a phrase somewhere—that people vote with their feet—by immigrating. Maybe that's me. I wanted less restriction, more freedom to try new things, so I came to America. When I get tired of New York, I'll vote again. I'll go someplace else."

6

It's Good for the Important Things:

To Leave Russia as a Jew

As late as 1742, after many European nations had long ago permitted their barriers against Jewish settlement to fall, Russia's Tzarina Elizabeth expelled the few Jews in her kingdom, declaring "I do not want any benefit from the enemies of Christ." Two decades later when Tzarina Catherine II authorized foreigners to travel and trade throughout her realm she appended the formula *kromye Zhydov* to her edict, "except the Jews." And yet before century's end, the tzars and the Jews would be thrown together. In successive annexations in 1772, 1793, and 1795, Russia laid claim to large segments of the decaying Polish Empire. Willy-nilly the tzars inherited hundreds of thousands of Jews for whom they had little use and less sympathy.

A succession of Russian leaders viewed this accidentally acquired population as the "Jewish problem," a harshly resented group whose separate religion, culture, and identity were to be systematically extirpated. Literally hundreds of laws singled out the Jews, ringing them about with crippling restrictions and disabilities. Tzarist opposition notwithstanding, the Jewish population in Russia continued to grow, reaching 5 million before 1900.

Russian Jewry confronted an ugly turning point in 1881. In March of that year, assassins murdered Tzar Alexander II. Opponents of the regime, espousing diverse radical programs, exhorted the populace to seize the revolutionary moment. The assassination brought into power a new regime committed to rooting out alien elements and sidestepping legitimate grievances by directing a diversionary campaign against the hated Jews. Government-sparked riots or pogroms threw Jewish communities in southern Russia and the Ukraine into turmoil. Thousands fled to the Austrian border town of Brody where Jewish volunteers helped many to depart for the United States. Meanwhile in Russia a tendentious government report blamed the pogrom disorders on the victims and resulted in the May Laws of 1882, a series of laws that further restricted Jewish rights in all important areas of trade, travel, residence, education, and occupation. These "temporary laws" also inaugurated a series of forced resettlements, herding the Jews into a sector known as the "Pale of Settlement." Additional restrictions sharply curtailed Jewish business and professional life. Unemployment soared.

At the same time tzarist authorities fanned popular prejudice, subsidizing the publication of about three thousand antisemitic books and pamphlets, including the notorious forgery, *The Protocols of the Elders of Zion,* which purported to show a Jewish conspiracy aimed at world domination. It did not take long in this poisoned atmosphere for the bitter fruit to appear.

Early in 1903, peasants in the city of Kishinev discovered the mutilated body of a Russian boy. The child's uncle confessed to the crime but the local newspaper, supported by the Ministry of Interior, called it a Jewish ritual murder. The ensuing pogrom on April 3, 1903 resulted in the destruction of 1,500 Jewish stores and homes. Far worse, eighty-six Jews were tortured and crippled and forty-five brutally murdered. Local police determinedly ignored all.

Similar rampages erupted across White Russia and the Ukraine. In 1906 Peter Stolypin, who had taken over the Interior Ministry, brought such pogroms under government administration, letting loose the furiously antisemitic group, The Union of the Russian People, to despoil Jewish communities. Between 1903 and 1907, more than 457,000 Russian Jews fled to America, part of a larger migration of close to 2 million Jews who journeyed to America between 1880 and 1920.

Despite their fears that such an influx would fuel American antisemitism, fellow Jews already in the United States responded to "the imperious call of a stricken humanity" and furnished significant help. In 1897 the most important Jewish immigrant aid institutions in the United States were merged into the Hebrew Immigrant Aid Society (HIAS) to coordinate immigrant assistance. HIAS provided meals, lodging, aid in locating relatives, medical care, job placement, even burial aid.

Established Jewish groups tried to scatter the arriving masses across the United States in the hopes that such dispersal would promote a neater and quicker assimilation. But New York City's ethnic milieu and broad-based economy exerted a powerful attraction. All efforts at persuading the new immigrants away from their "Promised City" of New York failed, and such districts as the Lower East Side of Manhattan and Brownsville in Brooklyn quickly took on the color of an Eastern European *shtetl* (small town) in the Pale of Settlement. These Jews, with their traditional culture and orthodox rituals, helped broaden the America's Jewish community's horizons.

But most Russian Jews still feared the New World. Those who clung fast to the traditions of Judaism feared that in this open materialist society they had heard so much about their rigorous national faith might be frowned upon; they feared what America's early Puritans feared: that they would be unable to maintain the discipline that comes about through community-imposed limits on individual action; without the discipline it would be impossible to cultivate a community of restraint. These Jews (whose religious world was bound up with the specifics of place and environment) therefore remained, locked into the unloving grip of their Russian motherland.

Another group decided to work out its problems through socialist change, and for awhile this group seemed likely to achieve its goals. World War I hastened the Tzar's fall and when the Provisional Government took power in 1917 it generously abolished all antisemitic laws. But the year closed with the displacement of this Kerensky-led government by the Bolsheviks.

Jews laid fond hopes on this regime. Its initial support for a secular Yiddish culture heartened many. The soviets even established a special section of Jewish affairs, the *Yevsektsia*. This was followed by a plan to establish the province of Brobidzhan in Western Russia as an autonomous Jewish region within the Soviet federation.

Yet for all this, as the Soviet policy toward Russia's 2.5 million Jews unfolded, it moved away from cultural pluralism in favor of radical assimilation. Josef Stalin dismissed Jewish national pretensions, remarking that Jews were only a "nation on paper." Religious study was prohibited, synagogues were closed, and special taxes were imposed on the clergy. Zionism too was clamped down on. These and other programs aimed at cultural amalgamation took effect, as Jewish children attended secular Russian schools and adults married outside their faith. Those Russian intellectuals and writers who were Jewish born seldom betrayed a consciousness of their heritage. Few wrote in Yiddish and fewer still addressed Jewish topics. By 1936, amidst his other purges, Stalin liquidated the Jewish leadership that had been set up in Brobidzhan in 1934.

World War II changed Russian Jewish life further. The annexation of territories between 1939 and 1940, combined with a large refugee influx, brought masses of more Jews to Russian controlled territory. Displaced by the Nazi onslaught, these refugees had little choice. With nowhere to run they sought haven in Russia, where at least physical survival seemed assured. For such Bolshevik grace they paid the established price: expropriation of private property, dissolution of communal agencies, and a severely restricted religious life. When Hitler's forces did invade the Soviet Union, local troops in the Ukraine, Belorussia, Latvia, and Lithuania often collaborated with their Nazi occupiers in exterminating Jews and dividing their belongings.

Babi Yar, where more than 100,000 Ukranian Jews perished, is one of those tragic sites whose fame rests on the horror that took place there. Yet efforts at memorializing Babi Yar's victims foundered. Nikita Khrushchev, postwar Communist party chief in the Ukraine, promised to erect a proper monument, but this was forestalled when Josef Stalin launched a new drive against the Jews, accusing them of assorted Zionist, imperialist, cosmopolitan, and American plots.

Sick, and close to death, Stalin pushed this campaign to its zenith in January of 1953 when the government accused a group of prominent doctors, most of them Jews, of planning to use their medical wiles to kill Soviet leaders. The resulting witch hunt swept many Jews from important positions.

For the next decade Babi Yar continued hiding its secrets amidst the Russian wasteland. In 1961 Yevgeny Yevtushenko published his famous poem indicting his country's silence.

> No monument stands over Babi Yar.
> A drop sheer as a crude gravestone
>
> . . . . .
>
> Wild grasses rustle over Babi Yar
> The trees look down sternly like judges.
> Everything here shrieks silently.
>
> . . . . .

Nikita Khrushchev, now leader of all Russia, denounced the poet for his temerity and for singling Jews out as particular victims of Nazi genocide. Composer Dmitri Shostakovich was also rebuked for making Babi Yar a theme of his Thirteenth Symphony. Today a monument stands over Babi Yar. It reads: "Here in 1941–1943 the German Fascist invaders executed over 100,000 citizens of Kiev and prisoners of war." The demand for recognition that it was Jews who died from antisemitism and not some generalized anti-Soviet fascism remains a muted shriek.

Although the Soviet Union nationalized the sacrifices of the Jews during World War II, it refused to let them become full members of the nation. Their identity cards—documents required of all Russians—were stamped "Jew", defining them as aliens in the only land they considered home. One had to show this card everywhere—to get a job, an apartment, a university appointment—and it left Jews open to discrimination and various restrictions. (They were, for instance, barred from the upper echelons of the Communist Party, from the military command, and from most foreign-service positions.) For many, their identity as Jews was something they would just as well hide, but could not; it was an identity kept alive by the state.

Soviet policies on Jewish religious culture heightened the dilemma, for while, on the one hand, Jews could not melt into the general population, could not forget their special status; on the other hand, the state prevented them from expressing their Jewishness in any meaningful fashion. Between 1956 and 1963, authorities shuttered three-quarters of the nation's synagogues, leaving fewer than one hundred houses of worship for Russia's 2.1 million Jews. The government refused to publish their sacred texts or to make available supplies for ritual observances. Books on religious law and Jewish culture grew scarce. Only a handful of Jews could stay away from work on their Saturday Sabbath. An entire postwar generation grew up with but faint knowledge of the practices and beliefs of traditional Judaism.

Other religious groups also suffered constraints under Soviet leadership, but they had their national religious organizations to sustain them. Jews had none. Other ethnic groups also felt eclipsed by the Russian Federated Republic in what theoretically was supposed to be a union of autonomous and equal Soviet republics. But they had the solace of their geography, their deeply rooted national customs, and their vital cultural institutions. Jews did not.

Increasingly this void came to be filled by the idea of Israel. The 1967 Arab-Israeli War, with its real threat to the Jewish State, brought many a Russian Jew to a turning point. Israel's war dance at the edge of a particularly disastrous precipice transformed them from remote observers to *engagés*, emotionally fixed on Israel. The Jewish nation's remarkable victory became a comforting symbol of endurance.

Before the war, the Soviet government permitted a small ripple of Jewish emigration to Israel for the purposes of "reunifying families." After the war, this was halted, and Russia severed relations with Israel. Anti-Jewish propaganda rose. Thousands of articles updating classical anti-Jewish themes portrayed Jews as fascists and Israel as a Nazi state. But many Russian Jews responded by openly embracing the Zionist identity so doggedly thrust upon them. Some fumbled with their Jewishness for the first time. The noted author Elie Wiesel observed that on a visit to Moscow he found young Jews

Professor Benjamin Levich waited six years before receiving permission to leave the Soviet Union. Founder of the field of physiochemical hydrodynamics, the sixty-three-year-old physicist is regarded as the most prominent Jewish scientist to have emigrated from Russia. (*Courtesy G. V. Wurtemburg, City College of New York*)

seeking "to return to Judaism, but without knowing what it is. Without knowing why they define themselves as Jews . . . [believing] in the eternity of the Jewish people without the slightest notion of . . . the meaning of its mission." The Russian existential Jew emerged. "We are Jews," one youth told Wiesel, "for spite." And they demanded the right to leave. To go "home" for the first time.

Soviet authorities did their best to dampen the immigration impulse by harassment and unpredictable refusals. No applicant could plan with any certainty on receiving a visa, although he stood an excellent chance of losing his job and rights just by applying. Early in the seventies the renowned astrophysicist Yevgeny Levich applied for a visa. His temerity brought him two years of cleaning latrines on Siberia's Arctic Coast before he was waved on to Israel. His elderly father Benjamin, one of Russia's most eminent scientists, also applied. Officials refused him outright. Only after six anguish-filled years did he receive his emigration papers. The head of a cybernetics institute, Alexander Lerner, applied for a visa and immediately lost his position. Authorities then refused his request. After putting in his application, ballet dancer Valery Panov paced his room for two years until he received a visa.

Anatoli Shcharansky was less fortunate. When he and his wife Avital applied for permission to emigrate to Israel, in 1973, the Soviets granted Mrs. Shcharansky the visa. The couple decided she would proceed and wait for Anatoli in Israel. An active advocate of free Jewish emigration and one of the founders of the Helsinki Watch Committee set up to monitor Soviet compliance with the human-rights provisions of the Helsinki Accords, Shcharansky's subsequent requests were repeatedly denied. Then, in 1977, he was charged with spying for the United States. Held incommunicado for sixteen months he steadfastly refused to cooperate in his own humiliation. At the trial—which received worldwide coverage—he pleaded not guilty and addressed the court with a bristling pride:

> Five years ago I applied to emigrate to Israel. . . . I am far from my dreams. One would think I would be sorry, but I am not. . . . I am happy to have witnessed the process of liberating Soviet Jewry. . . .
> . . . I wanted to exchange the life of an activist in the Jewish emigration movement here for a reunion with Avital in Israel. For more than 2,000 years my people have dispersed. . . . At present I am as far as ever from my people, from Avital, and many hard years of exile are in store for me.
> To my wife and my people, I can only say, "Next year in Jerusalem!" To this court which decided my fate in advance I say nothing.

Virtually all those in the first wave of emigrants went to Israel. Many were Zionists and religious Jews who considered the Jewish State a natural destination. But soon others, those less religiously committed, found themselves contemplating emigration. Increasingly, Jews in Russia, whether strongly leaning toward emigration or not, began to find that jobs, housing, schooling, and promotions were being withheld from them with the argument "why should we give you benefits when you will leave?" This, in turn created new pressures, eventually causing the fulfilment of the prediction. But of the emigrants who left after 1973, fewer left with only Israel in mind. A growing number sought a better life in the United States. By 1980 the number of new Russian Jewish immigrants in the United States reached 75,000.

Jews leaving Russia during this period could not apply for an American visa directly, as the Soviet government chose to maintain the fiction that Jews left only to join their families in Israel. The process of changing destinations did not start until they arrived in Vienna, the transit point for all emigrating Soviet Jews. The Hebrew Immigrant Aid Society, carrying on a tradition of almost a century of immigrant assistance, took responsibility for

In 1973 Anatoli Shcharansky applied for a visa to emigrate from Russia. Dismissed from his position at a scientific research institute he was denied the visa. He went on to become a leading figure in the "refusenik" community. Convicted of treason and "anti-Soviet agitation and propaganda" in 1978, he is not due to be released until 1991. (*Courtesy Greater New York Conference on Soviet Jewry*)

this part of their new lives. HIAS sent those Jews seeking an American visa to its processing center in Rome. Here HIAS offered classes in English and vocational training, ran an orientation program and provided basic assistance while it arranged to secure visas. HIAS agents also established contact with American friends and relatives for the incoming refugee families and weighed a range of considerations (reunion with relatives, religious needs, the Jewish population of various communities, the ability of Jewish communal groups to provide assistance, the special skills and needs of the immigrant, educational opportunities) before selecting American destinations for the immigrant families. In settling these immigrants HIAS tried to dis-

Project Ari, coordinated by the Federation of Jewish Philanthropies, provides
recent immigrants with professional counseling (*Courtesy Federation of Jewish
Philanthropies of Greater New York*)

tribute them as widely as possible, but despite these efforts, in a throwback
to a similar experience in the early 1900s, most Jews chose the traditional
clearing house for Jewish immigration, New York City, which held close to
30,000 Soviet Jews by 1980.

These newly settled immigrants received local assistance from the Jew-
ish-funded New York Association for New Americans. NYANA provided
help with job hunting, counseling, housing, medical insurance, and sub-
sistence expenses. But as a people who never had to search for their own
apartment, look for a better job, seek out a doctor, or choose a school, the
Russian Jews were often less impressed with the level of aid than with the
fact that it ended so soon. Intellectually, they expressed the realization that
they were on their own, their price for freedom; emotionally, instinctively,
they wondered at the price: unemployment, insecurity, and inner-city street
crime. It took getting used to, and they asked for patience. The editor of a
Russian-language newspaper in New York City explained:

> You Americans think that refugees from Hungary, Poland, the Soviet Union
> are all the same. We Soviets are not like the Eastern Europeans. We have

had 57 years of isolation and brainwashing. We are not just from another country. We are from another planet.

Some expressed a willingness to "take any job." But they brought fears from a society where a first job determined the track one's career would take; a manual occupation, they suspected, would keep them blue collar in America forever. Similarly others refused jobs outside the city. In Russia goods and services are in short supply outside Moscow and other principal cities. Moreover once a Soviet worker leaves Moscow or Leningrad he may not return without a new entry permit, which is often refused.

Adding a bitter leaven to it all was the sense of displacement. Actors, journalists, doctors, and lawyers, in one swift air passage, were without status. Telling a group of Americans that he was indeed an important journalist before landing in New York, a middle-aged Russian went on to speak of Aleksandr Solzhenitsyn. "Yes he is a man of courage, but he is not a friend. He is a very fervent Christian mystic. In his work," the man says knowingly, "Jews are always evil people." His listeners pay him the compliment of listening and he is for a moment returned to his station: a man of important views. But the conversation turns. "I need a job. I do not want to pack boxes. No one knows what I was," and he fears this will not change. "In America," laments another immigrant, "the doctors, and the butchers, and musicians are all the same. We are only immigrants." Physicians find their skills useless. "My hands," one surgeon says softly, "are crying." And American abundance makes the situation worse. "I see, but I cannot touch. Dreams, dreams," the new baker's assistant echoes Pushkin, "where is your sweetness now."

Most of the new immigrants did find acceptable jobs after six months or so. The doctors studied English and prepared for their rigorous American licensing exams. The professionals, with some help from the American Council for Emigrés in the Professions, were placed in decent positions, and the young men on the make found America's openness refreshing. Engineers, chemists, machinists, computer experts, and musicians, for example, landed relatively good jobs easily. Cab drivers, factory hands, and small businessmen made their accommodations, adopting an American standard of living, setting in place the foundations of a new life.

This new life brought some of the immigrants into their first encounter with Judaism. A surprising number showed interest in a faith that they had not actually grown up in. The Jewish community too showed interest in sparking a religious awareness among the Soviet Jews. Local religious schools (yeshivas) added special classes to absorb the newly arrived young. Special appeals raised money to provide the immigrants with Russian-language prayer books and religious guides as well as other staples of reli-

This youngster, celebrating his Bar Mitzvah, is a student of the Be'er Hagolah Institute, an Orthodox Jewish parochial school established entirely to educate "yaldei Russia" (the children of Russia immigrants). *Courtesy Be'er Hagolah Institutes*)

gious observance. Those abiding by Jewish dietary laws could claim kosher food allowances, and generous scholarships aided the needy with tuition fees in the private yeshiva academies. But in reversing a previous trend—in the early 1900s Jewish groups allocated much of their resources for Americanization, for programs consciously aimed at winning traditional Jews away from their religious culture—few in the Jewish community could speak with

Volunteers prepare food packages to be distributed to the needy for the Sabbath. (*Courtesy Tomche Shabbos D'Boro Park*)

confidence about the process of converting "paper Jews" into individuals conscious of their religious heritage.

Most of the Russian Jews settled in Brooklyn. The largest Russian community developed along the Brooklyn seashore in the Brighton Beach area. Euphemistically called a "changing neighborhood", this section was well on its transitional way from middle-class community to blighted slum—when the Russian immigrants discovered the salt air, the boardwalk, and the sea, so reminiscent of Odessa. Hundreds, and then thousands, streamed into the empty apartments and opened local shops, creating a neighborhood surrounded by familiars and known as "Little Odessa." Those seeking a religious environment settled in the orthodox communities of Borough Park and Crown Heights. Substantial numbers also settled in the Forest Hills-Rego Park sections of Central Queens, in the Washington Heights-Inwood neighborhoods of upper Manhattan, and in the Bronx's desirable Riverdale area.

Alex Bushinsky arrived in the United States in 1976.

"I once came home and I told my mother, 'Ma, I don't want to be Jewish.' I knew nothing about what being Jewish meant except to suffer for it.

A leaflet identifying Christian missionary work and assimilation as major threats to the Jewish identity of the recent immigrants. (*Courtesy Be'er Hagolah Institutes*)

It was not constant but after I was about eleven or twelve I knew it was there. I had some fights in school and kids—they don't hesitate—sometimes just to hurt me they say it like a name, a bad word, 'you are Jewish.' I knew that it hurt me to be Jewish. In the sixth grade I was thirteen and when you are sixteen you receive a passport. It's a kind of internal identity card that all adult Russians must carry. Your nationality is put on this card. I was very scared thinking that in three years I will have to carry a passport and everyone will know I am Jewish. That's when I told my mother I really don't want to be Jewish.

"I saw many disgusting Jews—old people who couldn't speak Russian, they just blabbered. I didn't like them, they were all short. Later I would meet tall, good-looking Jews and understand there were many kinds, but now I just thought of this type. I did not know a thing about Judaism. I knew that there were some holidays, but I did not know the significance; what they meant. I'm sure I violated every law and practice in Judaism.

"It is not just religion that you cannot practice; it is the whole Jewish culture and history that is hidden. My parents never told me about the bad times under Stalin. They thought it will get better and never told me about it. One family wanted to change their name because it was Jewish. They took the name Chmielnitzki. It was a famous name. The man was a Ukranian hero. But they had no idea that this man led a massacre of thousands of Jews in the 1600s. It's like a German Jew changing his name to Hitler.

"I did not feel angry at the people or the government. I felt angry at me, for being a Jew. It was my problem, not theirs. I was very patriotic. I wanted the best for Russia. In the Olympic games I was very interested in how Russia did. I wanted them to be first in space and to do better than America.

"After I graduated high school I applied to the university. A Jew can get into an inferior university where there are many openings, but the better universities will not take them. You knew that in Moscow certain universities did not accept Jews for sure and only a few others did let them in. I attended Gorki University in a large city. I was involved in sports and study, the regular student's life. I had Jewish friends, it seems to work that way. But we did not discuss immigration. In 1967 it was not happening yet.

"I was twenty-one and I had been in Moscow several times and I met people and we talked about being Jewish. I started to feel proud. But I understand that was really just a reaction to feeling inferior. I could not conceal it. I saw no way to assimilate. It would always be part of me. So I would be proud of it. You could protect yourself with this pride like a shield. But I did not have any *Yiddishkeit* (Jewishness) beyond this.

"I had graduated the university. I wanted to enter—well now it sounds funny, stupid, crazy, anything, but this is the fact—I wanted to join the army. It paid well, especially in Moscow. It didn't enter my mind that this particular army fights with Israel. Things like this, I didn't think about then. Now it is strange to me. I was almost twenty-two and I wanted to become an officer. You get better pay, good clothing, loose schedule, better apartment. Why not?

"Of course they rejected me. Of course, they didn't want Jewish officers. I suffered a lot because I was too stupid. They gave me hints at personnel. I didn't understand. I applied again. And again. I had good record, good recommendations, good diploma. They kept giving me hints thinking I could understand. I was stupid. I did not realize it for a long time. Finally I did understand and it hurt me very much.

"Before I was finally completely rejected, I started to work in Moscow.

I had lived away from my parents since I was sixteen and that was not a problem. The job was in a research institute, but a very backward place. I needed the work and I could not find a better appointment, so I took it.

"In Moscow I met a friend from Gorki, a brilliant physicist. Of all Russian school boys he won first prize in a physics contest. He won all types of awards and graduated from university at nineteen. He printed articles in the best physics journals. He used to get letters from big people writing: 'Professor so and so, could you tell us,' when he was still a student. We talked about being Jewish. Through him I met other people who told me about their problems and I became more sensitive.

"Still I was comfortable. Still I didn't think about immigration. I didn't want to learn. I thought I have problems to solve here. I do not want to leave. I don't want . . . .

"I was a year in Moscow. I tried to change my job. I couldn't get a good job. I tried three or four places. But I was a Jew and I could not get a good job. My friend was sharing my apartment. Suddenly he said, 'Listen. Why you are doing all of this stuff.' I said what are my choices. 'Get out of here.'

"I couldn't say a word. . . . I was shocked. . . . I said, 'Well, okay, what are you doing here.' I could tell he thought it out. He told me he was waiting for some people to join him and he was ready to go. I was still shocked, amazed. It was the first time I heard something like this. Just like this. If you are in a cage you must try to leave. To leave this cage of Russia. But my family, friends, country. It's like talking about angels. After you are acquainted with the concept and if you accept the premise the discussion makes sense. But only then. But once you start to think about emigration, it is a strong idea and it doesn't let go.

"After that I was rejected from three more jobs.

"I began to meet with other interested Jews. We read material about Jews. The atmosphere in Moscow was that you got your Jewish—really I should say Zionist because *Yiddishkeit* still was not there—your Zionist education from the air. You realized there was no place in this country for you. It passed around in the air. You thought about it and talked about it. When you think, you realize how abnormal emigration is. But it became a normal idea. If you are in a cage it can take a long time, but when you realize that you should escape it is so natural that nothing else is as natural. Try to get better food, better job, better apartment? No! Escape. I was afraid, but I really didn't care. This was no place for me. Not because of Zionism or *Yiddishkeit*, not any one reason, just that I knew I must escape. Where to was not important. From where, was important.

"I wrote my parents. It's true that letters are sometimes read by KGB but they can't search every letter and I hoped they would not consider me important enough to watch me and read my letters. I was right. So I wrote, 'I

Soviet Jews congregating outside a synagogue discussing current developments in the "refusenik" community. (*Courtesy Greater New York Conference on Soviet Jewry*)

don't like the situation, I want to get out.' They wrote back: 'We understand but your problem comes from not having a good job, and not finding a nice girl. This doesn't have anything to do with Russia.'

"I want to explain something. When you ask somebody why did you leave Russia, a person starts giving you reasons. This is not the right question and so you get the wrong answer. You leave Russia because you are not happy there. Usually why you are unhappy is very complicated. Jobs, private lives, school, personal reasons, friends all mixed together.

"First you become unhappy for some reason. Then you become sensitive and you realize you do not like certain things about Russian life. Therefore the real question is not why did you leave Russia. That is too difficult. Ask what bothered you in Russia. That is what people will answer anyway. Even if you ask why they left, they are really telling you only what they did not like in Russia after they became unhappy. If you are fundamentally happy or satisfied you accept many shortcomings. You may be aware of what you later consider a terrible problem but as long as your basic needs are met you are in principle happy.

"I can't exactly identify just what caused my unhappiness. Maybe my parents were right, that I couldn't find the right girl. I think I didn't want to

Soviet Jews celebrating an engagement. By 1977 all of those pictured here had emigrated. (*Courtesy Yuri and Golda Gershkovich*)

get married because I already thought of emigrating. When I became unhappy, things that had been around me all my life began to bother me, partly because if you are going to leave you better hate it so you shouldn't miss it later. This hatred developed very successfully because so much is bad there.

"Yes, it is possible here also. I heard a black man on the subway—he hated everything here.

"I couldn't get a good job. I am pretty ambitious and it bothered me that I could not find a good job. It is important to make a good career. If you don't, you cannot make enough money to support a family. And for a Jew in Moscow it was very hard to get a good job. When my whole future was in Russia I had to look through rose-colored glasses. Now I could be more objective.

"The medical system is poor. Except in the hospitals that serve the officials or foreigners. Surgeons still operate with instruments that came in lend-lease from America during World War II. These are still the best instruments available. In theory medical service is free, but that's in the clinics. Good care is expensive. You have to locate a good doctor and pay under the table.

"Everything is under the table and pull. If not, you have to stand on

Yuri Gershkovich lecturing to his high school reunion in 1974 in the USSR. Less than two years after this photograph was taken Yuri and the four other Jews in his graduating class had emigrated. (*Courtesy Yuri and Golda Gershkovich*)

line. For everything good there are lines. Sometimes these lines are for a mile and more. It can take hours. Here in America you have no idea of this. In Russia, for example, clothing is not nice or good quality. Sometimes a store will get a shipment of imported clothing and if people hear this they run to buy. They will pay very much to purchase something nice and pretty. For American jeans they will pay five or ten times the regular price. If you have friends or relatives with connections you can usually get things other people can't. Or you can bribe or buy on the black market. It's very big. A car can cost an engineer two- or three-years salary. And still you have to wait on line. Most of those waiting for cars are crooks. Only they can afford cars. A person on welfare in New York lives at the material level of a good engineer in Russia.

"The best opportunities for jobs, best food, best clothing and appliances are in Moscow. To live there you need a permit and they are limited. Moscow is one of the few cities a foreigner can visit so they try to polish everything and make it look good for foreigners. Right outside Moscow, ten minutes away, there are shortages of everything. It costs a month's salary to buy a suit and the clothing is so ugly and so badly made. That's why people will stand on line even for ten hours—yes, believe it—to get desirable clothing, and then you hear it is sold out. For anything good there are lines.

"Sometimes there are exhibitions from foreign countries. In the United States when you go to such exhibitions, if you see something you want you can buy it. There you can't ever buy what you see. It's painful, and I used to avoid going unless it was in my craft, computer technology. But other people went. Why? Because they gave plastic shopping bags to carry the pamphlets and sheets that they handed out. You cannot get these bags anywhere else. So they would go. The poor man who handed them out would be pushed and shoved. The people used these bags for lunch or shopping all year.

"We believe in Russia that who can steal, steals. We have a motto, 'To cheat the Soviet country is a matter of honor for every Soviet citizen.' Workers think nothing of taking home extra items from their factory. Everybody, not Jews only, everybody. We have another saying, 'They pretend to pay us and we pretend to work.' There is a book by Hedrick Smith, *The Russians*, that gives you many examples. His book is true. When I read it I feel yes, that is the way Russia is.

"People do not starve in Russia, but their material needs are not satisfied. When I arrived in Vienna from Russia I was shocked to see modern appliances. I never saw such things in Russia. And people in Russia blame the government for these shortages.

"You live two lives. You say one thing at work and another in private. There are party meetings, trade union meetings, Komsomol [young Communist league], stupid Russian elections. These are all required as part of your social life. Only in your personal relations can you really express yourself to friends. At work once or twice a week someone reads a passage from the newspaper to everybody else. This is called political information. The manager in my institute would start, 'Yesterday I was impressed very much with the speech of our General Secretary Leonid Breshnev. I was impressed with the depth of his thought, the level of his understanding and deep analysis he gave in his speech on agriculture.' Everybody knows it is shit. He doesn't believe it, we do not believe it, and nobody read this article. But everyone listens with respect. It's a jargon. You just speak. No one pays attention just like you get used to noise and pay no attention.

"It's a terrible waste. And you must attend meetings, demonstrations and parties. You don't want to. You hate it. But you can't miss it. It is—I call it—mandatorily voluntary. If you don't do Komsomol activity, like lecturing at work or in your neighborhood, you get zip raise. It's just like the elections, a joke. You get a card and they tell you to mark the name of the person you should vote for. They set up food stands near the voting places to get people to come.

"I began to consider leaving in '73 and I left in '76. I was in refusal [generally meaning that authorities refuse to grant permission to leave] for three years. Not from the state but from my parents. When I applied it took two months.

"I was already twenty-four and I reached as high as I would get. I knew I would suffer. My health would suffer in fighting these problems. I would never have enough money, and I felt this would not change because I was Jewish. I feared I would blame my parents and turn against them because they refused to give me permission to leave. They told me to think again. That I was hurting the family and my brothers' careers.

"It could happen. It has not happened yet. I promised not to go. Why should they suffer? Maybe they were right, the hell I know is better than the hell I don't know. But I got more unhappy. They didn't understand my unhappiness. I had to leave. I stopped all discussions.

"I ordered my invitation. It's a bureaucratic procedure. You can only leave Russia if you are rejoining your family in Israel. You have to be invited to come there by a member of your family. You get in touch with some organizations—and they get you an invitation. Then you write the legend, creating a story around the invitation. The KGB knows it's a fake, but they designed the procedure.

"I was afraid and nervous. My parents were scared and we kept everything secret. I quit my job and no one knew what I did after that. Even now after two years, nobody, nobody in my parents' town knows that I have left the U.S.S.R. The reaction of the people is not predictable. They might admire my parents or attack them.

"The most terrifying thing is the waiting. If you are refused you are in a terrible position. After you apply people are afraid to meet you. My relatives treated me like I was witched [bewitched]. I did not join the dissident movement. I did help them sometimes, but I have to point out something. You might think that some people apply to emigrate and others choose to stay behind and fight as dissidents. It does not happen this way. Everybody applies for emigration. If they do not get permission then they fight—to get out. If you are refused then you must fight. If not, you are ignored by the government, you do not get a job and you also get no help. If you fight you get food, help, clothes, material from other sources. Some refuseniks have eventually left Russia with world reputations and received donations and nice jobs.

"Some dissidents are very courageous; others want just to be heroes. For some refuseniks their best times are in Russia. They suffer with glory, they are like heroes. And some of the young ones are spoiled by this. Instead of getting an education they wait for permission to leave. They drink, smoke, take drugs and live like Bohemians away from regular discipline. They get support from those who advise them. But then, even after they leave, they cannot adjust. They are used to being relaxed, unemployed, undisciplined.

"I always thought of going to the States. The American Jews I met (mainly at the Moscow Synagogue) impressed me. They were so smart, so businesslike, so warm, educated, polite. I loved them. But in the end I went to Israel. Officially that is the only place to which you can emigrate but it is possible to come to America. Still, I felt if you claim you are Jewish you go to your country, join your own people, speak your own language. I was a moderate Zionist. And America was more distant. It was scary to think of getting a job without perfect English. My parents told me that competition was so high that I would not succeed. We thought of America as a prosperous country, but where a Russian would be a second-class citizen.

"Israel has to be a disappointment. You expect so much. All the happiness you did not have. I got a terrific job in computer programming. But when things began to change in the organization and it seemed that I might lose this job, I started to lose my good feeling for the country. I realized that my good feeling toward Israel was because I was happy in general. I had a good job, good status, a nice environment, and friends. When this was threatened my attitude changed. Later, in the United States, I was once on a plane with a woman from San Diego. I asked her if she liked San Diego. She said she hated it. Why? She started to tell me, 'Well you know I got divorced and. . . .' and I realized that she hated it because that's where she became unhappy.

"I learned about Judaism in Israel. I met a fine, very good man. He was Russian and he managed even in Russia to be religious. He was so righteous. He devoted so much time to teach me from the beginning. Of course this was not for money. Now I had a religion.

"Then I was invited by an American company to the States to try a job with the company. In Russia I was sometimes a technical translator and I came into contact with Americans. I kept up the friendships and now they got me an invitation to try out for a job and the company would pay my expenses for two months. I did not really expect to stay. I did not close the idea that I might stay, but I didn't think I would be so attracted to the States.

"I was delayed for half a year in Israel because of the incredible bureaucracy there. So I arrived here late. The same day I arrived they told me, 'Listen we waited too long so we cannot give you the job now. It is not available anymore.' They didn't feel sorry. They made thirty or forty thousand dollars—when I wrote to them that I made five hundred dollars a month, they wrote back you probably mean five hundred dollars a week. They felt I had money, that I could get a job just like that.

"I had only three hundred dollars with me. I was scared. I spoke to the

lawyer for the company. I told him I don't have money. He told me, 'If you want money why don't you just go to work?' I had no choice, I had to go to work. I bought a *New York Times*. I saw an ad with all my skills listed. I went there. It was an agency. The secretary asked for my résumé and in a few minutes an agent came out and said, 'Hi, my name is so and so I have arranged several interviews for you already, and I am expecting some more calls.' He gave me a list of nine companies—Irving Trust Company, Chemical Bank, Automated Concept, Sperry Univac, Salomon Bros., Royal Globe Insurance and some others. I got a job. Three days after coming to America I had a job. I was fascinated by working for an American company.

"My first exposure to New York impressed me. It turned out to be clean somehow. Later I learned it's not clean, but when I came it was clean. I expected huge piles of garbage but it wasn't that bad. I liked the tall buildings. They were gleaming from the sun. In the first two days I hated the city. I lost job. I had no money. Definitely I hated it. I felt insecure, terrible. But in five days when I saw I could get a job just like that, I started to work and half a month later I realized my prospects were much better here than in Israel. Within a month I got a second job teaching a class in data processing at a university.

"This was a new world for me. There were so many things I did not have: language, American education; I was an American immigrant, a Russian, and still I got a job. I decided to remain here (I usually like to say until things get worse,) because of the tremendous opportunities and the freedom.

"I was lucky. The Russians had copied all of the computer software from the States and I knew the necessary languages. Today I have a position as systems analyst. It is very satisfying. I have confidence in my career and I am satisfied with my salary. I have every right that you have except the right to vote and at the moment that does not concern me too much. I feel so comfortable, completely at home. I could not go anywhere after the States.

"I knew I wouldn't get a break in Russia because I was a Jew. It would be hard to get a good job, an apartment. Here, I got a job in a few days. It needed furniture. I got it in a week. Later, I wanted a vacation, so I went for twenty-four days. I took my paycheck and a little money out of the bank and I went across the United States, and saw the nice things. Terrific. It didn't take a year's salary. I appreciate it. I really do. In Russia you make peanuts, usually your parents help support you even after you are married. I was lucky. My father used to be a director of a factory and when I wanted to take a vacation he gave me money. Here I took fourteen different trips by plane. I changed reservations daily. Still I failed to confuse the American airlines. I even got a letter saying because of round-trip fares I am entitled to twelve dollars refund. In Russia I would not change anything (or I would

lose my trip). I would never, never get money back. It could happen that you wait ten years to have a telephone installed in Russia, really, ten years.

"I don't mind all the different types of people and the mixed cultures. The greatest thing in New York is that it is the capital of immigrants. An immigrant feels at home. In the first place he sees a lot of immigrants around. In the second place he realizes Americans have a good stereotype of foreigners, that they are professionals, and that they work hard and that they are smart. They don't care about your English. You are equal. You feel it. A foreigner and still equal.

"This is New York's asset. You can find any society. In my office you have Japanese, Chinese, Greek, Spanish, and Italian. More immigrants than Americans. Tens of different accents. They are all managers and you speak better English than they do. Of course you feel at home.

"There are a few Russian communities in New York, especially in Brighton Beach, Brooklyn. I did not live in that area of mostly Odessa Jews. I am not married and have no relatives here so I do not have a very strong connection with the Russian community. It's not really a community. People from Moscow, Leningrad, and Odessa do not mix in the States. It's not just a city. It's a type. In Israel there are circles by the year you come. The 1972 circle. The 1973 circle. Psychologically it is easy to understand. In the beginning it is difficult to adjust, to form your credo, your point of view. It is painful to have to go over this stage again with somebody just arriving. It is new for him and he needs to discuss his problems. You have been through it already. It is hard to go through the beginning again.

"I do not intend to persuade anyone from my family to come over, I can't promise them satisfaction. I can guarantee material things. I can support my whole family. But I cannot be certain they will be happy. I cannot persuade them, I just send letters telling how I live. They avoid the issue. Still I believe in several years they will be here.

"People ask if it is difficult to come from a Marxist Communist State and adapt to American capitalism. I would say Russians are more materialist than Americans. Could you believe that? For example, I still cannot understand that people voluntarily go to demonstrate or vote. In Russia we do not do anything voluntarily, we don't believe we can affect the destiny of the country. When you see thousands of people waving flags at Brezhnev at an airport welcoming him, they were transported there by State buses, from work. They were even given the flags. Here and in Washington I marched in some demonstrations for Soviet Jewry and the fact that people keep coming voluntarily amazes me. In Russia you do not do anything voluntarily or they think you are crazy. In this capitalist country you have volunteer work and charity.

"I was amazed that Americans do not work hard except where they are

The annual Solidarity Sunday march sponsored by the Greater New York Conference on Soviet Jewry. More than 100,000 marchers came to what has become the largest human-rights demonstration in the world. (*Courtesy Greater New York Conference on Soviet Jewry*)

building a career. The office empties at five o'clock. We are paid overtime, a lot of money, and still almost no one works. It looks like they do not need the money. When there was a big snow I was the only one to come to work. Many lived nearby—they could take the subway, the underground subway—like I did. Yet they lived in Manhattan and they did not come. In Russia you come. The weather could be even worse, you still come. Even if you are sick you come in and say you are sick and they send you home.

"There are problems in New York: crime, the race problem, and the weather, but my basic needs are satisfied. When I went to California I found nice clean communities and the climate is just perfect. Life looks much easier. It looks like this. I'm not sure it's exactly like this. I know someone who left New York and went to live there and came back in three months. She said people were too easy going there, not serious enough, and they are very materialistic. After three days in San Francisco I could not stand the idea of New York's dirt, climate and crowds. But I came back.

"The biggest problem in New York I think is fear of crime. People pay for a 'good' neighborhood. They live in ugly homes, in less attractive areas, and make many other compromises but the area is 'exclusive.' People are afraid and nervous. Perhaps many people do not even experience it, but they cannot escape an awareness of it from television, radio, the newspapers and this keeps them from doing things. There may be more crime here than in Russia (there is plenty of crime and street violence there too) but this shows me a level of freedom and civilization somehow. Really. But yes, it does make me tense. I have to be careful. That is the way New York is.

"It is overcrowded, dirty and the climate—I hate the climate. It is also very competitive, very tense. The city has a high standard of living. It creates new desires for things you never thought you needed before. It offers museums, theaters, everything.

"I am here now. I feel very far away from Russia. I have a very good job, a good salary. I am Jewish, I know *Yiddishkeit*. I am not afraid that this will keep me back. I am in America, in New York, and it is good, it is good for the important things.

7

I Was Afraid but More I Was Hungry:

Brooklyn's West Indians*

Dominican Republic

Curling along Eastern Parkway in Brooklyn, signaling its presence by its accents and wares, is the West Indian center of the city. It is not the only West Indian community in New York. Others dot upper Manhattan, Queens, and the Bronx. But it is the largest and most noticeable West Indian community in the city, perhaps because the West Indian blacks who flocked to New York in the 1960s and 1970s sought out an area in which American blacks had already settled and central Brooklyn's American black community goes back to the nineteenth century.

White Americans are likely to blur distinctions between native American blacks and black West Indians, distinctions blacks themselves have no difficulty making. Jervis Anderson, the Jamaican journalist, called attention to the variation in perception when he wrote: "To the majority of whites, however clean or careful their public rheotric, I have been a 'nigger' and to the American blacks I have been a West Indian. Each of these images has carried its special odium; each has entailed its special burden; each has created its special chasm."

Anderson expresses a theme heard repeatedly, if often less bluntly, in

* Although the term West Indies is perhaps more accurately used to describe the British territories that joined together in 1958 to form the West Indies Federation, it is used here in the broader sense, in line with popular usage, to describe all the islands in the archipelago between North and South America separating the Caribbean from the Atlantic.

other voices that call out for some notice to be given to differences within
the minority population. These voices point out that a country of one pre-
dominant race makes distinctions among those of its own race but amalga-
mates its minority segments. Caucasian Americans often see blacks or
Asians as groups who "all look alike," a phrase that more reflects the undif-
ferentiated judgment of the speaker than his perceptions. Differences in eye
color, skin pigmentation, hair texture, accent, and cultural background, although carefully registered within the group itself, seem indistinguishable to
everyone else.

The split between American blacks and West Indians, which Anderson
noted, is a valid one, based as it is on divergent cultural backgrounds. Although both groups have their origins in one of several African tribes en-
slaved during the seventeenth and eighteenth centuries, once in the Western
Hemisphere under different versions of forced labor, they naturally moved
apart. Further, most of the West Indian islands abolished slavery well before
the United States did (Haiti in 1804, Jamaica in 1834). Finally, in the West
Indies blacks made up a clear majority of the total population, easily more
in number than all the smaller blocs of other nonwhites who arrived later.
The case of Jamaica illustrates. In a country more than 90 percent black,
the middle class among them moved to control jobs in government, medicine, and education. Chinese, who were imported to do the physical labor
when slavery no longer existed, concentrated in land development and the
wholesale food businesses, while East Indians rose out of agriculture to run
retail shops. American blacks confronted a different situation. They rarely
enjoyed a clear majority, at least in any political or economic division where
it mattered. Further, immigrants to the United States avoided the South, so
that few came in at the bottom of the economic ladder to push blacks up.

Comparisons between West Indians and American blacks are old and
many. They come from the seasoned scholar as well as the quick-talking
student, with agreement more on facts than on interpretation. West Indians,
in most comparisons, appear to make more money and hold better jobs than
native-born blacks. An article in *The New York Times* in 1970 noted that
Manhattan's first black borough president, the city's black judges, and all its
high-ranking black police officers had come from the West Indies. Similar
success stories abounded in the business world. Carlos Hines, from Tre-
lawny, Jamaica, arrived in New York in 1956 when he was in his early
thirties. After working his way up from dishwasher to busboy, then waiter,
he opened his own restaurant in Greenwich Village, and then another uptown. In other fields, there are familiar names: Harry Belafonte, Sidney
Poitier, LeRoi Jones, Stokely Carmichael, Shirley Chisholm, Malcolm X,
Marcus Garvey, and many others.

In an attempt to characterize and quantify differences between West Indians and American blacks, Professor Oscar Glantz of Brooklyn College questioned several hundred New York students in the early 1970s about their expectations. He concluded that English-speaking Caribbeans were more likely than American blacks to value hard work. They placed greater trust in the New York City Police Department, and more often valued non-violence as a way to seek change. Of all the groups Glantz examined, only Jews indicated they placed greater emphasis on getting a college education. To questions concerning the possibility of finding a good job, the value of hard work, and the quality of individual freedom under the United States political system, West Indians responded most optimistically of all groups.

That they do better in the American system than native-born blacks seems clear. Their presence in high-paying and status jobs and in public office exceeds what their portion of the total population would lead one to expect. The explanation or interpretation emerges less clearly. In addition to cultural differences, the West Indians may acquire an edge simply by virtue of their having been immigrants. Several observers have suggested that newcomers to a country are often willing to live on less, delaying lux-uries for later. The new homeland offers a better earning opportunity than what they left and while their needs stay modest, they can put aside crucial savings for investment in business, education, and other long-term ventures rather than in consumables.

But there may be other reasons for West Indian successes. Professor Nancy Foner of the State University of New York, Purchase, has compared the records of West Indians (English-speaking Caribbeans, in this case) who immigrated to the United States with those of the West Indians who went instead to London. She concluded that the former did better. Three factors seemed important. First, the movement to America started earlier (by the 1920s about a quarter of Harlem's blacks were West Indian). Britain's influx did not occur until after 1951 when England's postwar labor needs caused the government to encourage immigration. A second factor Foner consid-ered important, although drawn from limited information, dealt with the different occupational backgrounds of the immigrants. Those who went to the United States included a higher percentage of professional workers than did those choosing Britain. There was still a third explanation for the vari-ation Foner found in the different racial contexts of the two countries. In Britain, Islanders encountered a mostly white environment while in the United States they were able to settle among native-born blacks. In England they tended to judge themselves (and be judged) by how well they did in comparison with whites, while in New York they more often compared themselves to and were compared with native blacks. Their residence pat-terns reinforced this comparison. By establishing themselves in black sec-tions of Brooklyn, Harlem, the North Bronx and Jamaica, they had more opportunity to establish businesses in the community, to judge themselves relatively successful, and to be further inspired by this perception of success.

The progress West Indians enjoyed did not endear them to many native blacks who, as early as the 1930s, labeled them "monkey chasers" and "black Jews." In the 1970s the prevailing epithet was "uptight." West Indians, for their part, complained that American blacks did not work hard enough, save fast enough, or take advantage of the opportunities available to them.

Many West Indians, and especially the well-educated ones, keep their distance from all but middle-class American blacks. Judith Brown, a college instructor just reaching thirty, looks back at her Barnard days in the tumultuous late 1960s: "There were the sit-ins and the demonstrations at Columbia but I remember staying pretty much out of them. The black Americans wanted to demonstrate to get soul food served on campus. Really! How could I identify with that? So I stayed with the Caribbean students and I made sure I kept the Jamaican accent. I made clear too who was paying my way. At Barnard in those days there was a kind of general impression that anybody black must be there on scholarship. I wasn't. My father was paying all the bills and I mentioned that fairly often. Now I see it was my way of establishing a separate identity, apart from American blacks. We saw their second-class status and didn't want any of it.

"I see the same thing with my students now," she continued. "On the campus where I teach—part of City University of New York—we have a Pan-African club. They are the black Americans. This club has nothing to do with the Haitian club. That may be understandable because of the language difference. But even the Caribbean club, which is English speaking and black, won't meet with the Pan-Africans. Then the Spanish clubs are separate too. Last year I talked with the adviser of the Pan-African club (I'm adviser to the Caribbean club) about a joint party. It never happened. Students wouldn't hear of it. Said they could never agree on which food to serve or what records to play.

"Even within the Caribbean club there are divisions. Last year I accompanied students on a weekend outing to the Catskills. The Jamaicans wanted reggae and the Trinidadians, calypso. From their perspective, it's not an unimportant disagreement. They see all these things—their accents and music and food—as their culture and they don't want to lose any of it. Why should they? Certainly there's no reason to amalgamate into a black American identity—they know that employers show more respect for West Indians.

"There's almost an aggressive self-consciousness that some West Indians want to push. That's one reason the Rasta movement has caught on with a segment of our young people in New York. People see the Rastafarians as radical, very antiwhite. They use 'ganja' or hashish, and they won't take regular jobs. The Rastas defend themselves by saying they are just protesting so much prowhite bias. In Jamaica most middle-class and upper-class blacks are viewed as culturally European. It's a difficult thing to get at and a white person might not see it, but for Jamaicans, it is very clear. The education system is still modeled on the British, and Europe was always on the vacation itinerary. That goes all the way back in Jamaican history. Middle- or upper-class Jamaicans like Italian and French art, music. But for the masses of the working class, that is not the identity they seek. They want something individual, uniquely Jamaican, and they find it in the Rastafarian movement. When they put their hair in corn rows, they are asserting that identity. In New York that becomes especially important to them and more and more are seeking that identity. It's like a religion with them. For the young ones that is very important. Not their parents."

West Indian immigration north has shown several swings during the twentieth century. In 1900, only 4,656 West Indians settled in the United States but that number grew quickly to more than 16,000 in 1907. That represented a high point, however, not reached again until the mid-1920s, just before the depression decade and World War II sent the numbers down again. After 1945 West Indian immigration began to climb again, reaching almost 13,000 in 1955. The following decade showed more rapid increase. In 1968, after the 1965 law had become fully effective, a total of 140,827 West Indians immigrated to the United States, a temporary surge before the number leveled off at around 50,000.

For most Islanders, the United States meant New York City. Steamship routes between the Caribbean and the eastern seaboard funneled most immigrant blacks into New England and the mid-Atlantic states. Others worked on truck farms and at construction sites in the southern states. New York City, with its sizeable black population, proved most magnetic of all, however, and 65 percent of the foreign-born blacks in the United States lived in the Empire City in 1930. Fifty years later one of every three legal immigrants to New York was West Indian. With a backlog of applications for visas, still others grew impatient and entered without documents or came as tourists and overstayed. Estimates of the total West Indian population in New York ran as high as 1 million, including illegals, making them more than one in eight of the city's peoples.

Jamaicans account for a considerable part of the West Indian immigration. Their consulate says a quarter, but most people consider this unduly conservative. Professor Judith Brown, the Jamaican who studied at Barnard in the 1960s, explains why her country, an island slightly smaller than Connecticut in both size and population, experienced a large exodus after 1972 when Michael Manley became prime minister:

In Jamaica more than half the population works in agriculture. The lack of jobs and the low earnings of those who do work cause many to consider moving, either to Kingston or to the United States. (*Courtesy United Nations, R. King*)

"Manley was appealing to perhaps 80 percent of the population with his anticapitalist rhetoric. Of course the talk was more radical than the actions. He nationalized no private property—only big companies and that with strict compensation. But still, the better-off were frightened—more by the threat of violence I think than anything else. People with big cars or nice homes were identified as capitalists and became fair game. The crimes against them were pretty frightening. Rape, for example, increased considerably. In Jamaica it was the ultimate class crime. Attack on upper-class

A large percentage of the agricultural workers are women, who earn so little that emigration offers an attractive alternative. (*Courtesy United Nations, R. King*)

women by lower-class men. It was a pervasive fear. My sister had just graduated from Barnard and she wrote our father saying that she wanted to go back to Jamaica. He strongly suggested she stay in New York. Out of fear, I think. Didn't want her in the house by herself.

"My parents' house was broken into. And it was the way it was done that scared them. Things were taken, of course. You would expect that. But the people who did it went further—broke a dozen eggs on the living room carpet. That seemed so unnecessary. Other wealthy people I know have had their houses broken into and then found things written on the walls—'We'll be back' or something like that. It's very upsetting and it causes many people to leave."

Although many middle-class Jamaicans prefer Toronto or Miami, some,

Although Jamaican men have been less enthusiastic than Jamaican women about job opportunities in the United States, they are coming in ever larger numbers (*Courtesy United Nations*)

citing family reasons or company loyalty, settle in New York. The Stanley family is one example. In Kingston, Michael Stanley had worked for eighteen years for a large American food company. His wife looked after their three daughters, a large house, and two full-time servants. Theirs was a quality life, not luxurious, but very comfortable. When Manley became prime minister in 1972, all that changed. Mr. Stanley's company was nationalized and he began looking for another job while he continued in the old one, fearful he would lose it. Preoccupied with the safety of his family, he began considering how to leave.

The decision did not come easily because emigration required leaving behind all one's personal property, including savings. But in 1977 the Stanley family changed its lifestyle drastically and moved to a furnished apartment in New York. Its tiny rooms and soot-covered windows compared badly with the light, spacious quarters they had enjoyed on their sunny island, but the family received special help in adapting. Friends acquired on several business trips to New York when Stanley still worked in Jamaica helped the family meet people and find schools for the girls.

By 1979 the worst of the initial adjustment lay behind and money had been siphoned out of Jamaica a little at a time. Friends from New York who went to Jamaica on business or pleasure trips drew on the Stanleys' bank accounts in Jamaica, then repaid them in American currency when they returned to New York.

What the Stanleys found jolting and difficult to accept was the racial prejudice. The wife of one of his white colleagues explained how she had been struck by the treatment of the Jamaican family: "They had so much to offer. What charm! They didn't have that chip on the shoulder that you see among so many American blacks and they just assumed that we would accept them. That's what made me feel comfortable I think. Then I realized that many white Americans just don't see beyond a black skin. We invited the whole family down to our place at the shore for a weekend. I really didn't think about problems that might arise because of their color. Perhaps I was naive. It's a completely white neighborhood on the Jersey shore. The girls brought a cousin so there were four of these leggy, svelte teenage girls who just looked marvelous in their bikinis. Well, nobody said anything to us that weekend—the neighbors just sort of avoided us—but the next weekend we really got told. No one would admit to feeling any objection himself. Each blamed it on the other. Our closest neighbor, who has always been very friendly, said, 'Old Joe Bechtel down the street was really mad about those people you had down past week. He said, "Where did they get those niggers?"' Then we met Joe and he attributed something similar to the next-door neighbor. And so it went. Can you imagine? Here were these well-educated, very sophisticated Jamaicans and all the neighbors saw was black."

The exodus of Jamaica's upper middle class is small compared to the outpouring of poor who pay no attention to the currency restriction. They have nothing to take out. Rosalyn Morris, who left well before Manley's rise to power, was one of the poor:

"I know I come late to America. Most people immigrate when they are young. I was forty-six. I try earlier but it doesn't work out. I always dream I come to America. When I was a little girl, I remember people come back from the United States. They look so nice. They dress so nice and talk so nice. When you not here, you give your life to come."

In many ways Mrs. Morris's story is not unusual. In Kingston she earned five dollars a week in 1968, not enough to buy her ticket out. Then she heard of a scheme that involved New York housewives, Jamaican lawyers, and women like herself. The 1965 immigration law included a work certification provision that permitted individuals to enter the United States to take jobs that could not be filled from the resident labor force; the employer in each case had to provide evidence that he had tried unsuccessfully to find a suitable worker from inside the country.

In 1968 about 40 percent of all those who came in from the Western Hemisphere carried a work-certification permit that they had purchased or arranged for, either individually or through a broker. Mrs. Morris had paid one hundred Jamaican dollars to a lawyer in Kingston and, in return, got a ticket to New York and placement as a live-in servant with a Yonkers family. For the year that she agreed to work, she received fifty-five dollars each week (plus room and board); the remainder of what she would have earned, under minimum wage laws, went to administering officials who had financed her trip and processed her papers. When her contract ended twelve months later, she could negotiate her own working and living arrangements. The job she was certified to do, the one that provided her with a visa for coming to the United States, she performed for only twelve months and two weeks.

The employment plan devised in the 1960s does not differ greatly from the redemptioner plan or even the indentured-servant system worked out in colonial America to bring employees to the Western Hemisphere. From the beginning of settlement, the American continents, lacking an adequate labor supply, offered the prospect of a better future to lure other nations' surplus. The indenture system, as it developed in the seventeenth century, provided for transportation across the Atlantic for men and women unable to finance the trip themselves. The ship captain, with whom they signed on, gave free passage in return for the privilege of selling their services for a limited time, generally five to seven years, after arrival. When their indenture period ended, servants took on all the responsibilities and privileges of any other free person. The system provided labor and at the same time helped populate the colonies.

The twentieth-century version of the indenture system, springing people free from poor conditions but this time bringing them to often overcrowded cities, proved particularly attractive to Jamaicans in the late 1960s. Some had unsuccessfully sought passage north for years. Their native English made them especially attractive as domestics for families that did not speak Spanish or French. The international exchange developed quickly out of entrepreneurship and needs on both sides. The 1968 statistics illustrate the point: slightly more than 17,000 Jamaicans entered the United States that year, almost 13,000 of them female. Of the adults, women outnumbered

4 to 1; 1 in 3 of the women was a "private-household worker." Among that number was Mrs. Rosalyn Morris, under a job classification that fits her well. It is work she has always done.

"All my years I been working—since I was thirteen. But I make so little. My mother was dead and my father was gone so I live with my grandmother. When I was thirteen I leave school to work in a college not far away. We say college for boarding school. My job was to clean and help feed the younger boys. Some of them was very young. I help clean and I feed the little ones. I make thirty cents a week and I have my room and board free. Once a year I get on a bus and go back to visit my grandmother in the country. About four hours on the bus it took—once a year was all I could go.

"Then I got a better job in the city—in Kingston—working for a woman, a very nice white woman. You see I have always been around white folks. All my life I work for white folks and never have any trouble. The only time I do not work for white folks was just before I come to New York. I work in a wholesale place owned by Chinese. I clean the lobby and the shelves. But to me, it never made any difference whether they was Chinese or white. The most I ever made in Jamaica was five dollars a week.

"After a while I started having children—the first in 1944. I was twenty. By 1958 I had five. I couldn't leave when they was little but I kept thinking. In Jamaica I only went to the third grade. My sister was older and she went more. Then we both had to stop to go to work. I wanted my children to have something different, something more than I had, so I decided to come to New York. When I finally got the papers I left the smaller children with my aunt—the youngest was ten but the older ones was grown. Lots of women did the same thing. Left their children with aunts, grandmothers. We help each other.

"I never expect to get rich in America. Friends who worked here and came back all said the same thing. 'Twasn't bad,' they said, 'but twasn't good.' I knew it had to be better than Jamaica. That's why I come.

"I come alone. No man come with me. I like being alone—choosing my own friends. Doing what I want. I'll never marry nobody again. When I take a vacation, I go where I want. Next week I'm going to Florida to visit some friends in Miami. I don't ask anybody. I never have much money. I have to watch everything but still I do what I want."

Rosalyn Morris's satisfaction with American life is quietly and firmly avowed, echoing the reactions of other Jamaican women of her age, reactions that are not as frequently heard from Jamaican men. Mrs. Evelyn Winston, with about the same number of years lining her face as Mrs. Morris, explains the problems her husband found when he came to Brooklyn from Jamaica: "In Kingston he had a good job—worked for a trucking company but he had gotten up to the point where he kept the books. With the same company for many years. Had some respect. Then he came here and had to become a mechanic all over again. He makes good money. It's a steady job. But he doesn't feel as good about it as he did about his job in Jamaica. Keeps saying, 'Let's go back,' but I won't go. I have a good job. I'm going to college so I'll get a degree. My children have the kind of opportunities they never had in Jamaica. Just last week my daughter was accepted at Mt. Holyoke College. We can't afford to send her, even with the scholarship they offered, but still it was nice that she was interviewed and accepted."

Evelyn Winston exudes the new confidence of one making her own decisions for the first time. The life she left in Kingston was not a miserable one. Her husband's job paid considerably better than Rosalyn Morris's but the two women express their satisfaction with their new lives in New York in similar terms. Neither plans to return to Jamaica for more than a visit.

Evelyn Winston's schooling in Jamaica had prepared her for hospital work (Jamaica's two largest exports are bauxite and nurses). A four-hour flight north, paid for by family savings and loans from friends, brought her to a job market where she could earn three times what she had at home. Until she found an apartment, her family remained behind and when they joined her she was stretching her day to cover three roles: full-time student at a community college; night-shift practical nurse; wife and mother to a less-than-contented husband and three teenage children. Admitting it was all hard work, she rarely complained, choosing to dwell instead on the parts of her life that had never before been so good—the pay and the expectation that it might get even better.

The same economic considerations, buttressed by political insensitivity and occasional repression, draw other West Indians to the cold winters of the north (where many count the sight of snow as one of their new thrills). Haiti, where the unemployment rate is often estimated at 60 to 80 percent, qualifies for the title of "poorest country in the Western Hemisphere." With more than 5 million people, its area and population roughly resemble Maryland's but all similarities end there. The island is 90 percent black and the rest mulatto; many (some say 86 percent) are illiterate. Middle-class Haitians speak French and embrace Catholicism but most Haitians speak Creole and mix their Catholicism with Voodoo.

Except for unusual spurts in 1791–1803 just before the achievement of Haitian independence and again between 1915–1934 during the United States occupation of Haiti, immigration from Haiti stayed small. Then, after 1957, when Francois "Papa Doc" Duvalier became president, immigration enthusiasm grew. During the mid-1960s when Duvalier's policies of repression and persecution became more extreme, many Haitian professionals and students came north. The influx continued into the 1970s but changed to include many semiskilled and domestic workers.

By the end of the 1970s more than 300,000 Haitians lived in the United States, with major concentrations along the East Coast, from Boston to Washington, in Chicago and most recently in Miami. In New York City, about half of the Haitians live in Brooklyn, concentrating in Crown Heights, Bedford Stuyvesant, Brownsville, and East New York. Another 30 percent live on Manhattan's Upper West Side and the rest reside in such Queens neighborhoods as Corona, Jamaica, Elmhurst, and Jackson Heights.

Haitian immigrants come from all rungs of the occupational ladder. That 10 percent are professionals (no other island in the Caribbean can claim anywhere near that number) adds credence to the claim of Haitian emigrants that their decision to leave their native island represents more than an economic exodus. In some cases they have risked their lives to flee political repression, dangers undertaken because they fear staying put.

One small boat, with sixty-five Haitians aboard, landed at Pompano Beach in Florida in December of 1972, presenting wealthy condominium owners relaxing nearby with a curious sight. After traveling eight hundred miles in nineteen days, they asked to be treated as political prisoners. United States immigration officials refused, however, saying they had fled only poverty and therefore did not meet the test for refugee status. Nobody refuted the point that they had known misery (the annual average income in Haiti is only a few hundred dollars) but the escapees sought to make clear other deprivations under a political dictatorship that punished criticism. Although conditions have apparently improved under "Baby Doc" Duvalier (who succeeded his father in 1971), Haitians tell macabre stories of the *Tontons Macoutes*, who continue as a kind of unpaid secret police often arriving unannounced to demand money, a house, or a woman. Senseless beatings accompany their requests, even those that are granted without hesitation. Victims who resist find themselves "jacked," an old punishment used against slaves in Haiti—the prisoner's hands are tied to his ankles and his body contorted into an excruciating crouch.

In spite of repeated stories of repression and maltreatment, Haitians evince little sympathy from United States officials. American policy towards Haiti has, in fact, zigzagged for decades. In the early days of Castro's government, the United States sought Duvalier's votes in the Organization of American States and had to ignore his violations of human rights, but then tempered its warmth between 1962 and 1964. Since then, as thousands of people have fled both Cuba and Haiti, the United States, feeling it necessary to prop up anti-Communist regimes despite their excesses, has made no move to treat the Haitians as political exiles, as it did the Cubans.

On the other side of the island from Haiti and nearly twice its size is the

Dominican Republic. Less densely populated, this Roman Catholic country speaks Spanish. One in eight of its people is white and three-quarters are mulatto, an official racial designation in the Dominican Republic, but with little meaning in the United States where mulatto Dominicans are grouped with blacks. Of the 10,000 or so Dominicans entering New York City legally each year, only about 1 in 50 reported professional status. Few came in as household workers (employers find it more difficult to use Spanish-speaking domestics) and fewer than 10 percent are craftspeople or skilled workers; like other Latins they are largely unskilled, often agricultural workers.

Dominicans define family more broadly than do American immigration officials. Children born of "free unions," legal marriages, or church marriages are all considered legitimate. Godparents frequently assume responsibility for their godchildren equivalent to that expressed by the natural parents. Since United States immigration law does not include provisions for extended families and children born to other than legally married couples, Dominicans often seek to reunite families with a variety of subterfuges. In 1979 two medical researchers, Vivian Garrison and Carol I. Weiss, traced a Dominican family since 1962 as it moved most of its fourteen members to the United States piecemeal. Only one came with papers to work; others were eventually called for. Two married in order to enter the United States legally. Some overstayed tourist visas; others "borrowed" papers or bought counterfeit documents, and the rest simply sneaked across borders with no papers at all. The saga of this one family, adopting a range of strategies to reunite its various members in the United States, illustrates the options open to enterprising immigrants as well as the limitation in the American law that recognizes only nuclear families born of wedlock.

Trinidad and its little island neighbor, Tobago to the north, figure less in the West Indian immigration picture, The two islands together are about the same size as Jamaica but with half the number of people (although the population is considerably more varied). The population is less than half black (the rest are East Indian or mixed) and the island's religious institutions reflect the fact that a substantial part of the population is from Asia. The Spanish *patois* of Trinidadians is tinged with the dialects of India and China, giving them a special lilt that, perhaps more than anything else, leads Rosalyn Morris, the Jamaican domestic who came to New York in 1968, to comment that "Trinidadians have more fun." In Brooklyn, where she settled after her year in Yonkers, she has ample opportunity to make comparisons among the West Indians. It is Brooklyn where the distinctions show most clearly.

"When I first got to Yonkers I thought that was New York. I had to take care of two children—about the same ages as my own two back in Kingston.

One day I said to one of the children, 'Is this New York? Is this what it's like?'

"And one of them said, 'This isn't New York. This is Yonkers!'

"So I decided that I had to go to New York. Took me three months but finally one Sunday I came. The thing I remember most about that trip was on the subway—I saw children in rags. Everybody around me in Yonkers dressed pretty nice. But here in New York were children wearing rags! It surprised me!

"After my year was up in Yonkers I moved out. The people I worked for were nice, but I wanted my own place. I had saved a little bit from the fifty-five dollars I earned every week so I came to Brooklyn and got an apartment. Some people I knew already lived here so they helped me. I already knew something about the neighborhoods. Rents were lower here, the streets seemed friendlier."

Rosalyn Morris's move to Brooklyn in 1969 is one story in the big migration of blacks to that borough during the decade of the sixties. In a ten-year period, from 1960 to 1970, Brooklyn gained 285,000 blacks bringing the total up to 656,000, while the white population (not counting Puerto Ricans) dropped by an even larger number (740,000), as people fled the borough for Staten Island and Queens. Black settlements spilled over into sections of formerly all-white neighborhoods and, to whatever extent integration came it resulted from black moves into white areas. Most whites in 1980 still lived in areas populated predominantly by people of their own race but the segregation was less clear than it had been in previous years. Rosalyn Morris and people like her help explain the shift.

Rural areas and small towns never attracted Mrs. Morris although she had grown up in the country. She prefers the excitement of the city where she says there is always something to do. Retirement, when it comes in another half-dozen years, does not conjure up visions of a small cottage with a flower garden. The constant traffic noise, the horns, the brakes, and the shouts outside her third floor apartment on New York Avenue do not bother her.

Rosalyn Morris will never buy a house in Brooklyn, she says. Her dreams can survive in rented quarters. But bigger checks and multiple earners in other West Indian families have made possible the purchase and renovation of brownstones along Prospect Park. Rows of quiet houses, with their immaculate sidewalks, remind observers that homesteading is not dead. Indeed Brooklyn has proved to be an enduring home-owners destination for decades for West Indians.

Although she lacks the great desire to own real estate that other West Indians show, Rosalyn Morris exhibits a conservative orientation common among Jamaicans. In economic matters she places her faith squarely in hard

A neighborhood celebration in the Crown Heights West Indian community features native-style music. (*Courtesy Brooklyn Rediscovery, a program of the Brooklyn Educational & Cultural Alliance, Jerry Spearman*)

work, complaining bitterly of welfare abuses: "I'm not opposed to all welfare. Some people need it. Old people. Cripples. But these young mothers with children, they should be put out to work. That's where I would be—always have been. When I was young with several children and no husband to take care of us, I didn't get welfare. I worked for what I could get. That's what I would do with these young mothers. Get them a job and put their children in a day care center. They're just sending up taxes for all of us. Besides it doesn't make them feel independent. They know they can't make it on their own. They don't even try."

Mrs. Morris makes clear that she has spent her entire life trying very hard to improve her situation and she has done it pretty much on her own. Though aware of a long list of Jamaican organizations in New York—savings associations, cricket clubs, and religious groups—she belongs to none of them. "I know they exist," she says "but I never needed them. I've always worked and when I needed help I went to my friends. I don't even go to church. In that way I suppose I am like my grandmother. I used to think she was religious—always going to one meeting or another: Wesleyan, Church of England, Gospel Meeting. She went from one to the other. Now I realize she wasn't religious at all, just social. Wanted to be with other people—wasn't God at all.

One of the city's most colorful festivals, the West Indian festival, held at the end of every summer, gives West Indians in Brooklyn a chance to create costumes that they have worn at important celebrations in their native islands. *(Courtesy Brooklyn Rediscovery, a program of the Brooklyn Educational & Cultural Alliance, Jerry Spearman)*

"My friends are the women I work with. At the Hilton Hotel for eight years. Clean rooms. They pay me all right. Almost nobody tips anymore because the rooms are so expensive. Sometimes I get a little extra, but not often. It's not the pay that bothers me. It's the boss. A woman. Much harder to work for a woman than for a man. They expect more. Oh yes!"

Rosalyn Morris's explanation of why she decided to become a citizen is entirely practical. "I never expect to go back to live in Jamaica. To visit, yes, but not to live, so I say, 'Why not become a citizen?' You know if things get difficult here in the States and somebody has to leave, the American government may begin to look around and they may say, 'You are a citizen. You are not.' Who do you think will have to leave? I think it is safer to be a citizen. Besides I love this country. Why shouldn't I be a citizen?"

Her daughter, the youngest of five and the only one to live at home, agrees with very little of what her mother says. "Oh yes, you love it," she chides, "but you don't even realize you're behind the color line—way behind. And it's not going to change. I am not an American citizen. I don't plan to become one and I'd rather go back to Jamaica where they don't have this big thing about color. I'm tired of being seen as just another black in a country where it is better to be white."

Sitting across the room from her daughter, this soft-spoken, middle-aged mother is all compromise and acceptance. "When I was young," she says, "I never thought about many of the things that are important now to my daughter. I didn't think about the distance between white folks and Negroes. I never thought about change. I worked around white folks. They treated me well and I thought I would work hard and give my children some of the things I never had. I never expected them to want so much—even to try to change the way people treated them.

"My daughter complains about life here—says there's a lot of prejudice—but she doesn't know how it was back in Jamaica. My three children all go to college here in New York. I never dreamed of going to college. She says there's a color line. She's right. But why worry about it if everything else is going all right? I heard before I come about how Negroes was treated here. Somebody even told me they threw us in the river. Oh yes! Certainly I was afraid—but more I was hungry and my daughter will never understand about that."

The New York Avenue apartment in Brooklyn where Rosalyn Morris lives with her daughter reflects an interest in acquiring things and caring for them well. The furniture is large, an Italian baroque coffee table taking up most of the floor space between two long plastic-covered sofas. Twenty-four inches of television screen flicker all day if anybody is in the house, the sound providing a background to whatever conversations the apartment hosts. The television noise has become so common, mixed with the street noises of autos braking and accelerating, of children screaming or parents calling out warnings and instructions, that Mrs. Morris no longer notices its separate existence. Occasionally she turns the radio on, above the television, without realizing that the two merge into one incomprehensible drone.

Her bedroom is dominated by a king-sized bed, leaving only a narrow walkway on one side while a large, ornate dresser and two matching chests fill the other side. The two dominant characteristics of the apartment are its colors—deep reds and yellows on all sides—and its fullness. There are no books, but magazines and newspapers from Jamaica attest to the continuing interest in the island and what is happening there.

With her tie to Jamaica so strong, why did she choose to emigrate to New York? She certainly could have picked another American city physically closer to home. With budgetary concerns and the problem of population congestion, both internationally known, New York should not, it seems, attract the immigrants it does. In Rosalyn Morris's case, the job contact was crucial since New York lawyers cooperated with those in Kingston to arrange her placement. If Kansas City attorneys had offered the same chance, would she have accepted? Probably not. She emphasizes how important it was for her to come to a city where she knew some people who were not family but friends. Ironically the fact that there were many blacks in the city pulled her, even though she knew well that she would be categorized within their lesser status. However great the prejudice and discrimination she would suffer on their behalf, their presence comforted her.

New York offers other advantages—familiar foods in corner stores that sell most of the dishes she knew in Kingston. Though these foods are rarely prepared as carefully as those she remembers in Jamaica, she enjoys being able to judge the difference, to criticize and compare those she gets here to the real thing. Mrs. Morris does not always shop at Jamaican stores—she is just as likely to buy her supplies from the Chinese fish market or the Jewish grocery on her block—but she relishes the special pleasure she derives from knowing the familiar is there. In a city of many foreigners, she has her own turf.

Most of the city remains as removed from her thoughts as if she were a tourist. Of politics she knows nothing beyond the current mayor's name. She has never voted and does not see why she should. Of changes in the city's population, its tax structure, its transportation, she cares little beyond what directly affects her. If the A train gets new cars she is pleased, but when the television newscaster hints at a possible fare increase, she is angry. Matching the Transit Authority's revenues and expenditures, either now or in the future, does not concern her. She will think of her own check book.

If the Empire City is the cultural capital of the Western Hemisphere,

Rosalyn Morris remains unaware. She never sees a play, hears a concert, or views an art exhibit. Her television set brings enough of the outside world into her life and the magazines she buys bring back memories of Jamaica. An occasional evening out—to eat and drink with family and West Indian friends—these are the pleasures she prizes.

Rosalyn Morris's has been a simple life, but one that satisfies her. Having been born in the countryside of a small island a thousand miles away, then having moved in middle age to a noisy, bustling city, she has found the two things she values most: a job that "pays enough" and the feeling she is home in an enclave that is not altogether foreign or unfamiliar.

8

I Didn't Choose America,
I Chose New York:

Varying Italian Perspectives

Finding New York's Italian neighborhoods does not require a map of the census wards. Shops filled with provolone, prosciutto, and pasta are a sure sign that one is already in one of them. Along Mulberry Street between Prince and Canal, down Sullivan Street where SoHo* artists have not completely uprooted them, Italians have lived for three-quarters of a century. Other parts of Manhattan that once drew Italians, especially East Harlem along 116th Street and the western sections of Greenwich Village, have bowed to new influxes. Puerto Ricans have claimed East Harlem and wealthy brownstoners have changed the Village. But the most famous Little Italy in America—New York's Mulberry Street—still holds its San Gennaro festival every September and for the feast of Saint Anthony, traffic is blocked on Sullivan Street every June.

Across the Brooklyn Bridge, Italian settlement is of more recent origin

---

* SoHo (for South of Houston Street) is in lower Manhattan and extends from Houston to Canal Street between Broadway and West Broadway.

but of much larger numbers. When Manhattan neighborhoods grew crowded and families acquired the money to move, they chose Red Hook and Bensonhurst in Brooklyn. After World War II, Brooklyn attracted even more Italians, and by 1970 large parts of Bay Ridge, Bensonhurst, and Gravesend, along Brooklyn's western bulge, reported census tracts that were more than half Italian. Since officials designate as Italian only those born in Italy and their children, ignoring others of the third and fourth generations, the actual Italian population is much larger. In Queens, to the north of Brooklyn, small pockets of Italians dot Long Island City, Corona, and Kew Gardens. On Staten Island, the Italian presence is more pronounced: in the names of the streets and the restaurants and in who becomes its college presidents and legislators.

New York's least populated borough, Staten Island has shown the largest growth in recent times in the number of Italian residents. That an Englishman Henry Hudson gave it a Dutch name, in honor of the Staats General that had sponsored his 1608 voyage, obscures an earlier visit by an Italian. Giovanni da Verrazano, sailing under a French flag, sighted the island in 1524, the first European to have recorded such a visit. Although he moved on to explore other parts of the coast, Verrazano took time to record his impressions. The native people were beautiful and friendly, he wrote, although the island was already crowded. Of all the early Italian explorers, none appears to have been more humane than this Florentine, who hoped the new continent would take the name "Francesca" in honor of his patron country's king.

Occasional adventurers and explorers from Italy gave way in the mid-seventeenth century to permanent settlers: a few Venetian glassblowers in Virginia and some Protestant dissidents on Long Island. By the time the colonies had wrenched their independence from England, set up government, and taken the first national census in 1790, New York City could point to a sprinkling of Italian names: 20 families along the southern tip of Manhattan. By the 1860s the number of Italians had grown to more than 10,000 and the community was ready to build the first Italian church in the city, St. Anthony's, at the corner of Sullivan and Houston. To the north in Greenwich Village, Italian shops sold delicacies and candles. Antonio Meucci, who preceded Alexander Graham Bell in inventing the telephone, hosted and employed Giuseppe Garibaldi in his Bleecker Street candle shop. Meucci's famous countryman did not linger, however, in New York. He returned to Europe to lead his native Italy to unification.

Each July more than one hundred men assist in carrying a giant monument, or giglio, in honor of St. Paulinus of Nola through the streets of Williamsburg, Brooklyn to Our Lady of Mount Carmel Church. (*Courtesy Brooklyn Rediscovery, a program of Brooklyn Educational & Cultural Alliance, Margaret Latimer*)

For many immigrants, familiar foods are very important. Stores specializing in ethnic delicacies mark New York's ethnic enclaves. (*Betty Boyd Caroli*)

For New York's Italians, the memory of these heroic countrymen holds special significance. Their statues dot the city. Garibaldi stands in Washington Square, Christopher Columbus at 59th Street, and Verrazano down in Battery Park facing the waterway he explored more than four centuries ago.

But the agreement that exists within the Italian American community on its national heroes does not carry over to many other issues. Nor did such agreement ever exist, even when these Italians were all still in Italy. In comparison with other countries of Western Europe, Italy was among the very last to unify. As a consequence, regional loyalties developed in place of national loyalties. Those who had always thought of themselves as Neapolitans and Sicilians had to learn to think of themselves as Italians. The changed loyalty did not come easily and often did not come at all. An often repeated comment has it that the lesser educated throughout Italy for a long time after national unity did not accept the word Italy as the name of their country but only as the name of the peninsula on which they lived, much as the Spanish think of the word "Iberia." When one patriot, enthusiastic about unification, in 1861 rode through a village shouting, "Viva l'Italia!" one man in the crowd, thinking a new queen had been crowned, turned to a friend and asked, "Who's Italia?" A European statesman, observing unification from outside, remarked, "Now that they have made Italy, they will have to make Italians."

In many ways, that making occurred outside Italy and even outside Europe, in the years during which hundreds of thousands of Italians poured out of the southern regions of Italy, most in search of work or opportunity. Emigration did not begin in response to unification. Thousands of miles of coastline had always provided relatively easy exit, and men and women with the desire to improve their lives had moved, first from one region to another, and then further on, to northern Europe and even Asia where Italians were reported making and marketing statuary and leather items in the 1850s. Cesare Correnti, writing in a statistical history of Italy in 1858, reported: "The number of Italians who are settling abroad or wandering there is large. Italian refugees, adventurers, tradesmen and doctors are scattered in all parts of the East. Peddlers and laborers are all over North and South America."

In the 1850s, when he was writing, Correnti may well have exaggerated what he saw, but thirty years later his words were borne out. After 1880, emigration from Italy, especially the South of Italy, grew rapidly. Men and women, worn out by malaria and cholera, discouraged by droughts and earthquakes, had been hoping for better times with unification. When instead the new central government imposed even higher taxes, the best alternative seemed simply to leave quickly. After 1880 two simultaneous developments in Italy's emigration changed its character and direction: the total number increased and the United States share of the total grew. Of the 135,000 who left Italy in 1881, only about 11,000 headed for North America; by 1901 those who intended to settle in the United States accounted for 1 of every 4 of Italy's emigrants. America, as a destination, took on special meaning, unrelated to geography. For many it represented a dream. One mayor of a small Italian village greeted visiting dignitaries with these words: "I welcome you in the name of all six thousand inhabitants of this town. Three thousand are in America and the others are preparing to go."

Many never intended to stay. Single men as well as married men, who left their families in the *paese*, made the journey in the belief that a few years of work in New York's construction gangs or Washington's lumber camps might provide them with a nest egg unequalled by any pension plan. Workers came back complaining about the climate and the bosses but not the dollars they had saved. Most men reported having lived on half their earnings; the rest they had sent back to Italy to buy small plots of land, or shops, or to pay off doctors and grocers. The repatriates often received strained welcomes in their villages on their return: mayors of small towns throughout Italy complained that the men had brought bad habits and many diseases; they drank too much and carried knives. Their dollars hardly offset, the mayors objected, the bad effect of leaving families without husbands and fathers.

Americans were even harsher. The "birds of passage" who went back and forth, staying two or three years, then returning to be with their families in Italy for a winter, found few champions in the United States. Their living habits were bad, reporters complained. They lacked the "civilizing" influence of women and children in their homes. Excessive drinking, noise, and filth were common. These were not the kind of immigrants that became Americans. When champions did appear to take the part of the birds of passage, they came from unexpected quarters. Woodrow Wilson hardly stood as the best defender of immigrants. Yet when someone complained to him that Italians had to be kept out because they took their dollars back to Italy, Wilson replied: "But they left the subways."

From the Italian side, government officials, when warned of the dangers of temporary emigration, responded: "But they bring back dollars." It was an exchange that fed both countries. The Italian government sought to increase the temporary flow by setting prices and conditions aboard the ships, providing for the remittance of dollars through Italian banks, and disseminating information about jobs in the United States. When the U.S. Congress decided to stop the traffic by imposing a literacy test that many Italians could not pass, the Italian government appropriated money for evening schools to tutor prospective emigrants. "This is a large source of income for us," one Italian senator said in the Italian parliament. "It would be terrible for us if it stopped."

The American government did stop the back-and-forth movement of Italians by passing the quota laws of the 1920s. When the apparatus for the restriction was finally in place, Italian emigration was cut to a fraction of its previous size. More than 100,000 in the early 1920s, Italian arrivals in the United States dropped to a tenth of that in the 1930s. An era had ended.

Nearly half of all the Italians in the United States in 1910 lived in the mid-Atlantic area, the belt running from Providence, Rhode Island to Baltimore, Maryland. Right in the middle of this concentration, New York

City was home to nearly one in four Italian Americans. It had been home since the 1880s and 1890s, when the great waves of Italian immigration occurred. The first generations of New York Italians shared their streets with all the other immigrant groups as well as with native-born Americans who had recently deserted dry farms for city lights. Some entrants, such as the Irish and Germans, stood ahead on the track, having arrived in large numbers several decades earlier. To the newly arrived Italians they appeared to dominate many businesses, as well as the Catholic church, and city politics. Other immigrant groups, the Eastern European Jews, for example, came at approximately the same time as the Italians. But more often the Jews came with higher education levels or more experience in a money economy or were more willing to discard old ideas about family and culture in order to capture their share of American gold; and so they moved up faster.

Each of the big nineteenth-century immigrant groups brought special skills and adaptive behaviors to New York: the merchant experience of the Germans and of the Jews; the political grouping and bargaining talent of the Irish; and the *contadino*-family emphasis of the Italians. Each shaped a new culture within different boundaries and on separate foundations.

Historically, Italians have protected themselves by trusting only those they know best: family and *paesani*. As a consequence, the obligations that arise between members of the same family or town have always been viewed as obligations of honor. When foreign armies overran parts of Italy, Southern Italians knew that though they could not count on their own armies to rout the invaders, they could at least count on their townsmen to make sure that individual insults were not without their price. Similarly, when local scandal ruined reputations—or threatened to do so—it was understood that families would rally to uphold honor. The code of behavior that developed was an intricate one, placing high value on the use of vendetta and a code of silence. Insults and transgressions, clearly defined, received traditional punishment. Family not only became the most important possession to protect—it was also the means of that protection.

But these loyalties did not extend beyond narrow borders. In the South, when law officials (either foreigners or Northerners) were imposed upon the local villages, local governance of the kind that mattered still stayed within an informal network of people whose families had worked alongside each other for longer than town records existed. Resistance and disobedience became necessary parts of survival; disrespect for outside enforcers imperative. Local residents employed nicknames for one another that outsiders could rarely identify and almost never translate; they used dialects and double meanings to confuse, and subtle gestures to mislead. (Sometimes nicknames replaced legal ones so completely that those on the birth certificate were practically forgotten except to the holder and a few of his family. This sub-

This small town in Calabria, in the south of Italy, is typical of those that Italians left to journey to America. (*Courtesy United Nations, J. Robaton*)

stitution purposefully complicated the task of draft officials trying to call up local men for service or tax collectors who had no list of nicknames.)

This labyrinth of concealments and subterfuges nourished such intense loyalty to hometowns that scholars described this narrow perspective as *campanilismo* after *campanile* or church belltower. It was used for people who trusted only those who came from under the same church tower as they had. Naturally, this attitude also expressed itself in popular adages: "Wives and oxen," one proverb went, "should both come from your own town."

This street market in Naples gives bargain hunters a chance to compare price and quality of produce and fish. (*Courtesy United Nations, J. Robaton/Pas*)

Even after they had moved thousands of miles away from Italy and from their own town's church tower, many Southern Italians could not slough off their strong feelings of *campanilismo*. Particularly in the largest American cities, attachments formed in the *paese* helped shape settlement patterns and determine job histories. In 1910, after some Italians had been here more than a decade or two, the Neapolitans still staked off their buildings along Mulberry Street while the Sicilian dialect dominated a few blocks away. On Houston Street shopkeepers were still carefully preserving not only their Genovese recipes for delicacies but their dialect as well. It would take more than just a few decades in New York to weaken regional differences, rendering them obsolete except for nostalgia's sake.

Another tradition that shaped the experience of Italians in America was their attitude toward work itself. All over Southern Italy, whatever the region, success had always had a special meaning, more related to family and to personal satisfaction than to money and mobility. Commitment to family well-being might demand sacrifice of one's self; it certainly put individual achievement in second place. Suspicion of self-improvement, a heresy in achievement-oriented America, remained the rule for the Italian *contadino*. For the observant Italian tourist in 1980, the difference is curious: "You Americans always want to talk about how much you make," a visitor points out. "In Italy we never do that. And at parties, you ask people what they 'do.' For us that's really rude. And what is most embarrassing is how you talk about how much progress you've made. Even your presidents brag about how poor they used to be. People come up to you—total strangers— and tell how they've improved themselves. When we improve ourselves, we don't want people to find out what we were before. We never talk about it—except to our closest friends who already know. Here in America, I never know what to say when somebody starts to tell me how successful he is. I am embarrassed."

Early in the century, Italian parents drew criticism for not pushing their children through schools into better jobs than they themselves held. Many did, telling their children again and again: "Mine will be the last generation in this family to work with our hands." The number of Italians graduating from high school climbed steadily and by the 1950s Italians began to be a significant factor in the enrollment levels of the city's colleges. But old ideas die slowly and not until the 1970s did Italians claim their share of seats in the City University. The change put new strains on family cohesion, as children outdistanced their fathers and sometimes their older brothers. Wives entering college from Brooklyn's Williamsburg section complained that their husbands, content with blue-collar (but high-paying) jobs did not understand them. The women's movement cut across ethnic lines, changing old relationships between spouses, and forging new ones between parents and children. As women attempted to define their lives in their own terms, old ways had to go. The long-cooked spaghetti sauce became only the most famous casualty; the others were more concealed but as deeply felt.

"My husband did not come to see me graduate from college last year," a forty-two-year-old mother of three noted. "Of course it was a weekday and he would have had to take off from work. Still, I really worked for that diploma and it meant a lot to me. Not even a dinner out to celebrate or anything. It was like he didn't want to notice."

No one fully understands why so many Italian American women enter college in their thirties and forties, but general agreement on the point indicates that this is the case. One professor in a City University college says: "Just count up the names of the older women in your classes—you'll see they're mostly Italians—the wives of construction workers and sanitation-men. With the money those men make, they can afford to have their wives in college." One mother of two tells why she entered college at age thirty-four: "I got out of high school and married the same summer. I never even thought about college—marriage was what most Italian families wanted for their daughters. It's what I wanted too. After my children were born, I was busy with them but they don't need me so much now. My husband makes a good living—we even have a summer place on Fire Island—so I said now I can do something I want to do. I love school—I have to watch that I'm not too enthusiastic in front of my husband. He likes to talk about what I'm reading, but he's not planning to leave his construction job. It pays too well."

The Italian man's preference for work he can see both saved and damned him. In the construction of buildings and subways, he reached a degree of job satisfaction that file clerks rarely experienced. "The only time I really felt close to my grandfather," one young Staten Islander recalled, "was when he drove me past a post office in Brooklyn. He had to stop the car and get out and explain how he helped build it—put the cornerstone in. The way he talked about it—he was so happy, so thrilled to be part of it. It was like it meant more to him than anything else he had ever done. And maybe he's right. There it was, forty years after he worked on it, and it still looked good. He did a good job—anybody could see that. I doubt I will ever be able to point something like that out to my grandchildren—forty years after I do it—so they and everybody else can look at it and say, 'Whoever did that did a really good job.' "

But pride in physical labor is a rural value, ill-suited to twentieth-century cities where a well-tended plot or a carefully made product no longer mark one's worth. For the Italian worker (by far the majority of pre-World War II Italian immigrants to the United States were unskilled workers experienced only in agricultural labor), the old values were hard to abandon. Not surprisingly, Italian success stories in New York came, for the most part, from fields that continued to emphasize physical labor: construction and food processing.

Italian Americans continued to boast their Italian intelligentsia: judges and magazine editors, professors and writers, conductors and internationally known musicians, but the biographies written of the most famous Italian Americans told of men who rose to wealth in a single generation, as a result of sweat and cleverness rather than study and perseverance. By the 1930s there were several such success stories but they were more significant as the stories of individuals who achieved than for any other reason.

Fiorello LaGuardia was one such story. He became the city's first "Italian" mayor (1933–45) though his link to Italian neighborhoods was tenuous. After 1950 the city's list of congressmen and state legislators included several new Italian names; by the 1960s Italians vied among themselves for the key to Gracie Mansion. In 1980 New York State elected its first Italian U.S. Senator, Alphonse D'Amato, although New York City voters contributed less than their share to the victory, Staten Island being the only borough to go for D'Amato.

Objectors lamented that no Italian name ever appeared on the Supreme Court list and that none ever got close to the White House. Blame was divided: some assigned it to Italian ideas about education and jobs, ideas that kept them out of the professions—especially law, the one profession that typically fed high political office. Others claimed a commitment to family imposed schedules that no successful politician could manage. Sunday dinner at home did not gain many votes.

When Italians did win high political office, some observers noted, they carried strong family loyalty with them. A television viewer on November 8, 1977, could not help noticing differences between the two candidates. Edward Koch, at his victory appearance, was flanked by his father and Bess Myerson. He kissed the latter. Mario Cuomo, admitting defeat to his supporters a few blocks away, looked into the television cameras as he introduced his wife and children. Then, very proudly, he kissed both his father and his mother. More pointedly, Alfonse D'Amato, in his 1980 Senate race, made family a cornerstone of his campaign. The candidates seemed to be saying that victory, if it came, would include family.

But some observers give little credence to the weight of family loyalty and responsibilities, pointing instead to voters who suspect that every successful Italian is crime-connected. "If you make it in this country and you have an Italian name," a woman publisher complained, "people just assume you're with the mob."

Italians had the bad fortune to immigrate in large numbers to the United States between 1880 and 1920 when the American temperance movement was at a peak. Perhaps no other element of their adopted country's mentality puzzled Italians more. From childhood they had taken wine as an enjoyable part of every meal—breakfast excepted. Drunkenness, or even overindulgence, was not tolerated but reasonably moderate drinking was no vice. The American movement to ban all alcohol, with the misleading name "temperance movement," therefore made little sense to most Italian newcomers.

When the Eighteenth Amendment to the U.S. Constitution became effective in 1920, prohibiting the legal sale of all alcohol, Italians regarded it with little sympathy. Recognizing the potential profits in liquor, they quickly moved into its manufacture, sale, and distribution. Other illegal ventures—in gambling, prostitution, and racketeering—operating along the fringes of bootlegging were also drawn in, as the same personnel and communication systems began to serve them all.

Most Italians stayed outside the illegal net, continuing to earn their pay with often backbreaking days of work. But in the public's mind, a few examples (Al Capone became synonomous with crime) tagged an entire people. The characteristics that Italians had nurtured because they strengthened the family—secrecy, the protection of honor, and the acceptability of vendetta—were integrated into an organized framework and became associated in the public mind with crime. The stamp was applied to all, no matter how far they stayed from crime. To many, an Italian surname perforce constituted a hint of association long after prohibition fervor had died out.

An Italian musician, shortly after he arrived in New York in 1979, explained how he learned what his Italian name meant: "One day I got a telephone call from a musician who works with me at Lincoln Center. He needed something and he wanted to know who I knew in the Mafia that he could contact. I thought he was joking so I laughed but he was completely serious. I had heard about that in Italy but I didn't believe it until I got here."

A middle-aged woman cleaning up the church kitchen after a meeting in Brooklyn discusses what it means to be Italian American: "I tell you. It is our curse. Because everybody thinks we're all criminals, we can't get ahead. Not in politics or anything else. The Mafia—it is our curse."

Only an occasional dissenter comes forward to remark on the advantages of the stereotype, inaccurate though it may be. A young Staten Islander, sitting with friends at a corner espresso shop, shrugs his shoulders when asked about Italians' identification with crime. "The Mafia? Does it bother me? Not at all. The Mafia is the one reason we get as much as we do in New York. It's the one thing about us that other people respect. I was down on a dark street in lower Manhattan a couple of years ago. Kind of a borderline neighborhood on the fringe of what they call Tribeca. The streets weren't well lit. Not much going on. I was walking along with a friend, pretty late on a winter night. These Puerto Ricans came up behind us. I was scared. There were three of them and only two of us. Maybe we were bigger and older but only two. I didn't even turn around and they kept getting closer. My friend sort of whispered that we better start running but there really wasn't any place to run to. So I started talking real loud in Italian. My friend doesn't understand a word of Italian but I just kept on, real loud and I threw in the word 'Mafia' a couple of times. Well, when they heard that word, it was magic. They scattered. Real quick. I never forgot it. I said to myself, 'Now that's power.' "

For most of New York's Italians, power does not come from associating with criminals, either real or fictive. They see strength in individual achievement, eked out in years of hard work and within a framework of family solidarity. To those who propose ethnic unity as a way to shorten the route, they respond unenthusiastically. It is not so much that the rules of loyalty to one's townsmen have endured but rather that the advantages of cooperation beyond narrow lines have never become apparent. Most attempts to unify into large power blocks founder. Joseph Colombo's Civil Rights League never got firmly based throughout many sectors of the Italian community. Mary Sansone's Congress of Italian American Organizations (CIAO) fell apart after achieving considerable strength and a large budget.

Sansone's attempt to unify New York's Italian organizations under the umbrella CIAO appeared for a time to be unusually successful. "Then it all fell apart," one outsider mused, "and it fell apart because of squabbles inside. Mary Sansone put it all together. Calls herself a social worker but she's one administrator. Real fireworks. I don't know how she got control of all those social service contracts but she was spending more than a million a year. In a few years it happened—all in the 1970s. Senior citizens' centers in Brooklyn and Manhattan. They were feeding hundreds every day. People came to play bingo or whatever. Then in 1978 it fell apart. You know why? One of her own people, one of her appointees, accused her of hiring some relatives, a violation of the nepotism laws. I think she had about twelve relatives on the payroll. So somebody else got all the money and she was finished. Now the interesting thing about all this is that she got crucified by her own people. Anybody spending that kind of money, that big a budget, is bound to look out for his own family. Everybody does it. But other people have a little more savvy. Instead of hiring his own son, he would call up somebody in a comparable position, say in a Jewish organization, and inquire about jobs available. It's just sort of understood that the other guy will hire your son and you'll give work to his daughter. That's how it's done. The Italians are too new to the business to know the rules. Sure you look out for your family but not directly. Not so openly, on your own payroll. Looks bad."

The lack of unity in the older Italian communities is exacerbated by the daily arrival of immigrants. Division between the old and the new of any group has marked every immigrant experience in New York. At the turn of the century, many tried to escape the "greenhorn" epithet by changing hairstyles, clothing, and accents as soon as possible. Being new in town was not an enviable status and there were always those present to remark on it when they saw the evidence. Among the worst culprits in the name-calling were members of one's own ethnic group who, having arrived only a few years earlier, had managed to stake out their own turf and now insisted on setting themselves apart, in the public's eyes, from their compatriots who had not yet shed old ways.

In no case is this split better illustrated than in that of the Italians. The

Northerners, who had arrived in larger numbers before 1880, had a special name for the Southerners, who came later. They found it in the victims' own lexicon. In Neapolitan dialect, *Guappo* (Woppo) means a young man who thinks a bit too highly of himself and dresses to show it. When such a person strutted the streets of New York in a fancy new suit he could hear "Woppo" from his Northern Italian neighbors or even from other Neapolitans. Everybody else heard it too and the word "Wop" became the epithet for all Italians, Neapolitan and others.

By the 1970s the word had changed, at least among young people, but not the antagonism between the recently arrived and those more firmly settled. "We were walking along," one young woman tells a group of her friends at a party, "and we saw these *Gheeps*. You could tell they just got off the boat by their shoes and their haircuts." She makes clear to her listeners that she was not favorably impressed and that she wanted to put as much distance, both physical and social, as possible between herself and the newly arrived Gheeps. The name is not entirely new—it was used in Brooklyn in the 1920s—but it was reactivated in the 1960s for use against the newest Italian immigrants.

Brooklyn, home to more Italian Americans than any of the other boroughs, shows most evidence of the split between new and old Italians. Since the passage of the 1965 immigration law, many new Italian immigrants have settled in one of the borough's Italian neighborhoods, especially Bay Ridge and Gravesend. "The farther south you go," one Brooklynite observes, "the more you find the new ones. Their center—that's along 18th Avenue where they have their big festival in September. Just go into one of those stores and ask them something in English. They'll answer you in Italian and they didn't learn it here from their grandmothers. It's the real thing. Right from Italy."

Newcomers find a mixed reception from neighbors who frequently express their resentment openly. Maria Manzone, a resident of Brooklyn for eight years, explains: "You'd think the Italians who've been here would try to help us. We're from the same country after all—sometimes the same town. But they keep saying that we have it too good. Too good because we didn't find the prejudice and hard times that their grandparents found. The funny part is that the grandparents are usually pretty nice to us. They talk real Italian. Not this mixed-up American-Italian that the children learned. The *signora* next door, for example, came here about sixty years ago. Had a hard life. Husband died when the children were small. She raised them herself. Always had to work. Now she's got a house and her son lives downstairs with his family. The son and his wife resent us—that we could come here and buy a house like theirs a few years after we got here. They say they had to wait so long.

"But it's not our fault. We just came at a different time. We work hard too. My husband was a tailor first and that's not easy work. Then when we had the money we opened our own drycleaners. I work there and the children help. We're in there six days a week, until late at night. We're not lazy—work for every dollar. But the people resent our success and they make fun of our ambitions. Think we are being superior when we send our children to college. I say, 'Why not, if we can?' Just because they had to wait years to see one of theirs in college doesn't mean we have to wait too. These are different times.

"They keep their eyes looking back, even on Italy. Have no idea how it's changed. Still believe that it's all old-fashioned with everybody wearing black. No washing machines—like the dark ages. They should go there and see. While they've been here, or their grandparents have been here, Italy has changed too. It's not so backward. We have cars and freezers in Italy too. But when I start defending Italy or explaining how it is, somebody immediately says, 'If you like it so much, why don't you go back?' It's not that I want to go back. We could not have done there what we did here—get this shop and buy a house and send our children to college. America has been good to us. But it hurts me when people talk so bad about Italy."

Mrs. Manzone's daughter Angela attends college. With friends, she often discusses her reactions to New York and to the Italian Americans she has met here. Only eleven years old when she left Mola (near Bari) in 1971, she lacks the enthusiasm that her parents show for staying permanently: "They want to live here for life. At least my mother. And my sisters are not going anywhere. Therefore it all depends on who I marry. If I marry someone who is American or of another nationality who lives here, I'll probably live here. If I marry an Italian from Italy who might want to go back, I'd go back. I don't feel strongly about it—not yet."

Angela's close friend, Giovanna Scrudato, favors Italy, perhaps because she has spent less time in Brooklyn. Her family immigrated from Formia (in Abruzzi) only five years ago: "I feel I would like to go there. Live there. I hope it will end up that I go there. After I finish college, maybe I will get a job that lets me go there—like with the airlines. To my city—it's so pretty. I don't like the resentment I find here among the Italian Americans. They tell us that we come here because over there we didn't have anything. That we just come here, make money and spend it over there. I don't think that's something to tell people when they come here to work. Because if they come here, they don't just come to find money in the street. They don't rob banks. They work for the money. If somebody works for the money, there is nothing wrong with going back to their country and doing whatever they want with it.

"Another thing the Italian Americans complain about is that we put our money away. They go out right away and buy a house, a fancy car. They go out to a restaurant every Friday and Saturday night while we eat at home and put our money away. They make fun of us. I don't like that."

The third of the young women, seated around Mrs. Manzone's dining-room table one winter afternoon, is Rosa Bianca. Most recently arrived of all, she came to America in 1976 from Catania. Prejudice, she feels, disappears quickly: "When I first came here I felt all this resentment against me personally. But with time, the accent starts to fade away and then prejudice starts to fade away too. I have to go with my parents all the time—translate for them. Some people don't like that. They say, 'If you're in the country, learn the language.' It takes a long time for somebody like my parents. People hold that against them.

"My father works for Merrill Lynch—he's a porter. There are lots of Italians there, also Spanish and Polish. He's picking up all different languages but not much English. My mother doesn't even work so it's even harder for her. She watches TV but she can't converse with a person in English. I think once you get rid of the accent so you can express yourself in English and they understand you, there is no real prejudice.

"As soon as we got here, we bought a house. With money we brought from Italy. It doesn't mean anything. People say, 'Oh you have it so good. You come here and you buy a house right away.' So what? They think everybody is so poor in Italy."

Angela Manzone agrees on this point: "People should go to Italy to see how everything has changed. Then maybe they can talk about it better. But hearing about it from their grandparents is not enough. Once I went to visit a family. The man was old. He said, 'Do you have a refrigerator in Italy?' I said, 'Bigger than you have here.'

"I have an uncle. He's going back after twenty-five years to see what it is like. He still believes there are no washing machines and he says, 'Well, you probably have a refrigerator but there's nothing in it.' That, I think, is the major difference. They really don't think there are appliances."

At the local college they attend, all are active members in the school's Italian club. They emphasize how it operates separately from the Italian American club. Officers of the two organizations rarely cooperate to sponsor joint ventures of mutual interest, and open warfare occasionally wrecks the tense truce between them. When this occurs, even formal, barely civil communications cease and members of both groups accuse the others of destroying posters and upsetting planned activities. The split is not the old geographical one between North and South or the result of class differences. It grows out of the tensions between Italians whose families have lived in the United States for a generation or two and those recently arrived. Both sides see the other as very different from themselves, separated by a gulf of American experiences that the Italian Americans accept as ameliorating and the Italians describe as destructive.

Angela Manzone's judgment is typical: "They have no culture—the Italian Americans. And the way they speak Italian makes me laugh. They use English words and make them sound Italian—like 'caka,' 'basketto,' 'carro,' 'pushare.' Those aren't Italian words. Whoever heard of them? But the Italian Americans think they know Italian better than we do.

"Their way of dressing is different. Everybody knows that. Fashion. In Italy people follow the style. If something is not the style, they won't wear it at all. But Italian Americans don't care too much about how they look. They feel free in how they dress. When I go shopping I try to find something that is imported from Italy. It's more expensive usually. I look at the material, too. I never buy polyester or dacron—they look cheap. But Italian Americans don't look at the material or the style. They are not so fussy as we Italians are.

"They get fat too. It's funny because people here think that in Italy everybody is fat. But it is not true. Sometimes when people get old or after they have a few children, they get a little fat, but young people—never! I never saw a fat child or young person until I came to New York. We eat spaghetti, yes, but only a little bit of it and not all the time—between meals and at night the way Americans do. It's a very different attitude. Nobody in Italy likes fat."

Ideas on dating differ too. Rosa Bianca explains what she has observed: "Teenagers with American parents have more freedom. I'm nineteen and my parents don't want me going out on dates. I go out but they don't know about it. They wouldn't approve. They say that if a girl has a boyfriend, she should be engaged. Not just go out on dates with boys she doesn't plan to marry. I'm the youngest—have two sisters—but I don't have it easy. My one sister—her boyfriend had to go to Canada because he couldn't find a job here. So he and my sister got engaged. She was only nineteen but they couldn't go out on dates alone unless they were engaged. Her boyfriend was from the same town in Italy as we were—his parents knew ours—but it didn't make any difference.

"I date mostly Italians who understand how this works—not Italian Americans. To tell the truth, I usually go out with my sisters and their husbands. We go to Italian places and meet Italians. But I have dated Italian Americans and they're really different. They think they're in a free country and they can do whatever they like. No respect at all.

"It's funny it should have ended this way because one of the big reasons my family came to New York was for me and my sisters. My father was an immigrant to Germany first. There were no jobs in Italy. For ten years he would work in Nuremburg for two months, then come home for two weeks or for a holiday, and then go back. When my parents had the chance to come here, they decided it was a good idea. My father never wanted us to go to Germany. Said it was too advanced. He's the old-fashioned-type man. With three daughters he was worried. I guess his friends were too because not that many took their families to Germany. My father's brother lived in New York. They wrote to each other. My uncle said, 'You are better off in America.' My father thought he would have control over his children here. A little more. That's what he thought."

Among their expectations—for more freedom or more control, for better education or job opportunities—new Italian immigrants rarely foresaw the possibility of conflict with Italian Americans. Yet it is a division that marks relationships at all ages.

Angela Manzone tells of observing the split among elementary school children: "I heard a lot of times the word 'guinea.' And my sister when she was in junior high school used to get called 'guinea.' By the Italian Americans. Just because we were new and didn't know English that well. We Italians tried to stick together so we wouldn't get called names and we got friendly with the Greeks, the Spanish, and the others who have just arrived. We get along better with them than with the Italian Americans. It's funny. They're the ones who give us most trouble."

The Manzone family and their guests illustrate typical immigrant experiences. Settled in Brooklyn, their eyes still turn frequently eastward, and they express dual loyalties. Enthusiastic about economic opportunities in America, they remember too well the relaxation of the long siesta in Italy. Families frequently disagree among themselves and, because of fast trans-Atlantic communication and travel, they need not make one permanent decision for an entire family. Their lives center on the old Italian American communities. They move into the parishes and the labor unions of their compatriots who have been more firmly rooted in American soil. Antagonisms inevitably arise.

For another group of Italian immigrants, little friction occurs with the Italian Americans. There is almost no contact. These are the artists and musicians, the writers and sculptors, whose motivations for coming to America are completely different. They settle in New York because it is the center of their world of working artists. Their friends are no more likely to be Italians than Russians or Japanese. They are almost always other artists.

Vito Calabrese is a musician. Sitting in his lower Manhattan apartment, he talks about how he happened to leave Italy for New York.

"I came here November 14, 1965. I was twenty-five. In Italy my life was not bad. In fact, I would say it was wonderful. I had played in different orchestras and had had a very successful career. After I graduated from the

For some Italian immigrants, the place they live is completely irrelevant except with respect to their profession or skill. For artists and musicians who come to New York because it is the center of their professional life, Little Italy holds little attraction or interest. (*Lewis Waldeck*)

conservatory in Venice in 1960 I did an audition with a Milan chamber orchestra and got the job. I lived in Milan for two years. Very rewarding artistically but I felt kind of a fish out of water, so to speak. I think anybody who grows up in Venice and then leaves finds it very difficult to adapt to an industrialized city like Milan. Too much of a jump. All of a sudden my life was very different. The streets became a problem because I never had to look for a traffic light in Venice—there were no cars. And the noise! That was the main problem. Venice has only boats and it's very quiet. In Milan I had tremendous difficulty to sleep at night because there was a tram passing by every half hour. Made a terrible noise. Even though I was living on the fourth floor, I could tell it was coming and I would wake up. I tried to change apartments but the landlady told me it was the quietest place around and that I would get used to it. Eventually I did and when I went back to Venice I couldn't sleep. It was too quiet! I had to turn on the radio at night to make some noise. And that is how I got used to noise and couldn't get along without it.

"In Milan my work was very rewarding. I played as solo with great conductors like Claudio Abbado. He is now musical director of La Scala. We went on tour in Germany where I played as soloist and got very good reviews. I did some recordings in Milan—it's a very cultural city. More important culturally than Rome. But I wasn't happy with my personal life. Milan is not really a beautiful city. In the winter it is very gloomy and the air isn't good. You can't see the color of the sky. So after two years my tendency was to go back to Venice. I was kind of homesick. It was a lonely life. I didn't have too many friends. For the first time in my life I had to establish all new friendships.

"When I heard there was a job back in Venice, I took it but after a while I left there too. The problem was that I had to do my military service. Somebody told me that if I went to Palermo to play in the symphony, the management there would arrange for me to do the military service and play in the orchestra at the same time. I did the audition for Palermo and got the job. It was a wonderful time. The city was nice and the people very pleasant. Unfortunately when I got my call for the army I found the orchestra management hadn't managed somehow for me to stay there and I had to do the army service in the other extreme part of Italy—La Spezia near Genoa. After a month or so in La Spezia, I was sent to Rome to play with the military band—spent more than a year there and that's when I met a lot of Americans. Musicians there studying on Fulbrights. Conductors. People like that.

"Well, those weren't really the first Americans I had met. As a kid living in Bari during the war [World War II], I saw some Americans. They occupied the city. Bari was bombed or a ship exploded or something and many people were killed. I remember seeing trucks of bodies of soldiers being hauled away. A lot of them were killed. I remember they were mostly blacks. Since then I learned that the United States still had segregated armed forces during World War II and that many of the blacks went to fight around Bari. But at the time I thought that most Americans must be black.

It didn't bother me—it was just something that I noticed. I remember that just in front of my grandmother's house there was a hotel and there used to be Americans there a lot of the time playing billiards and things like that. I used to hang around and they would give me chocolate. I had a good impression of Americans. They brought the good things. I remember corned beef for example. In cans. That was really something—we thought it was so good. A lot of dates, too. I don't remember exactly how I got those things from the soldiers. I think there was some kind of provision for the soldiers to pass supplies on to the population. We could go and stand in line and get supplies. My mother would go or my grandmother—somebody in the family. We were all living together—my uncles, aunts, cousins, grand-mother. A lot of us.

"My aunt had some relatives in America. Right after the war they used to send us clothes. Suits, shoes—things like that. They must have been used. I really don't remember. I was very young. But I remember that things were very hard. A very meager life. We liked to get those packages from America. That was my first impression of Americans—food from the sol-diers and clothes from my aunt's relatives. The impression was of a country that had a lot of money.

"I really never had any desire to come to America. When I started study-ing oboe, I remember my father telling me which instrument I had to study. That was right at the time we moved to Venice—after my father came back from the war. He had been a prisoner in Russia for many years and after the war he decided to move us all to Venice. He's a musician, too. All his family have been musicians as long as anybody remembers so it was easy for him to move. Anyway he told me to study the oboe because there was a very good teacher at the conservatory in Venice. For some reason I had wanted to learn the clarinet. Maybe because my father played in the band and the clarinets were the most noticeable instruments in the band. They played a lot of solos and were very important. But my father said it was better to study oboe because this teacher in Venice had fantastic students. They played all over the world.

"As a child the idea of travel caught my fantasy. I thought to myself that if I became a good oboe player I would be able to travel, but I didn't have any particular desire to come to America. My desire was to live in Italy and travel.

"In Italy people just out of the conservatory often spend a few years in a foreign country. Then they come back to Italy. A group at La Fenice in Venice had all worked abroad. My teacher had a student in Santiago del Chile and another in Mexico City. Those possibilities were in my mind— to maybe find a job somewhere outside the country for awhile. But actually when you study you don't think too much about where you are going to live. My preoccupation was to become a good oboe player.

"There was always that desire to travel. That dream. I remember my father said there were several of my teacher's students in England. I got very excited. It wasn't true at all, I found out later, but at the time I thought it was. Somehow England or the English-speaking countries struck me more, more than France, for example. England sounded like something very far.

"I came to New York as an adventure. And just for awhile. I had met an American girl in Venice and we planned to get married. She wanted me to know a little bit more about her country. Then it was a particular time in my life. I had just finished the army and I didn't have a job. I had many possibilities but nothing struck me. I didn't want to go back to Palermo although that job was still mine. I was offered a job in Milan with a chamber orchestra—not the one I had played with but another. That didn't sound too exciting. I had already tried Milan. In Rome there was the possibility of continuing to do freelance work at the television station. I had been doing a little of that while I did my military service. That paid very well and I liked living in Rome but it wasn't very rewarding artistically, doing commercials and music for television programs.

"America seemed like a great adventure and I was in a spirit of adventure. My idea was just to go and visit or perhaps stay for a few years. Not more than five. I was very clear in my own mind that this was just an adventure. I would learn English, hear some American orchestras, and work here for just a few years. Then I would go back to Italy.

"I remember the night I arrived in New York. All those lights. I really couldn't believe it. Magic. A little like that film by Fellini—*Amarcord*—when the people are in the slow boats and an enormous ship, all illuminated, appears. Arriving in New York was a little like that for me. I was up there flying—it's all dark below—and then you look down and suddenly it's all illuminated. This enormous area. Blinking lights. Incredible.

"I was unbelievably impressed by the enormous buildings and all the huge cars in New York. The traffic. Not at all like Milan. You could compare it a little to New York but New York is on a much bigger scale. In Italy I had heard about Times Square and Radio City. Those places were in my ears and I really wanted to see them. But when I saw them, the places were very different from the descriptions I had heard. Much bigger, much more exaggerated. Overwhelming.

"When I came here, I couldn't work for a few months because of the union. In Italy we have unions and you can belong but you don't have to belong in order to work. In New York the union controls everything—it's practically the law. You have to wait six months in order to join. Local 802. With a tourist visa (which is what I had) you can't join.

"To make a long story short, after two months here, I got married—not to belong to the union but that made it easier to apply for residence and then with the residence I could join the union. Then I could work. But even before the six months were up I got a call from a contractor asking me if I was free to go on tour. I said, 'Certainly I'm free.' I mean I hadn't been working at all for several months. The only problem was that I didn't belong to the union yet because I had not been here long enough. The contractor said that he would take care of that if I was willing to go on the tour. It was a last minute replacement and he was desperate. Couldn't find anybody.

"So I went all over the United States with that tour. It was the Robert Shaw Chorale doing *The Messiah,* and I learned some new English words. When I came back I was saying 'rejected' and 'despised' and words like that. All straight out of *The Messiah.*

"I didn't know much English at the time—not enough to communicate—and there was an Italian American in the orchestra who offered to help me out. He was really the first Italian American I remember meeting in New York. My wife was American and neither of us had relatives here. Our friends were Americans we had met in Italy. They all spoke Italian and my wife spoke Italian because she lived in Italy for several years. So I had gotten along pretty well those first few months with just Italian.

"Then I got the tour. That really taught me a few things. This Italian American had grandparents who had come over about fifty years ago from Naples and Sicily. One from Naples and one from Sicily. You could tell it immediately when he opened his mouth. He spoke the strangest mixture of the two dialects along with some Americanized Italian that wouldn't have been recognized in either place. I even had trouble understanding his meaning sometimes but I tried to be polite and not make fun of him or anything. He enjoyed showing off to the other orchestra members that he knew Italian and was helping me out.

"Then one day he started making fun of my Italian! He said, 'But tell me, Vito, are you really Italian?' I said, 'Of course I'm Italian. What did you think?' 'Because,' he said in this really funny mixture of languages that nobody in Italy would have accepted as Italian, 'you speak a strange Italian.' Well that was just about it. I really let him have it. I told him in front of a few people that what he was speaking was not even close to Italian and that he had no idea of what a laughable mixture he was talking. He didn't speak to me after that.

"That was a very hard tour. We were playing every night in a different place, and I was terribly disappointed with what I saw. In Europe when I went on tours it was to Germany, Austria, Russia, and they were all very interesting. Different people. Different languages and all that. But traveling across the United States was not like that. I found it very boring. Everything was very flat. No dramatic change of nature. When I came back to New York, I knew it was the only place. I was in other big cities—Chicago and

Cleveland. But I felt more at home in New York. It represents a small Europe. Different nationalities and different restaurants. I felt more comfortable here. You could say that I did not choose America. I chose New York.

"One reason I liked New York was all the activity. I couldn't get enough music that first year. The Cleveland Orchestra, the Philadelphia—I heard them all. Seemed to me I was going to Carnegie Hall every night. That was the year of the transit strike in New York. Nothing ran in January of 1966 and it was really cold. Down around zero I think but that didn't keep me home. I walked every night about fifty blocks to Carnegie Hall. No city in Italy could offer anything like what I heard that year.

"As soon as I got back from the tour I joined the union and began doing auditions for jobs. I knew then that as long as I stayed in America I wanted to be in New York. I felt there were lots of opportunities—maybe because so many of the people who were doing the hiring were immigrants themselves.

"I remember somebody said to go play for Leopold Stokowski. He was conductor of the American Symphony and always looking for new, young players. I telephoned and made an appointment. His apartment was up on Fifth Avenue—overlooking Central Park. I played for him and he seemed pleased. Then he started talking about my plans and he wanted to know whether I liked America. I said that I did. He was just making conversation—always very nice to young musicians just getting started. I don't know if he made a special point to be nice to foreigners but he was very pleasant to me.

"Then Stokowski said that he liked this country too but that he thought it had gone downhill since the first president was in office, and he turned to me and said, 'What was his name? I always forget.' Well I didn't know a thing about American history so I couldn't think of a single name, but Stokowski kept trying to remember it. He said, 'You know—it's the name of a city.' So I said, 'Philadelphia.' And he said, 'No, that's not it.' I said, 'Chicago'. And again he shook his head. Finally, between the two of us, we came up with Washington. Afterwards my friends had a good laugh when I told them the story—two immigrants trying to remember a little bit of American history.

"There are so many immigrants in the music world that I don't think anyone would say there has been much discrimination against them. Once maybe I heard somebody who was a New Yorker—a Juilliard grad—and couldn't get a job. He was complaining about all the foreigners coming in and taking the good places, but generally, I think, there is pretty much agreement that people who are good get the work. And they are getting the work. The other day I was going to a job on Long Island and all the musicians in the car, five of us, were all immigrants. There was a Bulgarian, a Russian, a Canadian, a Japanese, and me. That's not unusual—happens all the time.

"Each year I go back to Italy for a month or two in the summer. Rent a farmhouse in Tuscany or an apartment in Venice and just sort of soak up the atmosphere. If, for some reason, I can't go back, I really miss it. My family is still there and I want to see them, of course, but even if they weren't there, I would still want to go back to visit. Maybe that's because I can never decide that it's time to go back and stay. Sometimes I think about getting a job there, with one of the orchestras or even teaching in one of the conservatories, but I just can't make up my mind to leave New York. For a musician, there's too much here to walk away from. All the big orchestras come through and even though I don't get to hear them as much as I did that first year in New York when I wasn't working, still it's nice to hear a few.

"My friends are not Italian Americans. You know there really is a difference between Italians and Italian Americans. It's like two different worlds. My wife is a good example of what I mean. Her background is English—family came to America two hundred years ago so you can't get much more American than that. In Italy everybody thinks she's Italian. She speaks the language very well. She dresses and acts Italian. But in New York she can never pass for Italian American. One of the people I know who is Italian American said to me, 'As soon as I saw your wife, I knew she wasn't Italian. I didn't know what she was but I knew she was not Italian.' That made me think a little bit about the split that has developed. Italian and Italian American. They are really very different.

"We eat Italian food—pasta or something like that when friends come over and we always drink espresso. I don't think we own an American coffee pot. I can't stand the stuff. I don't know how people drink that. I remember on the plane my first trip, I was sitting next to an old Italian who was coming here to visit his daughter. He warned me about the coffee—had been here once before. Said it tasted like dirty water where somebody had washed socks. I sometimes think about that. It's a pretty good description.

"What would I have if I had stayed in Italy? More respect, certainly. Musicians have a lot more status there. Not here. We're about the lowest. In Italy you get called 'professor' and you get reduced rates on trains and things. More security, too. Musicians in Italy are paid by the state and paid very well. Health insurance—all that is taken care of. Less work there, too. Most of the big orchestras have two or three first chairs so that any one of them plays only about a third of the time. Even when they're playing, it's not so much work. In Italy rehearsals scheduled for 10 o'clock never start before 10:15 or so and they always end early. Here in New York you'd better be in your chair a couple of minutes before the time set to begin. I remember learning that right away. Stokowski had a reputation for expecting musicians to be in their places at least twenty minutes before time to start and he'd be up there in front checking off the names of people who didn't get there. But nobody told me this. Of course, technically it's against union regulations to require people to be there early so a contractor couldn't really spell it out. Maybe somebody hinted at the time but because my English wasn't so good, I didn't understand. So the first day I played with Stokowski I walked in about five minutes before rehearsal starting time. For me that was early! I never expected him to start right on the dot. I thought I was showing my good intentions. But he didn't like it very much and I heard about it. And of course his rehearsals and just about all the others I've been in during the last fifteen years go right up to the last minute. If a conductor tried to do that in Italy, the musicians would refuse to play. Start making so many mistakes that he would have to stop the rehearsal early. Here they really mean business. Lots of tension, too, during the rehearsals. Very competitive.

"Why do I stay? Well, maybe I won't. I never became an American citizen. There's no reason why I should. My wife is a citizen so I have all the rights. Except the vote, of course. The only inconvenience is when I leave the country. I have to go down to the Internal Revenue office and show them my check stubs and my last year's tax return so they know I pay my income taxes. They give me a little piece of paper and I have to be able to show that at the airport. Nobody ever asked to see it but I always get it just in case they decide to ask. I know they can keep me from leaving if I don't have it.

"It's nice to be able to go back and forth between countries. In a sense you have the best of both. I can relax and enjoy Italy in the summer and then come back and take advantage of everything going on in New York in the winter. People in Italy say my accent has changed and that I sound more American. People in New York know I'm Italian. I guess I belong nowhere. But me—I think I belong in both. I feel comfortable in both. And that's the way I'm trying to live my life—a little bit in New York, a little bit in Italy."

Vito Calabrese insists that he shares little with Italian Americans of the second or third generation. On the surface he may be right. His social activities rarely intersect with theirs. He counts none of them his friends. But nonetheless, when it comes to their core identities there is shared agreement that transcends social status or degree of Americanization on what it means to be Italian. At a September 1980 meeting at New York University, mental health professionals, speculating on what makes Italian Americans different and how long the distinction will persist, agreed that family was of unusually great importance, shaping decisions about where to live, how much education to get, and how to spend one's leisure time.

A university professor, grappling with the idea himself, asked students at a large metropolitan university to define what being Italian American meant to them. Their varied responses included one common denominator: a rich family life. Some of the students continued their discussion by including references to a complex culture that has gestures so perfected that entire stories can be told without words and a cuisine so distinctive that all the world knows some of its dishes.

Vito Calabrese includes references to family and a rich culture, but he continues: "Being Italian—it means being expansive and warm. That is how we came through generations of foreign rule and harsh government. We learned how to laugh and enjoy every day, one at a time. Not plan too far ahead. You Americans call that fatalism and you don't approve of it. You're all for hard work and careful planning. Very serious. Sober. Maybe we will never rule the world but most of us never wanted to. If we haven't done so well in America by your standards, don't measure up on all those charts and tables you draw up to show how many become doctors and lawyers and presidents, maybe you should ask us what we were trying to do. You might find we did pretty well on that."

9

Separate but Friends:

Chinatown's New Chinese

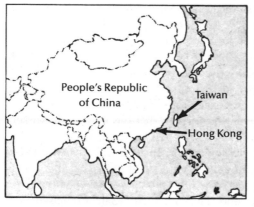

In 1902, when Prince T'sai Chen visited New York's Chinatown, he advised his countrymen to "move out of here and mix more with the people. Learn their language and their customs." The crowds along Mott Street listened silently and cheered politely when he left. But they did not move. Nearly eight decades later, Chinatown's center remains relatively unchanged, still impervious to the comings and goings of its immigrant neighbors. Reasons for this amazing stability lie both within the community and without, for voluntary segregation describes Chinatown's most fundamental aim while prejudice holds firm its borders from the other side. New York's Chinatown has stood for one hundred years, its most enduring ghetto.

When "time turned over" in 1900 the Empire City had many reasons for optimism. The rhetoric of reform and the power of newly acquired bigness—a result of the consolidation of the boroughs—added to the feeling that this new, twentieth century would be a better one. Anything seemed possible if only a few problems could be solved. One of the trouble spots, it was agreed, lay in lower Manhattan, south of Bayard Street, down to Worth, in the triangle formed by the crossing of the Bowery and Mott Street—Chinatown. Only a few thousand in a city of nearly 3.5 million, the Chinese could have escaped notice had they not been so distinctive.

233

Historians disagree on the exact date of arrival of the first Chinese on the Atlantic seaboard. A few Cantonese seamen, it appears, landed in Baltimore in the 1780s but Chinese immigration did not become significant in the East until after the California Gold Rush of the 1840s, when the first of those Chinese who were dissatisfied in California decided to venture farther east. The overland path became even more heavily traveled after several western states passed strong legislation restricting economic and social opportunities for all people from the Orient. In the 1860s California lawmakers excluded Chinese children from the state's public schools and required wage earners to pay special taxes in order to engage in either fishing or mining. Soon thereafter, Chinese men could not testify in court, either for or against Caucasians.

Such discriminatory state laws were part of an increasingly vicious national campaign to restrict or even cut off altogether Chinese immigration to America. Ironically this campaign coincided with official attempts by the United States and China to ease the free flow of people between the two nations, a move thought to be advantageous to the labor-short western states. The Burlingame Treaty of 1868 proved of temporary consequence, however, because the demand for Chinese labor in the United States fell off in the 1870s. After the completion of the transcontinental railroad in 1869, for which the Chinese reportedly had supplied 90 percent of the working force, opposition to "coolie" labor grew quickly. Led by Denis Kearney, an outspoken Irish-born rabble-rouser who insisted that the jobs of all workers were threatened by cheap competition from the Orient, many in the West became openly anti-Chinese. Vocal objections in time turned to violence. In Los Angeles's Chinese community, mobs killed nineteen men, and massacres occurred in other states. These physical attacks, plus laws that appeared to encourage second-class treatment (San Francisco, for example, passed legislation in 1870 prohibiting the use of sidewalks to persons carrying loads on a pole) sent Chinese men fleeing across the continent.

Some came as far as New York. Wah Ling, arriving in New York in 1880, explained to a newspaper reporter: "San Francisco no good place for Chinaman anymore." Then, in the parody of Chinese speech employed by the *The New York Times* in those years, Wah Ling is reported to have said, "White man flaid [afraid] to bling his shirt to iron anymore. Chinaman get pounded with stones by boys on stleet. He hear he can make money in New Lork and boys no pound him with stones. Tickets velly low now so he buy one piece of paper and come to New Lork." Wah Ling was correct about the cost of tickets. He and thirty of his countrymen paid less than forty dollars for the trip east. The part about stones remained to be seen.

By the time Wah Ling arrived, New York reported about 1,000 Chinese, many of whom lived in lower Manhattan. Most of the others had settled across one river or another, in Brooklyn or Jersey City. Anywhere else they simply would not have been able to rent quarters since many landlords preferred to let their buildings sit idle rather than rent to men who wore "pigtails," favored loose-fitting tunics, and ate a diet that reportedly included rats.*

Another source of prejudice against the Chinese was the composition of their immigration. Because many Americans were especially critical of immigrant communities that lacked what they described as the "civilizing influence" of women, the Chinese were particularly scrutinized when it was learned that their communities were sometimes 95 percent male. Asians held no monopoly on this prejudice—Italians, Greeks, and other European immigrants who had come over in heavily male migrations suffered similar attacks. But in Chinatowns, the discrepancy in the male-female ratio was the highest of any incoming group. This unusual settlement pattern, coexisting with the community's open acceptance of gambling, prostitution, and opium use, made the Chinese a special target for white Protestant neighbors intent on reform. The solution appeared clear, but drastic: keep the Chinese out.

In 1882 the Chinese Exclusion Act suspended the "coming of Chinese laborers to the United States" for ten years and set a fine of five hundred dollars and one year imprisonment per violation if ship captains disobeyed. The act, repeatedly renewed, literally stopped legal immigration of the Chinese until 1943 but numerous ploys were developed to circumvent the law. Since persons with professional or trade skills were still allowed to enter the country, a common ruse involved posing as a merchant rather than a laborer. Entry to the United States required a visa from China, but these were often given perfunctorily. Men with weathered faces from years of work in the fields got visas after insisting they were shopkeepers. One such man, apprehended in the southwestern United States and asked how he had come to have such thick callouses on his hands if he was a merchant, disarmed his questioner by replying, "From handling so much money."

Other schemes relied on false documents. Legitimate visitors to the United States were required to carry permits but fraudulent passes became common. In 1901 one Canadian printing press turned out hundreds (at fifteen dollars each) for laborers who planned their way to the United States

* The myth that the Chinese diet included rats was widely circulated and stirred up considerable anti-Chinese sentiment in the late nineteenth century. The press helped perpetuate it as did law enforcement officers. A New York police detective, on being asked whether or not the Chinese ate rats, replied, "Well, that's pretty hard to say but I don't think they eat them in this country. You will see a good many rats' skins nailed to the walls in the houses we go into but they say that they are put there for luck, just as we nail up a horseshoe." A reporter for *The New York Times*, describing a trip through Chinatown, said that he entered a dilapidated house and observed "a man, cooking something, perhaps a rat, in an iron pan," while other men lounged on cots smoking opium pipes.

through Canada in order to pick up these papers. Men who failed to obtain such permits arrived hidden in cargo. One shipment of sugar from Havana, Cuba, included eleven Chinese men stowed away among the bags of raw sugar.

But the "slot system" provided the most ingenious of the Chinese with a means of entry, its workings predicated on the practice by Chinese men of returning frequently to Canton. In 1881 *The New York Times* reported that almost two-thirds of the Chinese men living in the United States had already made three trips home, typically either in the late fall or early winter when jobs fell off. Family ties pulled especially hard just before the Chinese New Year, and one-way journeys from the West Coast cost only about fifty dollars.

After their immigration was restricted in 1882, those Chinese already living in the United States applied to bring in sons born on these trips home. Men who had not fathered a male child soon learned they could sell their "son slot" to a man of the right age, who posed as a son in order to come to America. Professor Betty Lee Sung of the City College of New York calculated that if sons were actually born in the numbers claimed to men visiting their wives in China, then the sexual ratio of births ran about four hundred males to one female. The 1906 earthquake in San Francisco breathed new life into the ruse. With the city's records destroyed, men who had been living in the city claimed American birth, thus qualifying them for citizenship, and then applied to bring in their sons.

Restrictions against their immigration and prejudicial treatment for those already here convinced the Chinese that their best protection against future attacks was isolation. They provided for their own needs by setting up organizations. By 1890 New York's Consolidated Chinese Benevolent Association (CCBA) met at 16 Mott Street, not far from its current address ninety years later. Although residents of the congested area refused to engage in American politics, they provided for their own kind of service center to settle disputes. The CCBA had roots in old Chinese customs, but it grew to meet the new needs of a poor population far from home. Men who died in America wanted their bodies sent back. Operators of gambling houses and brothels needed protection for clients and for themselves, and the Benevolent Association helped them all. Its head, known as the "unofficial mayor of Chinatown," had considerable power and earned in the 1890s a handsome salary of $9,000, almost twice what the City Council president earned. Family and district organizations, uniting men of the same surname or from the same region, functioned under the CCBA, finding jobs, lending money at lower interest rates than the banks, settling disputes, and serving the community in many different ways, thus reducing the need for contact with outside institutions.

Two secret organizations (called *tongs,* meaning, meeting halls or associations), the On Leong and the Hip Sing, already functioned in New York's Chinatown in the 1890s. Splitting the territory between them, one ruled the east side; the other, the west. Both protected illegal operations from police and from greedy competitors, while a shaky peace separated them from each other. In 1912 the On Leong and the Hip Sing clashed in a bloody fight for control, filling the pages of the city's newspapers with accounts of shootings and knifings. Calm emerged finally with a redefinition of territories, but periodic violent outbreaks continued to mark their relations. In 1933, after a particularly bloody battle, the two *tongs* signed an official truce in the office of the Consul General, who lavished credit for the agreement on the National Recovery Administration, a federal agency whose motives lay in the need to restore business activity in Chinatown. Men positioned behind the scenes ventured another, more credible explanation: the United States Treasury Department had threatened to close in on known gambling houses if representatives of the two *tongs* failed to work out their differences and end the war.

All the organizations of Chinatown, the *tongs* included, operated in a population that changed slowly before 1960. With the lid on legal arrivals, New York's Chinatown stayed fairly stable during the early part of the twentieth century while immigrants from other countries flooded Ellis Island. The Great Depression of the 1930s discouraged all newcomers. Then in 1943, in the midst of World War II, a war that allied the United States with China against Japan, pressures emerged to remove the restrictions on Chinese immigration. Strictly a public relations gesture, the idea of dropping the bar to Chinese immigrants never represented a change of heart; rather it was seen as a necessary step in undercutting Japanese propaganda accusing the United States of prejudice against Asians. The Chinese Women's Association argued: "It would matter little if the maximum [on Chinese immigrants] were 100 or 50 or even 10 so long as the privilege existed." One man, identifying himself as Chinese, admitted in a letter to a New York newspaper that he doubted his people could ever become "real Americans so far as the color of their skin is concerned" but he urged that they be allotted a quota as were other groups as a kind of penance for "indignities suffered by Chinese but not by any of the other Allies." In late 1943 Congress provided for a small quota (105) to enter each year.

Nonquota immigrants, including students, scholars, brides, and the children of Chinese Americans, continued to enter the United States in growing numbers. Some families encouraged their sons to go to America to study even though they realized that if the nation went communist, which it seemed likely to do, they would probably never return. In 1949 when Chiang Kai-shek's Kuomintang (KMT) army fled to Taiwan, that fear became reality. Chinese students in American universities found themselves abruptly cut off from families and funds. To pay their bills, they swept the floors of libraries and waited on tables, watching as one year turned into the next and the possibility of returning home became more and more remote. One mathematician, who later became a professor in a large university in the East recalled those lonely years: "People helped me, yes. I got so many degrees because people were always helping. But what could I do in Tennessee or Utah? Months went by when I did not see another Chinese. Now I live near a city with a Chinatown so I can buy the things I need. And see people."

Yet for most non-Asian Americans, Chinatowns, as late as the 1950s, furnished only colorful, exotic tourist stops. One midwestern college student, recalling a first trip to New York in 1958, remembered the guide's warning as he led a busload of out-of-towners down Mott Street: "Stay together," he said, "and watch me. If anything happens, watch which direction I run." The group had already visited areas with higher crime rates—42nd Street and Harlem—but the guide's most memorable warning came in Chinatown.

The 1960 census saw a significant increase in the number of Chinese Americans. For decades North America's Chinese population had remained relatively stable—less than 100,000. Then, partly as a result of the inclusion for the first time of Hawaii in the census count, the number climbed to more than 200,000. In the 1960s immigration from both Taiwan and Hong Kong also rose, due first to a 1962 presidential order to admit 15,000 Hong Kong refugees on a parole basis and then later to the 1965 law, which dropped the old quotas on Asians. By 1970, census takers counted 431,583 Chinese in the United States, and the following decade saw further increases as more than 20,000 entered the United States each year from Hong Kong and Taiwan.

New York's Chinatown felt the impact especially hard, as more and more of the newcomers chose to come east. Manhattan's Chinatown grew faster than any other on the continent and satellite communities sprang up in Brooklyn and Queens. Although Chinatown housed only about one-third of the city's total Chinese population, others came to Canal Street on Sundays and holidays to find the richest canned soy, the freshest *bak choy*, and the tastiest *dim sum*. They could choose from among a dozen Chinese newspapers, converse with every shopkeeper they met in their familiar Cantonese dialect, and forget, for an hour or two, that they were thousands of miles from their birthplace. Their use of Chinatown as a market and social center added to the congestion of the densely populated area.

The post-1962 immigration changed the face of Chinatown, bringing women and children into what had been a man's world. The families in-

A crowded residential area, New York's Chinatown draws thousands to the area for shopping and sightseeing, making it one of the city's more congested areas. (*Courtesy Center for Migration Studies, T.J. Marino*)

serted new vitality and optimism into an aging population but they also brought demands for new services. Chinatown's leaders faced problems at both ends of the age spectrum: the young required education and supervision and the elderly men, many without families (because their wives had been denied entry to America during the years they might have migrated) lacked a supportive network of relatives to help them in their old age.

Boys from Hong Kong were often doubly alienated. In the cosmopolitan city of the Orient where many of them had been born and all had grown up, they had largely and often willingly moved away from traditional Chinese cultural values. Even for those less eager to forget old ties, the very process of adjusting to life in the British colony, a colony with a rapidly changing population and a modern lifestyle, required that they do so. Yet in exchange, they expected to be supplied with the conveniences of modern living as well as other comforts of modern life. They found neither. Their nickname for Hong Kong reflected their disappointment: they called it "New Slum."

New York offered little better for many of the Hong Kong youth. American-born Chinese, wary of hurting their own opportunities in any way, did not always welcome the newcomers. In retaliation, the newest immigrants applied the disparaging name *jook sing* to them, meaning a bamboo stalk open at both ends—empty and lacking in content. The foreign born became *jook kok,* bamboo stalks closed at one end, roots significantly intact. The division between the old-timers and new arrivals was not unique to Asians. It marked most immigrant groups. Only the epithets were peculiarly Chinese and they rankled as much as "Greaser" or "Greenhorn" ever did.

As battle lines developed between opposing gangs, combat methods became more deadly. Guns appeared, though many who carried them lacked expertise in their use. Chinatown visitors were warned to look out for gang fights but not to panic. "They won't shoot whites," one guide observed, "because they know you'll come forward to testify. Chinese won't. They keep quiet. So if you're in Chinatown and a gun fight starts, just hit the floor and wait till it's over." But poor marksmanship complicated the matter as in an October 1976 gunfight that occurred on the Bowery, killing non-Chinese diners from Queens. Observers were unanimous in the opinion that had the gang members been better shots the only casualties would have been opposing gang members who happened to be eating in the same restaurant.

Gangs are not new to American cities but the feeling persisted among many people that Chinese gangs were atypical in that they did not emerge spontaneously as an outlet for bored, disgruntled youths. Some reporters traced the new Hong Kong youth gangs to the *tongs* that had functioned in Chinatown for decades. Others tied the delinquents to international crime organizations and even to foreign governments. Referring to the gangs as "the other Mafia," one newspaper ascribed their development to a number of causes. Home life often proved worse in America than it had been in Hong Kong: housing more dilapidated, schools more permissive, and parental supervision often altogether lacking as both parents went out to work. Economic need did not always push boys into gangs. In fact, some evidence pointed in the opposite direction—that delinquents came more often from the better-off homes in Queens than from the poorest blocks on Mott Street and that they were drawn more by psychological than monetary needs. Perhaps it was a combination of the two that prompted one gang member, who, when asked why he got involved in crime, replied: "To keep from being a waiter all my life."

Chinatown leaders, had they wanted to control gang activities as they had other elements of life in the community without intervention from city officials, might still have been unable to impose their authority. Most of the post-1962 arrivals had never known the rural, village life of China. They showed little respect for the old power center consisting of those emigrants who had left the mainland and taken control of Chinatown from its earliest settlement days. Hong Kong had provided these newer arrivals with a more international perspective, complex in organization and tough in methods of survival. In some ways they had moved farther from traditional Chinese life than had third- or fourth-generation Chinese Americans, raised in sheltered sections of foreign cities. The new immigrants did not nurture the strong attachment to family organization that earlier arrivals had been forced to perpetuate in order to gain such benefits as loans and protection. Older Chinatown leaders tried unsuccessfully to channel the youthful enthusiasm of the newcomers into martial arts and dragon shows, failing to realize that enthusiasm would soon wane. Chinatown's diverse segments illustrated a generation gap of the most extreme kind, exacerbated by thousands of miles and very different cultures.

One part of Chinatown gang life appeared clear: Hong Kong boys joined in very young. Quickly initiated into the intricacies of American law, which reserved especially lenient treatment for juveniles, gang leaders learned to assign the dirtiest jobs to the youngest. "Why should we get rapped," one gang member told an investigator, "when someone younger can do it for free?" The arrangement accomplished two objectives: it assured light punishment in case of apprehension and it furnished a rite by which to initiate new members into the club. By committing a felony, especially one involving weapons, a novitiate demonstrated his courage.

Membership lists became public information. In November 1977, the New York *Daily News* published individual photographs of several gang leaders, including some who had been killed. Each of the two dozen youths shown in the double-page spread were affiliated with one of the prominent gangs: the White Eagles or the Ghost Shadows. Some even consented to interviews.

Once considered the safest part of the city, Chinatown got a new image in the late 1970s. Newspaper headlines ("Terror and Gang War Rip Chinatown" and "The Destruction of Chinatown: How Gangs are Ruining a Once-Proud Neighborhood") frightened prospective visitors and customers. Chinatown businesses began to suffer. In spite of assurances that the fighting remained incestuous, outsiders came cautiously and less frequently, aware that a stray bullet from a poorly handled firearm killed as surely as one aimed accurately.

When business dropped off rapidly (some said by 35 to 45 percent between 1976 and 1977) restaurant owners began urging a cleanup. In the flood of articles that followed on the origins and organization of these Chinatown gangs, several journalists suggested in writing what many people living in the area had long felt: there existed a close relationship between the *tongs* and the gangs and that as a consequence the young delinquents of Chinatown were not simply an immigrant version of the American "boy in trouble."

In the late 1960s the White Eagles, who were at that time apparently the strongest of several gangs in operation, reportedly served the old On Leong *tong*. This *tong*, according to an 1898 book by Louis Beck, had from its beginnings attracted a "better class" of Chinese than did the rival Hip Sing *tong*. *Village Voice* reporters in 1977 went even further, charging that On Leong had ties to highly placed government officials in Taiwan. In the pyramid of power described by the journalists, one of whom claimed to have come from the Chinatown community, On Leong and the youth gangs through On Leong both served the KMT*, forming an international network that dealt in both legitimate enterprises, such as banks, stores, and land speculation, as well as the less legitimate heroin peddling and gambling operations of the East Coast.

The Whether or not these reports were accurate, the White Eagles fell from their place of power sometime in 1974, when On Leong leaders, evidently dissatisfied with their performance, replaced them with a new, rival group called the Ghost Shadows. The name of the gang provided an ironic comment on Chinese youths' attitude toward American society. It developed spontaneously, one version goes, in 1973 in response to a white, English-speaking newspaper reporter who asked a rival of the Eagles what their gang name meant. At the time, they were simply "Not the Eagles." But one among them was inspired to improvise a new name when the journalist mispronounced their name in Chinese. He volunteered to the American journalist that the first word in their name was "Ghost," a word that Asians derogatorily call all whites, thereby ridiculing the white journalist and the first part of the White Eagles's name. The second part was a play on the word "ying," which in Chinese means both eagle and shadow depending on the inflection it is given. As the journalist had mistakenly pronounced it, the word meant shadow. The reporter relayed the story and the city's most famous youth gang acquired its new name, Ghost Shadows.

The Ghost Shadows continued the extortion campaign that had served their dethroned rivals. One frightened restaurant owner, interviewed anonymously away from his place of business in order to avoid retribution, reported that most food establishments paid between fifty and four hundred dollars each month for protection, the exact amount being directly proportional to the size of the business and the fear of its manager. The gang's methods were direct enough, if not entirely explicit: "They never said I had to make extortion payments," the restauranteur noted, "but they said they need a contribution of four hundred dollars for someone in trouble and that they would need a contribution like that every month." In exchange the gang promised to protect the restaurant against robbery, broken windows,

---

* Sun Yat-sen organized the Kuomintang (KMT) political party in 1912. After controlling China for some years, the KMT was forced from the mainland in 1949 and now governs Taiwan.

and labor disputes. Almost no one dared refuse the arrangement the gangs offered, at least not for long. Momentary bursts of courage flagged as soon as a few broken windows or a hold-up showed the gang's intention and strength.

Then a change occurred. Spurred by the drop in business and by the knifing of Chinatown's former unofficial mayor in the summer of 1977, residents began to demand police help. They had never held much faith in either the honesty or the efficiency of law enforcers in China and they saw little reason to change their attitude in America. (If anything, the bias was reinforced by newspaper photographs showing known extortionists alongside the city's political leaders.) In 1977, a new fifth precinct commander, Allan Hoehl, took charge and vowed a cleanup. Local residents stepped up their cooperation; crime dropped and the gangs became less conspicuous. In 1978 police reported only one murder arrest in Chinatown, a drop from twenty-seven just two years earlier.

The dissatisfaction that had bred the gangs in the first place continued to be a problem in Chinatown, however, and fear did not die. One young college student, a resident of Chinatown, described leaving a theater: "I came out of the movie one night and started walking along when I heard 'bang! bang!' and turned around. There was a boy coming out of the theater and in his hand was a gun. I was so scared. I just tried not to look so he wouldn't think I could identify him."

When asked if she would testify against him if she could identify him, she replied, "Oh no, I would say I didn't see anything. If you testify they come back to get you. They always get you." Such demurrals feed the impression that Chinese gangs will remain untouchable so long as they prey only on their own people.

New recruits continue to replenish the gangs, also insuring their continuity. Among the recently arrived, many young people bring hopes and aspirations that seem too large to be satisfied except by criminal activities. Describing the disillusionment of her cousin who had just arrived from Hong Kong, one young woman said, "He got here two months ago and we enrolled him in English classes at night school. Gave him and his family a place to stay. It's crowded. They all sleep on mattresses in the middle of the floor. But he doesn't appreciate any of it. All he thinks about is money—lots of money. And he wants it right now. When he was still in China, we sent hundreds of dollars to them. Probably thousands. We worked really hard for that—we have a little restaurant in Chinatown and all the family works. Now he's unhappy and depressed. Doesn't show interest in anything. We think he will end up in a gang. We're all worried. We try to think of things to do with him—movies and that—but he's not interested in anything except money."

Initial disappointments tend to grow as the newly arrived Chinese look for housing. Most of them face a dilemma: should they look for something in Chinatown, where "key money" (payment demanded in return for the right to rent an apartment) can run as high as $3,000 or use the same sum, contributed by family members already here, towards a down payment on a house in Queens or Brooklyn? The latter alternative, although probably a better investment, is frequently rejected in favor of living closer to people who speak a familiar language and to shops that sell Chinese food and newspapers.

In many ways the decision to live in Chinatown remains a class matter, dividing manual workers with less education—who tend to choose the support and job opportunities of the ghetto—from better educated compatriots, who venture into other parts of the city. In Rego Park, Queens, or along Manhattan's Park Avenue, mink-coated matrons meet to play mah jong. They compare their children's progress in school and trade information on the newest restaurants. Married to professionals, with adequate middle-class incomes, they speak enough English for most situations and some of them speak English only. Chinatown is a shopping center for them, but only when it is not too crowded. "I never go down there around New Year's," one Peking-born woman says, "Too crowded. Too much noise and confusion."

The division is by no means clear-cut. Young, liberal, college-educated Asians began to move back into New York's Chinatown in the 1970s in search of their roots. Confucius plaza, a new high-rise apartment building, houses others who thought about leaving the area—shopkeepers and businessmen—but who preferred to stay close to their work provided they could find acceptable housing. Some returned after trying one of the other boroughs. For the most part, however, Chinatown's residents have remained the less educated and the more recently arrived.

National statistics on Chinese Americans show a curious split between the schooled and the unschooled. In 1970 completion of college was the norm for Chinese Americans. States with very small Chinese populations reported very high education levels. But in the areas of greatest concentration, California, Hawaii, and New York, as many Chinese as were educated were uneducated. Of all the states, New York was the most radically split: one in six Chinese New Yorkers has never attended school and almost half have acquired less than eight years of education but of the other half, one in five has completed college.

Jokes play on this division between the well educated and the unschooled. One engineer laughingly complained to a colleague: "I was always called Doctor and when I objected that I did not possess the degree, it didn't matter at all. They just told me that in the United States, Chinese are either Ph.D.'s or laundrymen and since I didn't take in wash, I must be a doctor."

New York's Chinese population does report a larger percentage with little education than any other state, partially explaining why the state's Chinese report lower incomes. In 1969 when the national median income for Chinese was $10,610, New York's Chinese showed only $8,316. Since restaurant and factory work was often paid "off the books," Chinese incomes were no doubt underreported. The statistic remains essentially valid, however, particularly in Chinatown.

New York's Chinese women present a special picture, special when compared with their countrywomen in other parts of the United States and when compared with Caucasian and black women. In 1970 about 50 percent of Chinese American wives worked outside the home; the equivalent figure for Caucasians was 41 percent and for blacks, 48 percent. Of those Chinese women who worked outside the home, 42 percent were machine operatives, usually in textiles, 25 percent filled clerical jobs, and 16 percent were professionals or technical workers. California's Chinese women tended to take service jobs, especially restaurant work, more frequently than did New York's Chinese women, who were heavily involved in the needle trades. The East Coast women earned more, on the average, and they continued to work longer.

Chinatown's older women generally keep working after the normal retirement age for nonimmigrant white women partly because their jobs are generally within walking distance of their homes. As many as three hundred small clothing factories dot lower Manhattan, ranging from small operations of a few sewing machines employing a dozen women to others staffed by several hundreds. These are today's "sweatshops," similar to those earlier in the century in which other immigrant women, especially Jewish and Italian women, worked. Rarely did these earlier immigrant women protest their situation too loudly, partly because they earned more than they had ever earned before and partly because they hoped to move on to something better or see their children do so. Chinese women are no different, though many realize they will work their lives away in these shops.

The sweatshops have their share of detractors and defenders although the women they employ generally speak well of them. One young woman, who labored in a dress factory before enrolling in a program to become an electrician's apprentice, defended employers for their fair treatment and remuneration. Their willingness to let small children perform tasks such as sweeping, sewing buttons, or rolling up bits of cloth was a favor to mothers, she said, who could supervise their youngsters while continuing their own work. A social worker in Chinatown also stood up for the small shops, saying that they would have set up in Southeast Asia, where labor was abundant and cheap, had they not found workers in Chinatown.

Whatever kind of work they do, Chinese women almost always have

Elderly women in New York's Chinatown continue to work in local textile factories well beyond the age when other women retire. (*Courtesy Margaret Defina*)

Asian husbands—96 percent in 1970. When younger girls seek to take non-Chinese spouses, their elders resist. Tensions inevitably mount and the concept of a generation gap, which took on such catchword popularity in the 1960s, achieves a special poignancy. In 1978, one father, alarmed that his two daughters were dating Puerto Rican boys, forbade them to continue the relationships. in November of that year, the two sisters jumped to their deaths from the roof of the apartment building where they lived on East 33rd Street in Manhattan. One was seventeen years old; the other only thirteen. The tendency of the Chinese to marry within their own ethnic group in America has a long history. For a century Chinese men had often remained single or lived apart from their wives and children. Their avoidance of interracial marriages occurred partly involuntarily, simply because many states passed laws barring such unions. (The U.S. Supreme Court did not void antimiscegenation laws until 1967, although some states acted earlier.)

The Little Italy Restoration Association (LIRA) was formed in 1974 to keep the area Italian. In 1981 a thriving Chinese laundromat next door to one LIRA storefront raised questions about how successful LIRA had been. (*Betty Boyd Caroli*)

When these laws were no longer enforced and when the male-female ratio of the Chinese American population evened out somewhat, most men and women continued to take Asian spouses.

During the 1970s Chinatown's most apparent change was its rapid growth. In the forty-year period after 1900 the population had doubled; in half that time, from 1940 to 1960, it would double again. By 1970, with the large wave of post-1965 arrivals, the population doubled again and the Chinatown Planning Association has predicted further increases for the 1980s.

This spiraling population pushes rents higher and edges boundaries out on all sides. With state and city office buildings blocking Chinatown's expansion to the south, growth has occurred on the north, pushing into Little Italy. The Italians, in uncharacteristic unified action, organized the Little Italy Restoration Association (LIRA) in the spring of 1974 to resist Chinese

Outdoor markets like this one in Shanghai are duplicated in New York's Chinatown, offering fresh fish and produce at low prices. (*Courtesy United Nations, A. Holcombe*)

Since China has no privately owned cars, the rush hour traffic is dominated by cyclists. (*Courtesy United Nations, A. Holcombe*)

This restaurant in Canton employs a female cooking staff. In New York City's Chinatown, the cooks are almost always men, a reminder that the early Chinese American immigration was mostly male. (*Courtesy Helga Busemann*)

expansion onto their turf. An Italian funeral director near Mulberry Street led in LIRA's formation, arguing that his people should not be forced to leave an area they had dominated for three or four generations.

Hostility toward new Chinese arrivals did not stop with the Italians. Chinese New Yorkers often sent money to help pay the costs of immigration for their relatives but then subsequently resented the crowding that the settlement of these new arrivals caused. Services, already severely strained, were spread thinner yet as the community tried to accommodate thousands of newcomers, many of them in need of a great deal of help in employment, education, and housing.

Just when the old associations—the CCBA, the *tongs*, and the family associations—could have been most helpful in mediating tensions for a troubled community, their power was being eroded on several sides. Newcomers showed little or no respect for the old rural ways that emphasized obedience to family. Even more important, the poverty programs of the 1960s fed money into the area, supporting groups such as the Basement Workshop, the Chinatown Planning Council, and the Chinatown Health Clinic.

Staffed by reform-minded young people, many of whom had moved to the area from cities in the Midwest or Canada, and supported by government dollars, these new groups challenged the authority of the traditional associations.

International developments and conflict between those who remained loyal to the Republic of China on Taiwan and those who favored the People's Republic on the mainland produced additional divisions in New York's Chinatown. Sentiment appeared to lean towards Taiwan in the 1950s and 1960s. Many of New York's Chinese had forfeited family land to the Communists and some had lost families in the fighting. Siding with Taiwan came naturally to these émigrés. Other Chinese Americans felt differently, but they had quietly nursed their own grudges against Taiwan for years, waiting for a change in American policy before speaking out openly. When President Richard Nixon visited the People's Republic in 1972 and the two countries opened offices in each other's capitals in 1973, many Chinese Americans believed that the official position of the United States had softened. Trade between the two countries grew. Those Chinese in New York less enthusiastic about the Taiwan government began to speak their minds, exposing a division in a community that had formerly appeared more united.

The influx of Chinese into New York in the early 1970s included some men and women who had never been favorably disposed toward Taiwan and who continued to maintain close ties with family and friends who stayed behind. Although they had chosen to leave the People's Republic because of the excesses of what came to be called the Cultural Revolution and although they deeply resented their treatment in mainland China, many of them, nevertheless, viewed the Cultural Revolution as a temporary aberration that had ended. They encouraged opening channels between the United States and the People's Republic for visits and trade. Because many of those fleeing the Cultural Revolution came from the more educated segment of the population and because they took work in New York as translators and teachers, they exerted a disproportionate effect.

The Cultural Revolution lasted only a few years after it evolved in the mid-1960s out of conflicts within China over defense, foreign policy and other issues. The objective, in Zhou Enlai's words was to eradicate "bourgeois" ideology in art, literature, and all other fields of culture: to revive the spirit of revolution among a population that had lost its enthusiasm. Students became soldiers in the campaign, especially those whose parents were workers, military officers, and party officials, and they set out to attack the four "olds"—old ideas, old culture, old habits, and old customs. Such an objective, interpreted broadly, permitted almost everything, including the ordering of straightened hair (because permanents were bourgeois), and al-tering traffic lights so red meant "go." Zealous youths saw corruption every-where, and they acted enthusiastically to wipe it out.

In those tumultuous years of the Cultural Revolution, Xiu Zhen first began thinking about leaving Peking. Students in the high school where she taught literature cut off her naturally wavy hair, accusing her of being a spy. The head of the school, a woman with very curly hair, got shaven. "We wore hats for a long time," Xiu Zhen remembers with a faint smile. "We had to. We looked terrible. My own students did not touch me—it was the others in the school. After it was over and I was living in Hong Kong, one of the Red Guards wrote to apologize. But I had left by then."

For Xiu Zhen, the Cultural Revolution remains a nightmare. In the New York publishing house where she now works, she speaks quietly of those years in Pcking: "For me it was very, very bad. I had relatives in Hong Kong, in Japan, in Germany. The Red Guards said I was a spy. Maybe I wrote some letters and mentioned something political but I was not political at all. I taught literature in high school. So they put me in jail. Everybody in this one room. I was there about one year and two months with fourteen other people. We didn't sleep there. We went home at night, but they made us work very hard. It was very cold. The windows were all broken and we had to put in new glass. Cut it with knives. Once our hands got very cold and we broke the glass. It cut our hands and they swelled up. The skin came off. Sometimes the Red Guards burned me with cigarettes. They kept saying, 'We have to wash your brains.'

"Then they took me to the countryside near Peking. I was there two years and one month. Every two weeks I came home for two days. Life was much better in the country. Nobody beat me. I grew rice and vegetables, flowers and corn. There was a school for us there. They said every professor and teacher had to learn to be a peasant. We slept in a dorm—every room had six or seven teachers. We ate together and the food was very good. The peasants treated me very well. Very good people but very poor. You Americans do not know what poor means. One peasant family I knew had seven children but they never called them by name—they used numbers. The mother would say, 'Come here, Six.' They went without shoes even in winter. Very poor. I had to work very hard. Carry water in a wheelbarrow. When I first went there, I could put only one bucket of water in the wheel-barrow. That was all I could manage. I was a literature teacher from the city. We always had servants when I was growing up. But soon I became strong. When I left I could carry six buckets—in one wheelbarrow!

"Then the government sent all teachers back to Peking. I went to a different school. That was in 1971 and three years later I left to go to Hong

Kong. I said it was because of my mother. She lived in Hong Kong and I said I had to go to her because she was sick. Of course that was not the real reason.

"In Hong Kong I was very careful. Many people came from the mainland and I did not know who was government. It was very dangerous. I was there two years. In Hong Kong the American Consulate has a system. If you have left the mainland you can apply for special permission to come to America as a refugee. It's not always easy. If they [Hong Kong government] find something wrong with you, you have to pay. They say you can't leave. Then you give them maybe two hundred dollars and they let you go. But when the family is large, that's a lot of money. And sometimes they hold the last one and they say 'Give more.' I know somebody in Hong Kong now. Her whole family's here, but she can't leave because the doctors there say she's sick. It's not true. They just want more money. So the family had to go to a doctor here and get him to say he will treat her when she gets here. Naturally they pay him to say it. Always we pay.

"I expect to become a citizen. At least my thinking is freedom. I don't worry anymore about the Cultural Revolution. I still have many problems but at least my life is freedom. I am sad when I think about my friends in Peking. When I become an American citizen, I will go visit them.

"Many of my problems are at work. Americans don't really like the Chinese. Then my language is a problem. I can't speak very well. Puerto Ricans are very mean to me. They think we are taking their jobs. I think that is the reason they are mean.

"Even with other Chinese I have problems. The Cantonese don't like us coming in. They don't say anything, but I see their expression. They only recognize Cantonese. Don't like us from Peking. It's very difficult to make friends with them. But I am glad I came to America. Today I am alive."

Xiu Zhen's life in New York is comfortable. She enjoys trying the best of the newest Chinese eateries and she purchases the most fashionable consumer goods—red-framed eyeglasses and the latest style wristwatch. In Rego Park, Queens, where she lives there are other Mandarin speakers and she finds many opportunities to use her first language. At her job in Manhattan, she improves her spoken and written English. Her memories of China are mostly pleasant (before the Cultural Revolution so abruptly altered her life) and all her references are to the area around Peking, where she grew up.

Other recent Chinese immigrants carry less pleasant memories, especially those who grew up in less comfortable circumstances. Wing Ng is one of these, a Cantonese woman whose family was poor. Sitting in an office on Mott Street, Wing Ng wears blue jeans and running shoes. Her English is strongly accented but understandable and she speaks staccato-like sentences, enthusiastically, emphatically.

"I've lived in New York a little more than three years. Came here in 1975 when I was twenty-three. Before that I lived in Hong Kong for three years. Before that—Canton. I came alone. Only me. No relatives. Nothing. My sister had a friend and the friend's mother lived in California. My sister wrote the friend's mother and told her that I really wanted to go to the United States, that I loved the country. So she became my sponsor. It was not easy to find a sponsor. I waited almost one year. Then I got some help from the YMCA, a religious organization. They have an immigration office in Hong Kong and I told them I wanted to come here and they took care of the visa. They lent me some money too. And I paid them back after I got here. My sponsor paid three hundred dollars to the YMCA and they took care of my air fare. Then when I got here I returned it.

"The reason I wanted to come to the United States is that I heard it is really freedom. That's the first thing. And the second was the education. It's hard to get an education in China. Only the United States can support you to get a good education and a good life. My childhood was not happy. Too many children. Poor. I don't want that again. I graduated from high school but nothing can get you into college. Even though you have good grades and a good record you can never get into college in China. I don't know how it is now but in my experience, when I was young, during the Cultural Revolution, there were no colleges to get into. Every student who graduated from high school in 1968, 1970, around that time, was sent to work in the countryside, to become a farmer. Even though he was a high school graduate, or even a college graduate, he had to go to the countryside. Leave his house, and go far away. I really wanted to go on to school, to learn something and I knew there was no chance to go back once I went to the countryside.

"So I left and went to Hong Kong. I could go there because my father lived in Hong Kong. My mother was in Canton. My family is split—I do not want to talk about that. My father is a manager in a company, not his own business. He works for a salary. He graduated from college, from law school and so did his brothers and his sisters. But my mother's family, they did not go to college. Not the sisters or the brothers. It's more difficult to go to college now than when my mother was young and always it was more difficult for a woman. If we had stayed in China my brothers could not have gone to college, no way. And me, not a chance. It is much more difficult now.

"In Hong Kong it is difficult to go to college, too. Only two universities. Too many people. Hong Kong is not nice to live in. Too much competition for jobs. The people in Hong Kong don't like the others coming in and taking the jobs. So the only jobs you can get are in the factories. The bosses make sure of that. They don't give the good jobs to people coming in from

China. No chance they give us. I was lucky. I got an office job, but all my friends had to work in factories or in construction.

"I came first to California. Los Angeles. Then I came here to New York. I had some friends. They told me there were more opportunities to find a good job in New York. To learn English. In Los Angeles everything is so far away. You have to drive in a car for hours to get anywhere. There's not that much chance to get an education, to go to school, because of the distances between places. I stayed there just two weeks and then I came to New York.

"When I got here I worked as a babysitter. I had a green card and I could have gotten another kind of job but I wanted to learn English. Even though you go to school, you are just listening a lot of the time and I wanted a job where I could talk English. So I found a job with an American family. They talked to me and corrected me. Told me how to do things. I took care of their little boy. He was seven years old and very easy to take care of. I took him to the park on his bicycle or to the museum. For me it was very interesting. My friend had the job before me and when she went to a company for a good job she left the old one for me. I kept it for only one-half year because I picked up English very fast.

"Later I read the newspaper and I heard of the programs at the China-town Planning Council. Training programs. I knew typing before. In Hong Kong I went to evening school and studied English too. The first day I arrived in Hong Kong I knew I wanted to get out so I went to school right away. That helped me when I got to New York, but the Chinatown Plan-ning Council program is fantastic. I always so appreciated that program. The government paid me eighty dollars a week to go to school. I needed the money since I was supporting myself. Sometimes I even sent money back to my family. This was a terrible time for me—a new immigrant. I had a language problem still and I found a different society here—all new to me. For the new immigrant, he doesn't know what is going on. Somebody has to tell him and the Chinatown Planning Council program is very good that way. I could join a program and learn what was going on in the new society without worrying about money. Mostly it's a program for young people. For the young it is easier to join the program. Also, the program has to find you a job and the companies don't want to hire older people. For older people, it is not so easy.

"After the Chinatown Planning Council program I got an office job— worked for a company for two years. Then I went back to school to get a promotion. It is better if you have education—a background.

"In February 1978, I started at City University, New York City Com-munity College. There are many Chinese people there, many different races. Many, many. I have helped about twenty people go there myself.

Told them it was a very good college, especially for data processing. I promised myself I will go on to a four-year college when I graduate but I don't know how long it will take. First I will get a job and then ask the boss to help me with my education. The only complaint I had with New York City Community College was that I didn't get any help financially. When I stopped work and went back to college I had been earning money—about $7,000 and they looked at that and said they would not give me any financial help because I had been earning a high income. That first year back in college was very difficult for me. I had to take any kind of job, just to get money. Type. Work in a restaurant. Whatever I could find.

"My brother came last year—the younger one. The older is still in Hong Kong. I found a sponsor for him—I took care of everything. He lives with me, of course. Sure. People ask me that question and I find it strange. Of course he lives with me. He's my family. We rent an apartment in Brooklyn—my brother, my friend and me. Chinese people like to stick together. Now my brother—he's twenty-three—he's doing the course in food service management at the Chinatown Planning Council. In Hong Kong he worked in a hotel and when he came here he got a job in midtown but he found he needed English just to understand the people so he went back to school.

"My brother and I find many freedoms here that we did not have in China. In China, if you wanted to go from Manhattan to Brooklyn you would have to get a permit from the government. In the subway station you have to show this permit, how old you are, all the information. Where you're going, why. Even to visit. When you buy a token you have to show the permit. If you are a teacher in a school, you ask your principal to write it for you. If you are a farmer, you ask the chief. If you are a housewife, you go to the community chief. I don't know when it started but it was always true as long as I remember. You can go shopping in your neighborhood or to your job but for anything else you have to have a permit and for that you have to have a good reason. If you graduate and get a job and they send you far away and you want to go back to visit your parents, that's a good reason. Always you have to have a reason.

"To buy things in China you have to have a ticket. For example, rice. You get an allowance of not too many pounds a month. Meat is hard to get. Vegetables are easy. For clothes you get a ticket also. Workers get blue jeans. Two pairs each year if you do hard work like miners. I don't know what the measurement would be here but you get like a certain number of yards or meters for the whole year. Inside clothes. Outside clothes. Everything. They all count as part of this allowance. Even bath towels are included and they are counted by the centimeters. Small towels don't count for as much of the allowance as big towels. Long sleeve shirts count more than short sleeves.

"Many people want to leave China but it is hard. In Canton, people have the best life because many of them have relatives overseas. Most of the Hong Kong people have relatives in Canton and they send food and the good things to them. Lots of good things come into Canton from Hong Kong.

"The Chinese people who get to New York are the lucky ones but still they have problems, especially the older ones. People between forty and fifty—it's too hard for them. Even small things they can't do because they don't have the language. One person is easy to support but often they have many and they have to work six days every week. The conditions in the factories are terrible. Dirty air, long hours, from eight in the morning to eight at night, six days! They are paid by the piece and only a few can make good money. I talk with them and they tell me they don't protest because they don't know how to talk back and they don't know the law. Most of the women go to work. Nobody stays home. Ninety percent of the factories are women. They work at least six years to get the social security. Hospitalization benefits are very important, too.

"The only thing I am not satisfied with here in this country is the medical support. It is terrible. One day I went to the hospital, for just two hours to the emergency room because I had terrible pains in my stomach. They took three bottles of blood from me and sent me home. The next day I went back and they said everything was normal. But the bill was more than three hundred dollars—it was, I think, three hundred and eighty dollars for just two hours in the emergency room! My goodness!

"Some women make good money. But remember today may be easy. You make a lot of money, but tomorrow you make only ten dollars and then the factory may close down entirely and you make nothing at all. I help people make out their tax returns and I know that many of them work very hard and never make more than five or six thousand dollars in a year.

"The men in the restaurants work only for tips. The restaurants hire only the young men. They don't want the older ones. The waiters can make eight hundred dollars in a month but they pay the tax for themselves. They even have to pay their own insurance and they have no security at all. I know a man who worked in a restaurant as a waiter. One day he hurt his ankle and went to the hospital. He got nothing! Nothing at all for four months! That's terrible!

"Chinese people have lower incomes because first, the language problem. If you know just a little English, you can go to an office and get a job cleaning up. It has more security, more benefits. But how are you going to get a job like that if you don't know a little English? And how are you going to learn English if you have to work twelve hours a day, six days a week and then come home and take care of your family? You have no time! No energy! You are always exhausted.

"You know for the Spanish-speaking, it is different. In the government, in the housing department, some people still cannot speak English. They speak Spanish but they get hired anyway. If we Chinese can't speak English well, can't read it and write it, nobody wants to hire us. But Spanish is legal in New York and Chinese is not. You can get a high school equivalency test in Spanish but not in any other language! Right? That's unfair! Right? It's the Spanish who get the jobs even though there are more Chinese coming in now. The post office, everywhere, you see the Spanish working.

"That's why the Chinese stay in Chinatown. They know their problems. They close themselves inside. Some of the people, especially the women, never go outside Chinatown. They can't shop or even say they have to go to the bathroom in English. Can't use the subway.

"Let me tell you a true story. I was going to Brooklyn and I met an old woman in the Church Avenue subway station. She was at least sixty years old, just walking around the station—it was about eight o'clock in the evening. She came up to me and said in Chinese, 'Are you Chinese people?' and I said 'Yes.' Then she showed me an address pinned to her dress and asked me how to get there. I understood when I saw the address that she should have gotten off one stop earlier but the train had skipped that station. She didn't know how to get back. When I showed her how to cross over and go back, she told me a terrible story. She said she had gotten lost two times already and that she was so scared. She worked in Chinatown in a factory—cut the threads in a dress factory—something she could still do even though she was old. She said, 'I don't know how to speak English. I don't know how to buy a token for the subway. My son buys the tokens. Each day he gives me two—one to go to work and one to come home. Going to Chinatown in the morning is easy because the signs are in Chinese. The streets and everything have their names in Chinese. I know when to get off. If anything goes wrong in Chinatown, I can ask somebody. But coming back to Brooklyn is more complicated.'

"That day and every day her son gave her five pennies for the trip home. He put them in her left pocket. Each time the train stopped at a station she was supposed to move one penny from the left pocket to the right and when all the pennies were gone from the left pocket she was supposed to get off. That meant she was home. That day she got mixed up because the train skipped a station so when she moved the fifth penny, it was the wrong station. That's why she was wandering around, lost. And there are many, many stories like this one.

"Maybe you don't want to call it a language problem—you can call it an education problem. Even if you have a degree from China, it means nothing here. Prejudice is not important at all. It's language and education that keep the Chinese people back. The reason they don't enroll in school you should understand. It's that they don't have the time after a long day.

At least ten hours in a restaurant or factory. And learning a language is not easy. Step by step. You need time.

"The language problem keeps them in Chinatown. If they move to Brooklyn they have trouble buying Chinese food and for the older people, it's hard to eat hamburger every day. You might like to eat Indian food or Japanese food once in a while but not every day, right? Now some people say that if the Chinese people got out of Chinatown, they would learn English faster but who would talk to them? If you don't understand your neighbors you can't talk to them. If something breaks down how are you going to talk to the landlord?

"So most people want to stay in Chinatown. Partly because they can get Chinese food there, and partly because of the language. Also to be near their families. It is getting very crowded. On Canal Street on Sundays now you can't turn around your body, so many people. I hope the government can help us, recognize the problem and get us more space. Build some new high buildings and fix the old ones. Apartments here are terrible. Bathrooms, kitchen rooms, everything together. Holes in the wall, plaster coming down. No heat sometimes. No doors, And people pay high rents. Before they even get them they pay fifteen hundred or two thousand dollars. You call it—key money? That's it. If they move out, they lose the key money.

"The streets in Chinatown are a big problem. They need to be cleaned up, but garbage collection is only twice a week and that is not enough when there are so many people. It's very crowded. Lots of people live there and lots of others come in on the weekends to do their shopping.

"As for safety, most people in Chinatown do not complain too much. They say it is as safe as most places in New York but I know that tourists are always getting robbed. I think the crimes are caused by—well, I don't want to blame it on one people. I have many friends—white, black, red— many people become my friends. I never say I hate one color of people because I don't, but I say that the Puerto Ricans still have a problem in New York. Many crimes here in Chinatown are caused by the Puerto Ricans. I have talked with a lot of Chinese people—women and others. They always tell me that they are scared more of Puerto Rican people than of the others.

"You can go to the police station and check the facts. You can read it in a Chinese newspaper. If you look at how many crimes are committed, how many purses are taken and how many houses are robbed, you will see that the Puerto Ricans are often the cause. A friend of mine was robbed by Puerto Ricans—they took her bag with forty dollars.

"There are Chinese gangs too and the Chinese people hate them. Young men get into gangs because there are no jobs. This was especially a problem before there were bilingual programs for them. Without the language, nobody would hire them. Now the gangs are not so bad. One thing that helped

change that was the police—the new captain—Mr. Hoehle. Everybody loves him! He gets everything very clear. Tries to understand the community. There are also more openings in the youth program and that helps. People are beginning to trust the police a little bit—just beginning a little bit—and that helps.

"Chinatown offers a lot. Many newspapers—there are twelve, at least. I don't read one all the time. I change. If I want to read the Hong Kong news, I buy one newspaper. If I want to know about another area, what's happening there, I buy a different newspaper. The speaking in Chinatown is many kinds: Mandarin, Cantonese and others, but the writing is all the same so we can read all the newspapers.

"Old people have it bad here and that is why my parents don't want to come here. That is my biggest sadness. When I know that the Chinese New Year is coming, it is very hard for me because my family's not here with me. My father is sixty-five already. He doesn't want to come here where he has no friends. To be a senior citizen here is not good—you can't go out. My mother is sixty-three already. I don't know if I'll ever see her again. That bothers me. When I sleep I always dream of my parents—my family. My sister would like to come here to live with me but it is hard. She is a worker, married with two children. It is very common to have only two children. Not when I was young—there were six in my family—but now most families are only two children. After two, my sister stopped. Her husband had an operation. They don't have to—it's not required—but many choose to do it. In a way, they have to because right now in China if you have more than two children, there are penalties. Nothing is supplied for you—food or anything—so it's better to have the operation after two. I agree with that. Too many people are starving in the world. Right? Why not keep the ones who are here strong and healthy? That's my mind.

"I don't know how my life will go. My parents don't want me to marry with a non-Chinese person. For my own opinion, I will tell you that I probably will not because everything is different. When I came here I was more than twenty years old. The eating, the living, the loving—everything was different. I want to keep to my ways. The Americans—it is not that they are bad but they are different. Most of my friends feel the same way—my Chinese friends. We cook Chinese and we speak Cantonese. I have many American friends. It is not a problem to have non-Chinese friends. Getting married to a non-Chinese—that is the problem. It is your whole life. It is hard to say it in words but my mind is this: we are two cultures—American and Chinese. We can be friends but we should be separate. That is the way I feel."

From the office where Wing Ng sits, she can look down on Mott Street where Prince T'sai Chen passed nearly eighty years earlier, offering advice

to countrymen to disperse and mix, with little apparent effect. New York's Chinatown remains an enduring ghetto, reinforced by thousands arriving each year, willing to face its discomforts in order to live among familiar accents.

10

Their Children's Country:

Modern Greek Odyssey

Greece emerged from World War II ill prepared to meet the challenge of rebuilding its war-ravaged society. Not only were Communist and Monarchist factions fighting each other, but much of the nation's industry was closed down and the once-proud center of Western civilization was reduced to a barter economy. Hundreds of thousands of displaced persons depended on public aid for sustenance.

The option of leaving these woes behind was available to very few. Much of the rest of Europe also stood in disarray, and the United States, operating under a thirty-year-old policy of immigrant quotas, alotted only 308 slots for Greeks. Special refugee legislation passed in 1948 temporarily raised this number, but charged those additional places against future allocations. As a consequence, when this program ended, there were no quota slots left for Greeks for the remainder of the century; by one calculation a Greek applicant in 1950 could not expect his visa until 2014. Only the periodic passage of special laws kept Greek immigration alive through the fifties.

It had not always been so hard to win sympathy for the ancient home of the democratic ideal. Admittedly the American imagination has to be

261

stretched too far to grant Demetrios Sicilianos his conceit that Christopher
Columbus was a Greek explorer. Few, however, debate the critical influence of Hellenic thought and culture on American life. Commencement
speakers and high school principals conventionally lead their audiences on
expeditions tracing American law and philosophy back to Greek sources,
and politicians as far back as the Revolutionary generation have pointed to
ancient Greece as the model for early democracy. "The mention of Greece
fills the mind with the utmost exalted sentiments," President James Monroe
wrote in an annual message in 1822.

By 1822, however, precious little remained of Greece's early glory. Centuries of Ottoman rule had reduced her to a Turkish satellite of minor global
significance. Even her proud Eastern Orthodox Church had suffered from
the corrosive effects of outside interference. While Turkish rulers followed
Moslem custom and placed both religious and secular authority under the
authority of the church, they intruded into its affairs shamelessly. In the
seventeenth century, for example, Turkish officials raffled off top church
positions to the highest bidder.

Not until the 1800s, under the influence of the same Enlightenment
ideology that fueled the American Revolution, did disaffected elements in
Greece begin a successful drive to recapture Hellenic independence. Led by
a group known as the Hetairists, the Greek Peloponnesus revolted in 1821.
The painter Eugéne Delacroix would faithfully portray the ruthless civil war
that ensued, in which the passion of centuries-old animosities led to the
massacre of large numbers of defenseless Turks and Greeks for little military
gain. Resolution came only after Britain, France, and Russia intervened to
secure the revolutionary victory. But even in victory, "mother Greece"
stood stripped of Crete, Macedonia, and the Aegean Isles.

Those Greeks who came to the United States in these years included
sailors, explorers, gold miners, occasional settlers, and students brought over
by American Protestant missionaries to study in American seminaries. After
1850, when the two countries developed a commercial connection, Greek
agents could be found doing business in the port cities of New Orleans,
Savannah, and New York.

Greek immigration did not turn significant until 1890, in the face of a
critical economic reality: Greece's ability to produce sufficient food and
trade for its expanding citizenry gave out. In the late nineteenth century
Greece became heavily dependent on currant exports, which replaced silk
raising and olive cultivation as staples. Currant sales rose spectacularly in
the 1870s after disease wiped out French vines and currants became a substitute for French grapes. When the French crop recovered by century's
end, currant sales plummeted. Other problems—poverty, soil erosion, crop
failure, and overpopulation—scourged the agricultural economy. Peasant
life, difficult in the best of times, turned harsh, and the small farmers felt

cut off from a government apparently indifferent to their troubles. And the military situation, always precarious, claimed so many years of compulsory service that the emigration alternative began to seem more and more appealing. In 1848, 1 Greek had arrived in the United States. With young males pouring out of the ports of Patras and Piraeus in 1891, more than 1,000 came; by 1910 one-quarter to one-fifth of Greece's total labor force had left, more than 183,000 going to the United States.

The newcomers came largely from rural farm villages. They brought with them little formal education and few industrial skills. Yet, as immigrants they avoided America's farmlands in favor of the burgeoning industrial cities of the Northeast. Greeks took jobs in tanneries, slaughterhouses, coal mines, and on railroad construction gangs. Many settled into textile mill occupations in places like Lowell, Massachusetts, earning between six and fifteen dollars a week. Industrial America provided such jobs aplenty and impoverished sons of the Peloponnesus came in increasing numbers to fill them, mostly in New York, Chicago, and Lowell.

The early Greek immigrants did not intend to settle permanently in the United States, only to stay long enough to gather some dollars and return in enhanced circumstances. With World War I this situation changed. In 1915 Greece's King Constantine noted that despite the gratifying recent return of as many as 42,000 Greek males to join in the war effort against Turkey, his subjects were again leaving Greece; this time for good:

> At first . . . the men went alone. Their idea was to make a modest fortune, return to their families in Greece, buy a little farm or a shop . . . and live in comfort . . . among their own people. But . . . many of those [now returning to America] . . . took their families with them. . . . For them it was no longer an experiment. . . . They had been to America once. . . . They knew where to go and how to get there. So when they sailed . . . it was as prospective Americans . . . quitting their mother country forever.

Determined to sink roots for an American future, Greeks began to climb out of menial labor, investing their earnings in small businesses. At first they stepped onto the lowest rungs, peddling from pushcarts or opening shoeshine parlors. Some soon achieved much more than marginal success, establishing flower shops, fruit and vegetable stores, and confectioneries. But the trade that became most commonly associated with Greek Americans was the restaurant business. One step up from common labor and peddling, immigrants opened coffee shops and eateries preparing Greek-style dishes. Hard work and long hours by all family members made it possible to wrest profits from many of these modest restaurants.

More than half a century later, new Greek immigrants continue to place their hope in hard work and small business. Helen Christakis, standing outside Macy's department store on Manhattan's 34th Street selling hot dogs from her cart, represents this spirit well. Her working day stretches from early morning until past dark: "If you come early the spot belongs to you, so you have to be here every day in the morning." Husband Theo wheels a similar cart. "Too many hours work," he says, exhausted from pushing his portable business eighteen blocks. "We are on the street," Helen explains, "so our kids can go to school. They don't know that we can be more worth than a office man."

The years separating the Christakis family from the earlier immigrants witnessed the development of a stable Greek American population in the United States, as both immigration and repatriation diminished to very low levels after World War I. Fearful that this would weaken ties to the old traditions, the Pan Hellenic Union worked to promote the teaching of Greek, the maintenance of Hellenic culture, and the vitality of an American-based Greek Orthodox Church. Like similar attempts among other groups, however, these efforts were not particularly successful, as time and American experience wore down the old ways. War, however, still had the power to arouse loyalty to the motherland and Greece's resistance to Mussolini's invasion during World War II stirred these emotions. Many who had long before stopped identifying with Greece now felt a powerful obligation to close ranks to help the civilian population in Greece. More than three hundred local committees sprang up to coordinate aid efforts. The well-known Greek émigré Spyros Skouras sparked a $10 million drive for the Greek War Relief Association.

Greece itself was thrown into turmoil during the war. For three years a puppet government ruled at home while a government in exile in London fostered vain hopes for liberation. In the meanwhile the people suffered frightfully. Italian and German invaders systematically killed thousands, wiping out entire towns and villages. More than 1.1 million people were left without food, shelter, clothing, or medicine, while Axis occupiers rifled the treasury, reducing the economy to a shambles. After World War II, civil war between the Communist and Monarchist forces delayed the return of stability and held back progress. Consequently in the 1950s, after its Western European neighbors had built modern industrial economies, Greece was still predominantly agricultural. As late as 1959 per capita income stood below $300 a year.

By 1955 the number of Greeks emigrating reached 30,000 annually, with approximately 1 in 4 destined for North America. To circumvent the restrictive American quota, Greeks increasingly chose to enter through the back door. Between 1959 and 1972 an estimated 23,000 Greeks "jumped ship" (the simple expedient of abandoning ship after it docked at an American port) and this represented only one of several unorthodox routes to the United States. In the same period the total illegal Greek immigration prob-

Two Greek women returning from a day of farm labor on Chios Island. Although only one-fourth of the total land area of Greece is arable, most of the people still work in agriculture. (*Courtesy United Nations, M. Tzovaras*)

ably exceeded 100,000, 65 percent of these undocumented aliens eventually settling in what became the world's largest Greek community outside Europe—in New York City. George Castamanis, talking in a Queens restaurant, tells how he came to live in this city:

"I jumped a boat in Baltimore and made it to Oklahoma. My plan was to reach Hawaii. It's an island with different kinds of people and that's where I think I can disappear and nobody can found me. I worked there one time on a ship and I like it there.

"I go on a bus from Oklahoma to California and from there I'm going to take a job on a ship and go to Hawaii. But happens somebody knows my plans. I see some men from the army, and on the bus they are looking at me and looking at me. I figure they are thinking this man he jump ship. I got right off.

"I come from Salonica. It is the second largest city after Athens. It is the most beautiful city, Byzantine-style churches and castles. We lived in the center of the city.

"My father worked for the Ford Motor Company in Detroit. In 1933 he was sent to Greece to work for the company and there he married my

mother. But in the war the Germans kill my father and I was with my
mother and two sisters. Those were very hard times. People were starving.
We was a little lucky; mother was a cook in a restaurant and she brought
home things from the restaurant. We used to give everybody in the neighborhood.

"I stopped going to school very young. After the Germans, came the
Communists, and we have civil war so I cannot go back to school. It was
worse than when Germany was there. People was dying and starving and I
had to help out.

"After the civil war my mother's family—she have brothers in Athens
and Corfu—write we should come to be closer with them. My mother have
three little kids and she alone so we all move to Athens when I am eleven
years old. Right away I start to work. I sell toys and other things for my
uncles. I do this until I am twenty-two years old. But I get tired of this. My
friends and me, we talked about a better life, about going somewhere else,
away from Greece. Greece was not so modern, still only small business. We
don't know what is better life anyway; we want adventure. I think Greek
people they are always in adventure. If you go to Africa you find them. In
places you can't believe. In South America. All over. They go on a ship
and they get off somewhere. We decide to go to Europe in 1962.

"My mother don't like my idea too much. But I want to see other country, how it looks. Most Greeks who go to another place go to Germany
then. I was, too, going somewhere so I go to Germany for five, six months.
I work as a ship hand in Hamburg for Greek ships. I travel to America, ten,
fifteen times.

"To say the truth I don't know why I left ship in 1963. I hear many
stories about people leaving ship in America, start to work, get better life. I
want to work somewhere where you don't jump and shake when the sea is
not so calm. I try America. See if I like it. I leave the ship in Baltimore.
Then I go to Oklahoma. Then I plan go to Hawaii. But I get scared, and I
stay in Oklahoma.

"The Greek priest in Oklahoma City came from Astoria, Queens. He
told me if you want a better life with a lot of Greek people you better go to
New York. There are a lot like you—young. Thousands of Greek girls. Just
don't go to Greek places because the immigration [officials] always going
back and forth. Don't make trouble. Then no police will stop you for identification. So I go to New York.

"I bring a little money. I could do any job. New York has a lot of jobs
around. I survived.

"One day, the first week I'm in New York I went to drink coffee and I
met somebody from Salonica and he took me to live for a while with his
family in Manhattan. Finally I got some money and came to Queens.

A woman drying grapes to make raisins in the Greek Peloponnesus. (*Courtesy United Nations/Tsagris*)

There I meet my wife in a dancing place. She was an American, but I did not marry her so I could become 'legal.'

"Once before I marry I want to go back to Greece so I went to the same ship company from which I left the ship in Baltimore. I tell him I like to be again with the ship. He told me okay, I would like to take you, but first go to immigration, tell them the whole story and if they don't lock you up or send you to Greece, they will give you twenty-nine days to still stay. Then come to me and I will give you a job on the ship.

"And I was a little upset so I go downtown to immigration. I am ready to tell them I jump ship. I speak very little English so I ask someone at desk how do you tell that you are here because you leave ship. She doesn't understand. She tell me something. I go to other desk. For ten, fifteen minutes I go up and down the floor to ask how I can be again the way I used to be. So I can't found the way. So I left from there and I start again working and all that. I even talk to a lawyer and he found out that I could stay legal in United States because my father was American.

"So I got married. Her name is Hilda Flores from Puerto Rico. We stay

Approximately 100,000 people of Greek descent live in Astoria, Queens. This commuter is reading the Greek-language *National Herald*. In the background is the Triboro Bridge, which links Queens, Manhatten, and the Bronx. (*Nick Manley*)

in Greece three months for honeymoon. She have the kids very well. I send them to private Catholic school in Long Island. Every summer I send them to Greece. Twelve years ago I got divorced. No reason. I went to Salonica and marry a girl from there.

"In America, Europeans are the best people I think. Gentlemen and everything. We work hard. I live in Woodside, Queens for twelve years. It used to be European, very nice. But lately it gets worse, lots of noise, not clean. South Americans now with loud music. We Europeans work hard. I work to make money to go to Greece and to send my kids to a good school. I have to work seven days a week and all holidays. Spanish and black people they think we are money hungry. That's not true. They don't work this much, then they still want their kids should have the same like my kids. Okay, but let them work hard like me. Sometimes sleep at the job, work two or three shifts to make the money. Italian, English, German, Greeks, I think I understand them better. We are European people, we can say hello.

"I was in restaurant business. I found jobs all over with Greeks. Today you see me in this restaurant. Tomorrow maybe you don't see me. Lose job and get another job. I work for friends. But two times a year I leave job and go to Greece for a month, and month and a half. When I come back I go back to job if it's there, if not I get another one.

"Greeks work much more harder here than in Greece. There they don't work. They don't know what is work. They want to make money even more than here, but not like here to work Sunday, holidays and weekends. They are more relax. Americans, they have so much they don't know how to keep it. I remember how it can be when people starved in Greece. I know what is bread.

"Whatever work I do, I do so much. I expect something from my life. I destroy myself for my kids. Here Americans say first me then my kids. We are closer. We live with mother and father. We work hard to get a better life. I saved money and I bought a house in Athens and a villa near the sea. It was a few years ago. Very cheap. Now it is expensive.

"I been in many places. Washington, North Carolina, Oklahoma, California, but I like New York. After you live in New York you cannot go no place. Night time you like dancing, movies, theatres, clubs, parks, a lot of different TV stations, you have it.

"A year ago I went upstate to look at a restaurant for a business. We were disgusted with noise, dirt, pressure, and the busy life in New York. We thought to buy a place outside New York. To live like a person like in Europe. It was too quiet. Too boring. We came back to New York.

"I could go back now to Greece. But not to work. America is a place to work, not Greece. Today Greece is much better. They say it's like U.S.A. But not forever. Maybe next year or in five years, or maybe ten, but every ten years, they have a fight, a war or trouble in Greece. America is not like that; it is secure.

"To say the truth when somebody leaves his country and goes to another country—me too—then they have two countries. In Europe there is never security. We suffer there. The Germans kill my father. America, until now—until now—is a great country. We have problems but for jobs it is a very great country. We live here very nice. Therefore, I am American citizen. We can do anything. I have good opportunity here. I like here. I go to Greece I like there, I feel more Greek than American. Mother country is forever. I tell you in America they fix up something. No one pressure you to forget your country or your religion.

"But I must go back. I work too much. I am going to give up some things to go back. Even if it is not as rich as here in United States I will pressure myself to live there. I work enough. I don't want to work anymore. I am tired to work. I can go there and come back two, three months a year to make some money. Like they say Germans are mechanics in America,

Jews in business, others in other things, Greeks in luck. They surprise people who don't expect them to be success. There is a lot of bread here and Greeks get more than we expect. One old woman tell me, 'I came here and there was heating, plumbing, bathrooms. I think I'm in paradise.' But we work for it."

As in the earlier, pre-World War I situation, Greeks arriving after 1965 often came with the idea of amassing savings and returning to Greece. This back-traffic continued to be considerable, filling small towns and villages in Greece with repatriates from America. The village of Skoura, ten miles from Athens, is not untypical; in the words of an observer, "It is a suburb of New York."

In 1979, almost 20,000 Greek Americans living in Greece received social security checks monthly. "We live from America," a Skoura villager exclaimed. Every month a Sparta bank sent a truck to Skoura to cash the checks that local retirees received in the mail.

These Greek American retirees have helped considerably to raise the standard of living in rural Greece. American savings bought homes and brought modern appliances to areas that a decade earlier were just installing plumbing. But relatives, friends, and children won over by American ways and comforts were left "on the other side," and the feelings of loss are considerable. "We have lots of bread," said one local retiree in a bittersweet tone, "but we don't have the children."

Depopulation was plain for all to see. Two thousand people used to live in Skoura; in 1979 the number was five hundred. More than one hundred homes were unoccupied. What happened to the original promise to return? To raise children who spoke the pure Hellenic tongue? George Mariakis, a Greek journalist, writes: "After ten years they have made a certain amount and they think why not stay and make some more. Their hair turns white, their children have grown up, and before long it's hard to come back." Men who lived to comb gray hair and buy a piece of land near their beloved Mediterranean knew that it had been accomplished by way of America and it was a sobering awareness. It was a fact that they respected and they spoke well of their second home, of their children's country. Responding to a simple question with his own simple answer, an immigrant explains:

> You ask me which country I like better, United States or Greece. The only way to find out is to cut my heart and you'll see it is split, United States on one side, Greece on the other.

Throughout the postwar era the pressures to emigrate—low wages, unemployment, and political instability—continued to play on the Greek population, but two critical events significantly increased the number of Greeks coming to the United States: the lifting of national-origins quotas on American immigration and a military coup in Greece. Thus, between 1946 and 1960, the period before these changes, only 46,000 Greeks entered the United States. Over the next fifteen years, from 1961 to 1975, total reported immigration (ignoring undocumented aliens and Greek nationals arriving from other countries) climbed to 142,000.

On April 21, 1967, after a three year constitutional crisis and a bitter debate over the issue of Cypress, a military junta overthrew the constitutional monarchy in Greece. Led by Colonel George Papadoupolous and other junior officers, the junta suspended key articles of the constitution, closed the parliament, forbade political activities, and eventually sent King Constantine into exile.

George Pappas escaped the colonels to come to the United States in 1967 and found his new home a welcome change.

"I never saw such a country, such a city. You feel like a different person. You hear so much about the history and the people and now you are here. So much technology. So many people. I was happy to see so much. Never did I see a country with opportunities like here. Look at me. I came with no language, with nothing actually. I have difficulty asking for a meal, a hamburger, a hot dog, now I do okay. I am proud of this country.

"I come here on Saturday and on Tuesday I start to work in a machine shop. I find out you find the dollar here but you have to work a little bit hard to find the dollars. I working hard, save every penny. After six months I have the opportunity to put down $3,000 to buy a house. On the Independence Day for Americans, July 4, I move into my new house. Then I work hard to buy chairs and beds and spoons. My dream, you know, is coming true."

In 1967, the year George Pappas left Greece, the Tetis family also began considering emigration, especially after the tanks rolled through their beloved Athens. Like many Greek men, Thomas Tetis was accustomed to spending his nights in the local *Kaffeneia* (coffee house), discussing politics over syrupy coffee. Playing cards for small stakes with other men filled his hours with simple pleasures until one and two in the morning. It is a practice with old roots. In the *Symposium* Plato described a scene in which Socrates, Aristophanes, Alcibiades, and other Athenians drank, joked, and exchanged light conversation until the "crowing of the cocks." (As late as 1979, Athens had more clubs, taverns, cafes, and bars, relative to its population, than any other European city.)

When Thomas's twelve-year-old son Alex returned to school after the coup he learned that the colonels had decreed short hair cuts for all boys. So strict were the rules that street police carried shears, stopping an occasional long-hair to scissor an "X" on his head. Alex recalls the experience:

"My philosophy professor—in the first year of high school we study philosophy in Greece—was very strict about the hair. He sent me home because I avoided shaving my head so short. My mother came to the school and she said, 'He has sensitivity on his head, gets colds all the time, that's why he can't cut it.' This did not work. 'Maybe in grammar school this excuse will save his hair,' the professor said, 'not here.' So my hair went on the floor."

Except for her son's pride, Alex's mother, Hari Tetis, did not really mind the junta. It finally put an end to the ceaseless street demonstrations and sharp political debate. She considered it unseemly for Hellenes to fight and argue among themselves. The new regime brought quiet, discipline, and stability. It restored the order Hari was raised to respect.

At the center of that order stood the family. Imprecise in its scope—it included aunts, uncles, assorted cousins, and godparents at the least—it was very clear about two things: the preservation of family tradition with honor and its allegiance to the idea of marriage. Every member of a family carried responsibility for its honor, but Hari recalled how women were regarded as most vulnerable to allurements that might bring dishonor on the family. Throughout her teenage years male relatives closely watched and guarded her. Always she remembered the tradition that if a girl was dishonored it called for a retaliatory "honor crime," often the spilling of blood. Even in contemporary Greece persons acknowledging honor crimes are often acquitted in court.

When Hari married Thomas, neither considered marriage a personal, private affair. On the contrary, it represented a family arrangement brought about not by romantic serendipity, but by clear-eyed elders reckoning in family calculations. Parents sought "fitting" matches for their offspring and then engaged in hard bargaining to seal the marriage, whose development would revolve about the birth and upbringing of children. Female virtues included industriousness, hard work, self-sacrifice, and respect for male authority, but none denied that the size of a girl's dowry played a considerable role in her desirability.

By 1967, when Hari's own son reached his teens, this static world was changing, in part, under the influence of Greek TV, which transmitted the freer and looser styles of foreign cultures. The young absorbed these changes quickly, perhaps too quickly, Hari felt. Many men and women in urban Greece no longer made arranged marriages, which pleased her, but the looser morality and growing sexual freedom did not. Maybe then, Hari thought, the junta might prove to be a good thing. But still she and Thomas worked so hard and brought home too little money. What kind of future could they promise Alex?

Hari's brother Peter Nikos, already in America, felt the family should join him in New York. He kept writing Hari about the easy life in New York, the well-paying jobs, and all the comforts of America's higher living standard. Peter was also Alex's *koumparos*, or godfather. In Greece, *koumparos* is not an honorific status, it carries actual responsibility for the child's welfare. Peter's letters voiced concern about Alex's educational opportunities in Greece. Alex was just starting high school, but Nikos feared that after graduation Alex would not make one of Greece's only two major universities. "Bring him to New York," he wrote, "there is plenty opportunity to get an education here."

Thomas and Hari hesitated. Was it fair to interrupt Alex's Greek education? (It went without saying that if they did go to America it would be only for a period of time, definitely not for good.) But would he still keep to the Greek ways? Could Hellenism persist amidst America's freedom and modernism?

The revolution had produced dislocation; Alex's future seemed less secure than it once appeared to be. Thomas was earning a meager living. In the late sixties, America boasted a soaring economy and newly loosened immigration laws. The calculus of interests, hopes, fears, and strains favored emigration. The equation emerged as the "Tetis Five-Year Plan." They would go to the United States for five years, make some money, watch Alex enter a reputable university, leave him with his *koumparos* until he finished his schooling, and they would return to Athens and open a business. Peter Nikos sent them the required letter of invitation sponsoring their immigration under the fifth preference category reserved for brothers or sisters of American residents.

Alex Tetis, today a black-haired strapping 6'4" accountant with a winning smile, is studying for a master's degree in Business Administration. He remembers: "The first thing that struck me about New York was my uncle's wealth and the size of the city. He met us with this huge Buick Electra and drove us from the JFK airport past the Verrazano Bridge. Holy cow, this is something! He had this beautiful house in Bay Ridge, Brooklyn. It had color TV, stereo, everything. (He has just sold the house to return to Greece. My mother can't get over it. He brought us here. Now he goes back and we stay here.)"

The father, Thomas Tetis, recalls his arrival with a rueful smile. He was prepared "to take over the world and live easy." America was "the country with everything for an easy life. It turns out no. It turns out no."

In the first nine months Thomas shifted from job to job with spans of disheartening unemployment in between. Finally, after weeks of scouring the Greek language papers for work and having young Alex pick through the classified section in the English ones, he landed a job with a construction firm. Before he was hired the manager warned him about lateness and absences. Thomas told him not to be concerned; ten years later he talks with pride of never having taken a "sick day."

Tetis is in the broad tradition of his people. They came to New York prepared to work and prosper only to learn that its blessings were more mundane than the letters said, but that jobs, often hard, physically demanding jobs, were available. They filled menial occupations in machine and construction shops, greasy spoons, and restaurants, washing dishes, cleaning floors, and waiting on tables. The way up was slow and deliberate, often by becoming a cook, a manager, and eventually perhaps a restaurant owner. The blue-collar job was the foothold for the hard climb to success and respectability. But for their children they demand more.

In this they follow the experience of preceding generations of Greek immigrants. Those arriving earlier in the century often took menial jobs, but helped their children pursue college and professional educations. Their offspring rank high among second-generation groups in educational attainment. Only the children of Lithuanian, Japanese, and Russian immigrants earn higher median incomes, and few other groups show higher rates of self-employment or lower proportions in laboring jobs.

"My aunt's son quit college," Alex recalls, "to work on ships. Sometimes he made $700 a week. 'No no that doesn't work. Don't go there,' my mother says, 'be a gentleman, work in an office.'" Thomas tells his son: "Don't be a worker like me so you are bossed around. Be something. Don't get your hands and shirt black from work and sweat. Be a gentleman with education."

No less than others, the Greeks have their rivalries within the group, between those long settled and well assimilated, and others more recently arrived. But among the post-1965 immigrants a tight, sustaining community spirit exists. "I never thought it would be like this," Thomas Tetis says. "In Greece everybody is independent, a lot of arguments over politics. Everybody has their own opinion. Here they stick together. They help the new Greeks who come. We are a great community. I am proud."

Greek Cypriots, especially, found themselves welded together, stridently opposing American arms for Turkey during Richard Nixon's presidency. Many non-Cypriots joined this protest movement despite the fact that Cypriots and Greeks were not particularly close in Europe. Irish, Cubans, Mexicans, Croats, Jews, Poles and Puerto Ricans often transported their national loyalties to America. It was therefore not surprising that Greeks did so too. The distrust of Turkey that marked Greek attitudes in Europe remained sharp in New York. "You have to understand," says Thomas Tetis, "we were under their boots for four hundred years. We remember what they did; it cannot be forgotten. There is hate." The American Greek community launched an intense lobbying effort to pressure American policy into opposing Turkey, especially after the Cyprus issue erupted anew in the seventies. Even the elderly, who ignored American politics before, were moved to take pen in hand and sign petitions. Close to 250,000 telegrams flooded the White House demanding an embargo of Turkey.

In the 1970s when interest in ethnicity produced a new grammar of "identity," "consciousness," and "diversity," Greeks did not fail to make a case for equal attention to their own needs and problems. In the atmosphere of ethnic competitiveness that dominated New York's politics during these years the larger and more powerful ethnic groups were able to secure funding and support for their efforts; smaller groups often lost out in the shuffle. One mark of Greek power at the local level was the establishment of the Hellenic American Neighborhood Action Committee, largely out of government funds. Another was HANAC's ability to assemble a mostly Greek staff of experts to work in the community dealing with economic and social problems. HANAC also conducted a social and demographic survey of the city's Greeks. Aside from flashing the conventional rhetoric of ethnic assertiveness—"HANAC suggests that the best way of meeting . . . [people's] needs may, in fact, be by meeting ethnic needs and that pluralism is healthy for the society as a whole,"—the report proved to be a candid, sophisticated self appraisal, especially revealing on undocumented Greek aliens and on the special world of Greek senior citizens.

The single most powerful institution for Greek Americans remains the church. With 97 percent of the population belonging to the Orthodox Church in Greece it has not changed as much as religious institutions elsewhere. As late as 1976 the American Archdiocese wrote proudly: "The Greeks never knew nor ever approved the separation between Church and state." Combining Christian teachings and Hellenic culture, the church represents a seamless union of Greek ethnicity, supporting and fostering both ethnic and religious traditions. In the United States the church assumed a leading role in opening Greek schools, conducting courses in the language, history, and culture of the home country.

In his daily life and the privacy of his own home, a Greek observes his religion too. The sign of the cross, made from right to left with the thumb and three middle fingers together, is a common ritual. It helps a person resist evil, brings heavenly blessing, and signifies respect and gratitude. Many Greeks keep a private altar at home, burning incense and an oil lamp before an *ikonostasis* as a personal worship service. Family differences and disputes are referred to this altar. In times of stress and pain it serves as a font of faith and reassurance.

A Greek Orthodox service led by Bishop Theodosios of Ancona on a visit to
the United States. Behind him is Reverend Angelo Gavalas, pastor of the
Three Hierarchs Church in Brooklyn. (*Courtesy Three Hierarchs Church*)

Alexander Tetis notes some differences between the church in Greece
and America:

"In Greece when you saw the priest you bent down and kissed his hand.
He always had a beard. Here the church wants priests to fit in with everybody so they shave. I don't go to church often. When I was a school boy in
Greece everybody in the high school had to go to church every Saturday.
Only a doctor's note could excuse you. Here I go to church on major holidays only. I take communion. I fast when I am supposed to but I am not as
close to religion like in Greece. When my mother tells me to go to church
more often, I tell her when I get to be her age I'll worry about making peace

Archbishop Iakovos, Primate of the Greek Orthodox Church, celebrating the midnight service of Anastasis (Resurrection) on the Saturday night preceding Easter Sunday. This is the holiest period in the Greek Orthodox faith. (*Courtesy Greek Orthodox Archdiocese of North and South America*)

with my maker. Even she only goes every two or three weeks. We are not, like Catholics, required to go every week.

"Our communion is also different. Orthodox do not take it as often as Catholics. When you do take it, it is very serious. You fast. You eat no animal products for three days before, and two days before, nothing made with oil. The day before you eat only natural foods like fruit or bread. Before communion you make confession, usually at home before ikons; confession before a priest is less common. You pray for forgiveness. Also you ask close relatives to forgive you if you did something offensive to them. After communion you may not spit for twenty-four hours. Every bit of food that you start must be finished, all drinks must be completely emptied. Nothing is left over from a mouth that took communion.

"Religion is a very conscious part of a Greek's life. In Greece before the revolution the church was involved in all major political decisions and in the social life. Even here if a new business is opened the priest comes to bless it with prayers and water. At the beginning of the school year the priest blesses everyone with prayers and water. At every civic function comes the priest with his water. Archbishop Iakovos [primate of the Greek Orthodox Church in North and South America] is very powerful here. Greek businessmen, political leaders, lobby groups, community heads all advise and receive advice from the church."

Easter is the most important holiday on the Orthodox calendar. It is a three-day affair preceded by forty days of Lenten fasting and introspection. The last few days are spent in hectic preparation of sweet Easter breads and other foods. Good Friday is a powerfully rendered day of sorrow and fasting and midnight Saturday ushers in the celebration of Resurrection. The church stands dark with the priest holding the only illumination, an altar candle. After his blessing he calls out "Christ is risen." All join in singing these words and one by one congregants light the candles they are holding until light floods the church. These candles are then carried home with great care and reverence. Sunday climaxes the period with a feast. Families roast whole lambs and dye eggs red for their feast that follows. Says Alex Tetis: "It's good for the spirit; it makes you proud."

Beneath the church's apparent unity some dissension has developed over degrees of Americanization. What author Stephanos Zotos refers to as the "emergence of an American Orthodoxy . . . less dogmatic and more realistic" has resulted in a split with more formalist, tradition-oriented worshippers. This division was exacerbated when Archbishop Iakovos signaled his approval of ecumenicalism:

> As the youngest Church in America we lived in relative isolation yesterday.
> . . . Yesterday we were a Church of ceremony and pomp. Today we are a
> vital Church living not in the past but in the present.

The church in Greece criticized this ecumenical initiative. Consequently, some of the most recently-settled Greeks ignored the American church and established their own unaffiliated churches. In this diversity the Greeks paralleled the experience of Jews and other groups, with more recent settlers maintaining that they have brought a more authentic religious practice than that of their Americanized coreligionists. By 1980 more than ten such unaffiliated churches were holding services in Queens.

New York Greek culture produces an adequate, comforting social life wrapped in Hellenic custom. Weddings, baptisms, popular weekly dances, night club shows and vernacular movies sustain the community's old attachments. Cocktail parties remain a foreign institution. Long, exuberant dinners with friends are the chosen alternative. But the *kaffeneia* culture of the old country has changed in America, as friendly chatter and light gambling over thick black coffee became more intense and less amicable. In the few *kaffeneias* that exist in New York, gambling is the major attraction with a gambling-den atmosphere overtaking the old neighborhood club style.

The family remains the social fulcrum in the Greek community. The ancients created a goddess—*Hestia* (meaning hearth)—to guard over the family, and the tradition of family as a sacred relationship persists. "Only the family," the Reverend N.D. Patrinacos has written, "has sufficient powers to keep humanity separate from animality." Tradition equips it with authority to carry out these obligations. Parents receive respect, honor, and primary consideration. The pursuit of family welfare is placed far above the idea of individual fulfillment. The importance of the family chain and the reciprocal obligations of its members are passed on with folktales like the following:

> A husband and wife lived with their son and an old inlaw. After deciding one day that the old man was too much a burden in the crowded household they sent him to live in an old shack in the forest. Every other day the wife prepared some leftover food and sent it over in an old basket. One day they found their little son making a similar basket. They asked him what he was doing. He explained that he was preparing it for their old age, so he could send them their food. The next day the family brought the old man back, recognizing their callousness.

Daughters are especially protected, not usually allowed to date until age twenty or twenty-one. Males enjoy more freedom, but strong opposition awaits the son or daughter seeking permission to marry a non-Greek. This pattern is particularly strong among those from the small towns of Greece, but it is not uncommon in the working-class areas of Brooklyn and Queens. It has produced pockets of Greeks who are isolated and narrowly inner directed. Social functions, dances, and parties are frequently 97 to 99 percent Greek in attendance.

Greece is not a multi-ethnic society and the cultivation of diversity is not part of the heritage immigrants bring with them. As a Greek resident of Astoria put it, "We have no tensions with other groups. We just don't associate with them." Still, Greeks in New York City learn the prevailing attitudes. "Puerto Ricans," the Astoria resident allows, "have a reputation as the bad guy and that's their reputation in the community. Blacks also. In Greece there are no minority groups."

Whatever their social and economic background, Greeks take pride in knowing about their history. "In Greece," says Alex Tetis, "even workers know the elements of Greek history. Not like here where many people do not know the two sides of the American Civil War. There everybody knows about the Battle of Marathon. Especially if there is a grandfather in the house. He takes the children on his lap and teaches them everything he

Astoria and other Greek sections remain essentially village communities where neighbors stop to talk on the streets and patronize local stores. Residents claim with pride that it is easier to find Greek foods of every variety in Astoria than in Athens. (*Nick Manley*)

knows, every bit of history. My father sat with me often to tell me his experience, his lessons, his philosophy. Yes, we discuss these things."

The old Tetis family's five-year plan to stay in America for only a few years and return home has been revised. Thomas worked for a number of years but money did not accumulate as quickly as he had anticipated. When he did save up some money he used it as a down payment on a house in Bay Ridge. With the passing years he moved closer to a pension. While Hari kept reminding him of their original plan he became aware that he had new attachments. Hari was less ambivalent. "Hey," she would tell him, "we made our money. We can do something with our lives. In Greece we go out a lot, not like here just once in a while to Astoria. Let's go home."

Alex, their son, has also developed American ties. "To tell the truth I would like to go back, but it's a sort of dilemma. My opportunities are here. There is more use for my credentials here. But now that Greece is in the Common Market my education could be valuable there too. But our five-year plan has now grown to fifteen or eighteen years. My father will stay until he qualifies for social security. Then he will go back. He tells me: 'I want to retire, buy a house on one of the islands and have your mother cook me fried fish caught just that day.'

"Myself I am torn. My roots are here now. I write to my friends there. I read the Greek paper. I keep up to date on Greek affairs. But I am used to the pace of Manhattan and Brooklyn, not the Athens borough Anodafni. I am used to the comforts. Some do come with a plan and return exactly on time. No deviations. Another friend of mine left right away. He couldn't take it. He just said, 'I'm going home,' and left.

"If I go to Greece now I could be drafted. My mother is always telling me to pay the $700 so I could buy out my conscription. It used to be $300 and she keeps warning me that the price will go much higher. Once I buy it I can go back without any worries. Now if I were to go back I could be picked up on the streets and drafted. However, there are special times when you can go, like at the end of August, when if you go as part of a Greek social club or church group they won't take you."

New York Greeks live in their ethnic enclaves, still choosing their olive oil and feta cheese carefully and cooking with the best ingredients they can find. Every March 25, they treat New Yorkers to the spectacle of the *Evzones,* in which elite Greek palace guards with their skirtlike *foustamelas,* balloon-toed red slippers, and red skullcaps, march to celebrate independence from Turkey. They take small steps toward the new ways. No, Greek women are "not slaves here," a first-generation immigrant tells an observer. "That isn't true. I am the boss in my house, but I don't hit my wife with a club or anything like that. We are partners. I drive the car, I take care of the bills. I speak better English. But she's got rights. She wants to buy something, we talk about it."

Change, however, is the rule for all immigrants. Let Alex Tetis finish:

"I decided after all the years here that I will become a citizen. My mother also became a citizen, but not my father. I was very impressed when we were sworn in. The judge told us that his parents were immigrants. He said that we should not forget our old country. 'That's where you are from and that is your culture—apply it here. Go to visit, teach your experience to your children.' I felt that this judge was very understanding. I appreciated it.

"When we left my mother said, 'You are an American citizen now. If there is a fight with Greece with which side are you going to fight?' I told her and I meant it: 'Whoever is right.' "

11

Dr. Martinez's Daughter:

A Honduran in Manhattan

Honduras

The honey-colored woman walking along 53rd Street in Manhattan is not easily placed. Her race, her station in life, even her age are not obvious. An Oriental slant about her eyes contrasts with reddish-brown hair that is slightly frizzy, no doubt from repeated use of a straightening iron. Yet her bone structure and thin lips seem almost Caucasian. Slim as a teenager, she exudes the poise of a mature woman.

At 8:35 A.M., on a Friday morning, a casual observer might guess that she is heading towards one of the many midtown advertising offices. But her bright red mandarin jacket is too flamboyant for Madison Avenue. An actress? But theater people do not mix in morning rush-hour crowds. A self-confident air argues against her being either a secretary or a waitress, but she is not quite tense enough to be her own boss. The fine leather in her shoes contrasts with her skirt, which hangs unevenly, suggesting that she may have shortened it herself and then not taken the time to press out the wrinkles.

Gloria Martinez enters the subway at 51st Street and paces up and down the platform. Apparently oblivious to the press of the morning crowd around her, she walks back and forth, her eyes fastened on the littered cement floor. She stops several times, as though about to find something of interest on the toes of her shoes. Then she resumes walking. Of the people around her, no one pays the slightest attention.

282

The diverse mixture on the platform includes a great variety of individuals: expensively dressed men on their way to important offices who all but ignore young boys in too-large sneakers on their way to anyplace but school. Secretaries who have worked many hours to achieve an appearance of no effort in their grooming stand beside women in their early sixties who have clearly dressed quickly, perhaps because they no longer wake up with youthful expectation and instead have begun to see each new day as no more than one more day toward retirement and the end of this dreaded subway ride. The diversity eludes simple description just as does Gloria.

It has become a habit with Gloria ever since her arrival in the city in 1965 to pace subway platforms without pattern. She would not characterize it as a habit, however, insisting that she hates repetition of any kind. Boring. Terribly boring. Even having the same breakfast two days in succession annoys her, and she has purposefully varied small details of her life—the route to the subway or where she shops for food.

But living in New York requires living with the monotony of subway rides and waiting undetermined amounts of time between trains. The initial enthusiasm with which she once greeted each morning's adventure in the underground maze of tunnels that makes up the city's subway system has worn off and only the practical acceptance of this cheap, fast travel remains. Now the system takes her uptown at about the same time each day, but to avoid acknowledging a habit she varies the coach she enters. That way, at least, she does not see the same faces every day.

When Gloria leaves the subway at 167th Street, she walks two blocks to a building marked "Golden Years." Inside, strong disinfectant odors of freshly scrubbed floors mingle with the smells of food cooking. The one long ward through which Gloria passes contains only the barest necessities: iron beds, unshaded lightbulbs, worn linoleum. Only one or two of the residents in this home for the aged have made an effort to mark out his or her own space with something personal: a photograph or some flowers. The other tables along the beds contain the same impersonal items: a box of paper tissues, a drinking glass, a pad for ordering meals.

Gloria enters the office on the left and changes into a white lab coat to begin testing and labeling specimens sent in by the resident physician. In her working clothes, she is more easily placed—a Central American who is not the first in her family to attain professional status.

The path to this Bronx laboratory trails back more than three hundred years to Western Africa, where slavers kidnapped Gloria's ancestors and placed them on a ship bound for Barbados. A Caribbean storm wrecked the vessel near the French island, St. Vincent's, and the passengers who survived went there to live as free men and women. Already living on St. Vincent's were a tribe of Indians who called themselves "Garifuna" but, according to one anthropologist, Christopher Columbus renamed these eaters of human flesh "Caribales." That name changed again later to "Canibales," and the English word became cannibal. The Carib Indians were reportedly fierce warriors, a reputation they well deserved. They attacked not only the European explorers who came to the island but their more docile Indian neighbors as well. One tribe, the Arawaks, succumbed entirely to the Caribs—the men were reportedly all killed in battle and the women were taken as wives. Assimilation with the Caribs did not come easily for the Arawak women, who preserved their own language for centuries and used separate vocabularies among themselves. Men and women understood each other, but Arawak language was for women only.

The Africans mixed with the Caribs, resulting in what has become known to outsiders as "Black Caribs," but the people themselves continued to use the name "Garifuna." After the British took St. Vincent's from the French in the 1790s, the natives fought British rule violently. Even though the English brought superior weapons to the fray, they could not totally subdue the Carib Indians. Finally, in desperation, the British governor decided to rid the island permanently of this troublesome group, and he arranged to transfer all five thousand of the Black Caribs to the Spanish island, Roatán. Hostile natives made the deportation difficult and expensive, costing the British Empire, according to some historians, millions of dollars. After a few months in Roatán, the Garifuna went to the mainland where they settled, about 1800.

Gradually the Garifuna stopped warring and settled into agricultural occupations along the coast. To their language, which mixed the African and Indian vocabularies of their ancestors, they added a few words from French, English, and Spanish but well into the twentieth century their speech remained more African than anything else.* Garifuna rituals retained the mixed flavor of both continents too. On Christmas and New Year's eves, the Black Caribs performed a dance called the *jugugo*, with men and women dancing separately all night. The next day masked male dancers, wearing colorful knee pads, did the *yancunu*.

In 1980 there were reported to be about 12,000 Garifuna along the northeastern Honduran coast, where they work small farms or occasionally sign on for tours with merchant ships. Their isolation preserves their distinct quality. Most of their tiny houses lack electricity and telephones, so the people continue to live simply as they have done for decades.

---

* A ten-year-old boy, arriving illegally in New York City in 1977, claimed to be a refugee from Uganda, and Spanish interpreters, puzzled by his speech, believed him. Later a curious Honduran went to see him and recognized that he was a Garifuna. He was returned to his family in Honduras.

Like other parts of rural Honduras, education levels remain very low. Many people cannot write their names. The rough terrain makes travel from one section to another difficult and teachers are reluctant to take assignments in remote areas. A standing joke among urban Hondurans claims that rural teachers must be paid in cash because they cannot write to endorse checks. As late as the 1950s, teachers could present certificates of aptitude, rather than proof of education, to qualify for their jobs. Education was for the very few.

In one small Garifuna village along the northern coast of Honduras, Gonzalo Martinez, Gloria's father, was born in 1914, the last of fourteen children. His father died a few months after the boy's birth and his mother, a shrewd woman who could neither read nor write, resolved that this last son, if none of the others, would have an education. Her husband had left many acres of land under her control, land that he had accumulated gradually under a type of arrangement similar to the notion of squatter's rights. The government permitted people who could not afford to purchase land to use certain plots for indefinite periods of time so long as they cared for the land and made it productive. Areas available under this program were not the most fertile but hard work made them productive.

Gonzalo's mother ran the farm alone and, in the good years, put aside a few *lempiras* for her dream. Of the older children, one taught himself to read and write Spanish. The others remained almost as unschooled as their mother. Upon reaching adulthood, each married and settled in a small house near the large family home. The matriarch house was not only the largest of her brood, it was the biggest in the entire village. Size did not provide modern conveniences, however. Her kitchen had a rough stone fireplace for cooking, a few wooden shelves for storing old utensils, and a heavy, unpainted table. The house had no running water or inside plumbing. Yet Gonzalo's mother took pride in its size and comfort. It was all she needed, she said, that and her one educated son.

By the time Gonzalo was nine, he excelled at soccer and when he was fifteen one of the national teams that tour Honduras invited him to join. Remarkably, remote villages might lie outside the national communication systems but soccer scouts got through to search for new talent. When they spotted young Gonzalo, tall for his age and exceptionally well coordinated, they offered him a place on one of the minor squads. Later, at nineteen, he joined the country's top team.

Dark and good-looking, Gonzalo Martinez became a national star. He played well, and his Garifuna ancestry gave him a romantic flair. Reporters sought him out for interviews; young people hung around the locker room doors after games, waiting for a close look at him or for his autograph. One of his first trips outside the country took him to Costa Rica where the man-

Northeastern Honduras, where many Garifunas still live, has been one of the last areas of the country to modernize. (*Coutesy United Nations*)

A major exporter of produce, Honduras employs many men at unskilled, agricultural work. (*Courtesy United Nations, Jerry Frank*)

agers of the local soccer team watched him play. Within hours they offered him a full scholarship for medical school in Costa Rica if he would join their team.

Six years later, medical diploma in hand, Gonzalo Martinez returned to Honduras and applied for a research position with the country's largest, most prestigious firm. United Fruit's main business was exporting produce but it operated in many other areas of Honduran life, having become a national conglomerate with powerful political ties. La Lima, a small modern town near San Pedro, was its showplace, featuring wide streets, large parks, modern schools and well-equipped laboratories. Some of the company's researchers dealt only with agricultural problems—soil content and its change over time—but others investigated common medical problems, especially tuberculosis and intestinal infections. Dr. Gonzalo Martinez headed for the super modern city and one of its bacteriology labs.

For his first two years with United Fruit, Dr. Martinez lived in bachelor quarters provided by the company. Then in 1942 he met a young lab assistant, Elisa Brown, a Bay Islander whose family history could hardly have been more different from his. She came from another of Honduras's minorities.

More than 90 percent of Hondurans are mestizo, a mixture of Spanish and Indian. Another 6 percent are Indian. The Garifunas and the Bay Islanders, two tiny pockets of only a few thousands each, keep to themselves. Both of them arrived under very different circumstances. When the British Empire abolished slavery in the 1830s, thousands of people, both black and white, fled Jamaica and Grand Cayman to go to the Spanish countries of Central America. When they settled on the tiny islands off the Honduran coast, they retained their Protestant religion and their English language. Most engaged in fishing. Very conscious of their English roots, they projected a sense of superiority and self-importance to other Hondurans who viewed them as reserved and very controlled.

Dr. Martinez found Elisa Brown's poise and aloofness extremely attractive, a contrast to the earthiness he accepted in his mother and sisters. A few months after their first meeting, he proposed marriage. Her family tried to dissuade her, arguing that she could do much better than an uncultured Garifuna. But Elisa refused to listen. Even after her parents announced they would never attend a Roman Catholic wedding, she continued with her plans. In a prenuptial conference with a parish priest, she promised to bring up her children in their father's religion.

Gloria Elizabeth Martinez was born in 1943 followed in two years by a sister, and then, two years later, the two girls had a baby brother. Gloria's mother spoke English with her children during their first years but eventually she gave that up and worked to perfect her own Spanish. Gradually she erased almost every trace of her English heritage and completely immersed herself in her husband's culture.

The Martinez family lived in a comfortable, modern house in one of the best sections of Tela. Other United Fruit professionsal—doctors, lawyers, and business executives—were their neighbors and friends. Experiments in bacteriology gained Dr. Martinez a reputation as one of his country's outstanding scientists. He enjoyed the sort of popularity and success in medicine that he had won in soccer in his youth. And his marriage succeeded, too. Elisa was the perfect companion and mother.

Dr. Martinez's life abruptly changed in 1952 when Elisa died unexpectedly after minor surgery. He tried to curtail his grief in order to help his young children. He learned to braid the girls' hair and prepare their breakfasts, but his work suffered. Moreover he missed companionship. He decided to remarry.

"At first, before my father married Marta, she seemed like the perfect stepmother but afterwards she really changed. Became sullen and so resentful. I suppose I was at a difficult age—just twelve and my sister was ten. Our father wanted us closely chaperoned the way other middle-class families did—all parties with adults present and our clothes very proper. When he was a boy, he had never had any of that. I mean everybody married very young and there was a lot of freedom among the Garifunas, but he wanted something better for us. Marta wasn't interested. She bickered over petty things—the color of a belt or a hairstyle—and she gave little attention to our choice of friends or our use of leisure time. My father would get angry and they would argue about us. Finally he saw that it wouldn't work and he decided to put my sister and me in boarding school. The problem was his salary. It was big but it wouldn't pay for two boarding schools.

"Since then my father has told me that he regretted his decision. He even called it cruel, but at the time it seemed the right thing to do. Many people ask why my father didn't rely on his family for help. He had several sisters and his mother was still living. But the answer was pretty clear to anybody who knew his family. None of the sisters had an education and two of them never married although they had children. That's not too unusual in Honduras. Lots of people don't have real marriages—they just live together. It goes back to the lack of judges and priests. If nobody came through to marry you, you just lived together. My father wasn't ashamed of his family but he didn't want us going back to live with them. Of course my mother's family was no help at all—she had completely broken with them when she married my father.

"First he inquired about better paying jobs in the United States. When a colleague mentioned an opening in bacteriology in New York City, he applied. One phone call later, the job was his with a salary four times what he had been earning. He calculated carefully and decided that he could afford boarding schools for us in Honduras, support his own household in New York, and still pay for frequent trips back to visit us.

"He chose the schools carefully—Roman Catholic for my sister and me. Not so much for religious reasons, I think, but because he thought we would learn better manners there. For me, a convent run by the nuns of Maria Ausilia D'Ora, who were known for their strictness. My sister got a more fashionable school just outside the capital, Tegucigalpa. A lot of diplomats sent their daughters there. My brother was only six when our mother

died. I think he was most upset by it, so my father decided to let him stay
for a while with one of his married sisters and go to public school. My sister
and I were supposed to join him at our aunt's for the school holidays.

"The arrangement never really satisfied anybody. My father was unhappy with it and my sister begged to be transferred. I tried not to complain,
not because I liked the school but because I didn't want to cause my father
any worries. Everything he did was for us.

"The nuns at Maria Ausilia spoke very little—never showed any joy or
love. They made us undress under a sheet if other girls were in the room.
Tent dresses were issued to wear to showers. I never saw anyone without
clothes—including myself. The school didn't even have a full length mirror.

"My marks were very good. I obeyed all the rules. Got my assignments
in on time. No one had to scold me, but I wasn't happy. I had my own
private escape. Whenever I felt particularly lonely or uncomfortable, I'd take
my sketchpad and go out under a tree on the school grounds. Or maybe I'd
sit down with my secret 'writing' book. I'd write poems about confusion and
choice. And I dreamed about becoming an actress. Occasionally I got a part
in one of the school plays—that fed my dream to become an actress.

"Those five years passed in one blur for me. We had our holidays together and sometimes my father came back for a visit. Twice he invited us
to New York. Once in 1958 when the city was all decorated for Christmas.
I'll never forget it—seemed to have a million lights. Electricity was always
so expensive in Honduras. We had never seen anything like it. Another
time we came to New York in the summer and my father took us for long
walks to all the different neighborhoods. I felt like I was traveling around
the world just going from the Lower East Side to Little Italy and then to
Chinatown. Back in Honduras I tried to draw pictures of what New York
was like but it seemed so far away—foggy. I never got a clear picture.

"All of a sudden in 1960 my father wrote that he was coming back to
live in Honduras. I still don't know why he decided to return just then.
Maybe he thought my sister and I were older, more mature and Marta could
get along with us. Maybe he just missed us. He never explained.

"After he moved back to Tela, he wanted me to go to medical school
but I just couldn't accept the idea of studying that many years. I still had
that dream about becoming an actress but of course I didn't tell him. For a
few months I helped him in his lab. Then we compromised. I agreed to do
three years of medical technology so I'd be qualified to work in a lab.

"In Tegucigalpa, where the university was located, I had more freedom
than I have ever had in my life. The boarding house where I stayed was
supervised by two sisters—widows about sixty. They set strict curfews and
meal schedules but I had plenty of time to myself, too. And I loved it.
Made up for all that time in the convent. I met lots of people. One of

them, Carlos, was special. He was an engineering student and sometimes we spent evenings with his friends but other times we just enjoyed being together. He taught me to smoke and drive a panel truck. I loved trying those things—very risky, I thought. I guess the risk was most of the fun. I often had a nightmare that my father was standing on a street and I drove right by him in the blue panel truck, a cigarette in my mouth and Carlos snuggled up on the seat beside me. My father would have had a fit!

"My father's friends seemed to be everywhere. The city has only a couple of hundred thousand people and I had this feeling they all knew Dr. Martinez. It was really this fear of disappointing my father that led me to break up with Carlos. He was planning a student demonstration with some of his friends at the university. They wanted me to keep the panel truck nearby in case they needed to get out in a hurry. I didn't have to carry a sign or anything—just keep the truck ready. But I couldn't do it—kept thinking that I might get arrested or get my name in the newspapers. The other students were really angry with me but I wouldn't do it. After that Carlos and I stopped seeing each other.

"When I graduated I had to make a choice. I was twenty-one and I had two possibilities. I could either marry or I could go back and live in my father's house. There wasn't anybody around that I wanted for a husband and I couldn't face living in the same house with Marta. Getting an apartment on my own or sharing one with another girl was out of the question. My father wouldn't even consider it. I guess if I had had the same choice ten or twenty years earlier, I would probably have married just anybody in order to escape going back to my stepmother's house. But in 1964 I thought of another solution. I would go to New York. I knew a little about the city and I had met some of my father's friends. It seemed the perfect solution— I could always say I was going to study medical techniques. Ironically the most radical solution, emigration, was the easiest to explain!

"If I thought I had freedom at the university, New York was double freedom. My sister and I got our own apartment. That was exciting. And then the city was so big that I didn't even have a nightmare about meeting my father. Being Dr. Martinez's daughter in Honduras was a disadvantage. Everybody who knew him or had heard of him expected me to act in a certain way. In New York, nobody cared who my father was—except a few of his close friends, and they helped me. One of them gave me a job my second day here.

"I have never been thrilled by medical laboratories but I was excited the first day I went to work in New York. Even at the university in Tegucigalpa, the best equipped in Honduras, we didn't have the fancy x-ray machines like the ones I got to work with in this little lab. And there were always plenty of supplies—tissues, disposable trays, towels, things like that. In medical school we were always told to save, conserve, not use so much. And sometimes when the supply ran out, we had to wait weeks for replacements. In New York I could just go over to the closet—it was like a warehouse—always full.

"My sister and I stayed with friends for a couple of weeks and then we moved into a tiny apartment on the corner of Madison Avenue and 97th Street. The bath was so small we used to joke about leaving the door open so we had enough space to dry ourselves. Otherwise, we'd hit the wall trying to pull the towel back and forth across our backs. The apartment was small but we had two white telephones. I guess that was extravagant but telephones always held a special fascination for us. Both of us remembered those years in boarding school when a call from our father meant going down to the local town hall. That one room received all the communications for the entire town. And the reception was so bad! We used to have to shout two or three times before he understood. In New York in our apartment we could each take down a receiver and place a call to him in Tela. Then his voice would come through so clear—he seemed to be in the next room. We never got over it.

"The block where we lived was very mixed. Over on one side those rich Fifth Avenue women were shopping at Gristede's or sending their maids to buy things for them. But if you walked half a block the other direction, the barrio began. We shopped both sides. Used our convent English on the west and our Spanish on the east.

"Most of the Spanish-speaking people were Puerto Ricans and they laughed at some of our words. We don't really speak Garifuna but we use a few of the phrases. But we had a lot in common with the Puerto Ricans—food and music.

"There were a few American blacks too. I learned to call them blacks because that's what they wanted but I hate that word. I wish they would use Negro or African. That's what they are. I never felt close to them at all and they could take one look at me and know immediately that I wasn't one of them. If they heard Spanish, they assumed I was Puerto Rican. Of course white New Yorkers never knew where to place me either.

"We had this circle of friends—Spanish-speaking but from different countries. We went to poetry readings, plays, concerts or sometimes just sat around at a party and talked and ate and drank. No matter how poor we were, we always had food and wine. We were all very different but we felt close together—all aliens in a big city."

To an outsider, Gloria's friends lived poorly, in the worst neighborhoods of upper Manhattan and the Bronx. One among them, an agronomist by training and an actor by avocation, moved from job to job because he was an undocumented alien. He had come to New York as a tourist and, like thousands, had overstayed his visa. Taking whatever job he could find, he worked as an ambulance driver, liquor store clerk, and peddler. Anyone passing him vending his scarves and belts on 34th Street would have been surprised to learn that he could converse in Spanish, Portuguese, and English about the poor soils of his native Honduras or the difficulties of performing Pirandello. He paid no taxes but he demanded few services.

And there were many like this man. Nobody knew how many. As a group, they lived in an uneasy network of shifting contacts. During the week they lived their days as badly paid, unskilled workers or tradesmen, exploited by the shrewder among them who took advantage of their illegal status. At night or on the weekends, however, they might meet socially a leading singer from the Metropolitan Opera or their country's representative to the United Nations.

Gloria moved more easily than did some of her friends in this uneasy network because she had entered the country legally. Her papers were in perfect order. Yet because so many of her friends lacked her freedom and because she had become involved in their efforts to stay, she often forgot that her own status was different.

New York's freedom brought other responsibilities besides that of helping friends. For the first time in her life Gloria had to learn to manage her own finances, without the help of her father. And she learned to cook. In Honduras she had remained unfamiliar with kitchens because someone else had always prepared her meals: the convent, the boarding house, the family's cook. But in New York she learned to shop for familiar items and then prepare them for herself. It was an adaptability she recognized in many Central Americans, who called it living for the present and forgetting the future.

That meant spending all the dollars she earned and sometimes she spent more. When friends needed cash, they came to her because she earned more than most of them. Frequent trips back to Honduras cost money but she insisted on going twice a year. And large telephone bills came in each month.

In New York's world of Latins, Gloria and her sister made friends with a great variety of individuals. The experiences and language they shared dwarfed huge differences in education and aspiration. One of the men they met, a mechanic in a Bronx garage, began to date Gloria's sister. Within weeks he had introduced Gloria to his brother, a clerk in a novelty store. The Paz brothers' family were Garifunas still living in rural Honduras. They had probably never heard of Dr. Gonzalo Martinez. No one in their family had attended school for more than three years and most could not write their own names. Day laborers in the poor farmland on the northern coast, they earned less than a dollar a day.

But Roberto Paz and his brother had an ambition that the others lacked. In 1966 they entered the United States illegally (seamen on a ship, they simply left it in New York and did not return). Those first few months in the United States they took odd jobs for cash. Then someone offered to sell them identification papers, social security cards, and birth certificates. Papers and numbers supposedly came from Spanish-speaking people who had died or disappeared, but Roberto suspected some were stolen or forged. With the documents that he purchased for $150, Roberto applied for employment. Each month he sent money back to his parents, often $50 but sometimes more. The Paz brothers could hardly believe their luck. Their only hope was to remain in the United States and continue to earn dollars.

In the shifting kaleidoscope that mixed immigrants in New York, the differences between the Paz family and Dr. Martinez's daughters were obscured. Temporarily they were thrown together. In Honduras Gloria and her sister would never have met the Paz brothers except in circumstances that would have clearly marked their differences. In New York, they not only met. They married.

After her marriage to Roberto Paz in 1969 Gloria began to appreciate the wisdom of her father's warnings. He had flown to New York especially to dissuade the girls from the marriages. Arguing that they could do better than marry these less educated men, he urged the girls to postpone the weddings at least for a while. Even better, he suggested that they return to Honduras for a few months to think things over and get their lives in some perspective. He had worked so hard, he said, to get them out of the world of the uneducated. Why would they insist on going back? But the sisters remained firm and the weddings took place on schedule.

Four months later Gloria realized that she had married a childish, temperamental man who had little respect for her dreams and shared none of them. He ridiculed her table manners while she was embarrassed by his gulping down his food. Objecting to the way she spent money, the way she dressed, the friends she invited to their apartment, he made her life miserable. But at the same time she recognized all this, she also learned she was pregnant. She would not leave the father of her child.

"After our son was born in 1970, the marriage really went to pieces. Roberto would leave the apartment for days, sometimes weeks, and come back and tell me I couldn't do anything about it. He knew I wouldn't consider divorce and he bullied me, knowing how powerless I was in a foreign city. At home in Tela I could have called on my father or my brother to help work things out. In New York I had only my younger sister and she was having her own problems.

"I went back to work when my son was only three months old and that caused more problems. Roberto wanted me to work—we needed the money—but he also wanted me to do all the household things that I did when I wasn't working. He pouted when the laundry wasn't done or when one of his favorite beers wasn't in the refrigerator.

"But everyone admired Roberto's ambition. He moved up very fast. From the clerk's job, he moved to section chief and then manager of the whole store. And he always kept up his night classes—no matter whether he was living with me or someplace else. First, he got a high school equivalency and then he enrolled in Bronx Community College.

"We fought a lot over money. No matter how well he did, I always earned more. Lab technicians make more than people in his kind of sales. And we needed both pay checks. One thing that used to make me mad was the amount that he sent back to his parents. Fifty or one hundred dollars a month—often my money. Of course my father didn't need money, but I didn't see why I should have to work so hard to send money to Roberto's family.

"When things got really bad, I escaped the same way I did at the convent. I bought a cheap easel and set it up in one corner of my kitchen. The room was so small I had to take out the table, but I managed. Whenever I wanted to shut everything out—tired feet, a crying baby, or Roberto—I'd pick up a paint brush and try to remember what it was like in Honduras. That's when I began to write songs. "Honduras Bonita" and "Para Que Odiarte" are my two favorites. And I still dreamed about becoming an actress.

"It's funny because I could have left New York anytime I wanted to. My father would have sent me the money to go back to Tela. But with all the problems I have had in New York, I'm still not ready to leave. There's such variety here and so much opportunity to try different things. So when I was writing songs about Honduras or painting pictures of the countryside, it didn't mean I wanted to go there.

"When things got really bad between Roberto and me, I filed for divorce. I had tried to avoid it at first. I didn't want people back in Honduras saying, 'Martinez's daughter is divorced.' But in 1975 I signed the papers. I guess you could say that is one of the things about me that New York has changed. In Honduras I never would have considered divorce. In New York I not only got the divorce, I talk about it. When I go back to visit my father and people ask about my son's father, I say, 'Oh we are divorced.' Even my son talks about it.

"The problem is not really the church. I was raised a Catholic but I am not religious. The nuns at school tried to make us religious but they failed. I started to go to confession because I liked one particular priest but after he left, I never went back. In New York I have never gone to mass even once. But I pray every day. You know the Garifunas put great faith in their dead

ancestors—think they can intervene in every day matters. Well I don't pray
to dead ancestors but I pray for protection. Safety. Behind all my love of
New York, I still think of it as a kind of jungle where lots of people get
hurt. In bad neighborhoods where most of my friends live, more things
happen and people have no place to turn for help. No insurance against
thefts. Most of them don't have their families—mothers, aunts, and sisters—
to help out with the children. When the children get sick, it means we have
to take off work to care for them. Raising a child alone is very difficult in a
big city.

"Well, after my divorce I couldn't manage. The city seemed so full of
problems. I felt completely alone and responsible for my son's safety. Maybe
it was cruel but it seemed the only thing to do at the time. I sent him back
to live with my father. My brother, also a doctor, lives near my father.
Between them, I knew my son would have a strict upbringing. Safe.

"A few hours of overtime each month help me earn extra dollars for my
son's expenses. My father could take care of it but I want to do it myself.
My son and I talk every week about his school friends, his music lessons,
his soccer games. He's already a good soccer player and I like to keep up
with his games. Even when my telephone bills cost more than my groceries,
I keep calling. I don't want him to grow apart from me the way we did from
my father.

"Just last month I began to realize that this arrangement won't work
much longer. I'll have to bring him to New York to live with me. I don't
know how I'll manage, especially now that I'm finally getting the chance to
do some acting.

"A New York Theater Ensemble production this summer will mean rehearsals for me every night until midnight or after. But I want to do the
show. Leroi Jones wrote it—a history of slavery in America. It's called *The
Motion of History*. The subject interests me as an outsider, not a participant.
Jones chose me for the part over lots of other people. Somebody said 700
people auditioned for 25 roles. I think I got the part because he thought I
looked African. Certainly not for my speaking ability. It's my first English
play—I've done lots of Spanish theater but no English. I have to do several
different roles. That's funny when you think about it because I can really
change my appearance to look African, Indian, Spanish. Whatever I want.
In one scene I am a slave being led out of Maryland by Harriet Tubman.
For that part I put on kerchief and talk southern. Then in the last act I have
a big speech. I put on my dashiki and talk Third World, 1970s style. Of
course I had never heard of Harriet Tubman or most of the other people
mentioned in the play. I've learned a lot of history. And I can change easily
from one part to another. If I put on a white shirt, you'd think I was Negro,
but in beige I can pass for Indian. Some people even wonder if I'm part

A professional Spanish theater company, the Repertorio Espanol was established in New York City in 1968. It performs contemporary Latin American
plays and Spanish classics, as well as other plays in Spanish translation. Here
three members of the company perform Lorca's *La Casa de Bernarda Alba*.
(*Courtesy Repertorio Espanol, Gerry Goldstein*)

Chinese. In red, you can't place me at all. That's an advantage in this
play—I think that's why I got chosen. Anyway it's a wonderful opportunity
for me."

At 5 P.M. on a Friday in May 1977, Gloria Martinez takes off her white lab
coat and puts on her red mandarin jacket, checks her makeup and smooths
down her hair, which in spite of repeated exposure to a straightening iron
tries to curl up and kink around her face. She picks up the large straw bag
and walks towards the subway entrance.

As she heads towards Greenwich Village, in a different train from the
one she took this morning, Gloria reviews details for the concert she will
give this evening at Greenwich House. The group that will be performing
the songs she wrote is the best Spanish group she could find. She has insisted that they be used even though their fees are high. Her share of the

evening, including rental of the hall, musicians, and refreshments, will come to $325, more than she takes home in two weeks of work. But she did not hesitate to join with her Latin friends to sponsor this evening of original music. A talent scout or a reviewer might like one of the pieces and lead them to a publisher or a recording studio.

When Gloria arrives at Greenwich House on Barrow Street, only two musicians are on stage setting up their drums. She begins arranging the table at the back of the hall so refreshments can be served at intermission. The building's super keeps insisting that food belongs at the end of the concert but Gloria remains firm.

At 7:30 P.M., when the concert is scheduled to start, the hall is empty. A few of the musicians' friends wander in and out. Slowly, gradually, after awhile, the room begins to fill. First the non-Latins, who are the only ones to come less than thirty minutes late. The others, according to a non-spoken rule, adhere to a strict distinction between Latin and non-Latin events. The latter demands punctual attendance at the announced hour. The former uses a different timetable. Everyone knows where this evening falls.

At 8:15 P.M. the music starts. Gloria settles back in the last row to listen and to watch the audience for reactions. Nervous and tired from a day's work and from hours of anticipation and preparation, she appears cool and poised. The nuns at Maria Ausilia D'Ora would be pleased. If asked, Gloria Martinez (she never used her husband's name) will answer that this evening does not fit into any particular scheme for a developing career. She lives for the present. She adapts.

Even the next few years remain unplotted. Her son will come to live with her and then perhaps they will go to Spain so that she can study Spanish literature or theater. Changing countries helps develop talents, she thinks. But in the end, no one operates completely outside his own country. Because she believes this so strongly, Gloria is sure she will return one day to Honduras to open a theater or do research into her Garifuna roots.

She leans forward in her chair to listen to the words of her song: "I would rather be your lover. . . ." The hall is full of Gloria's friends, some of whom have known her for fifteen years. Yet none of them knows quite what Dr. Martinez's daughter is thinking.

Epilogue

Even before these stories could be published, they had changed. Rosa Marcos Guerro, the *chola* from Peru, became an American citizen after having refused to do so for years. Her reason was simple: she could not get documents for her mother to leave the country and then return unless she, Rosa, became an American citizen. Il Soo Kim, the Korean airlines executive, left New York for an attractive new position in Saudi Arabia. Kim does not think of the move as permanent. He expects to return to New York within a few years. Bertha, the young undocumented alien from Ireland, was refused reentry when she tried to come back to New York after a vacation in Cork. She is working in Ireland. Vito Calabrese, the Italian oboist who wanted to live "a little bit in Italy, a little bit in New York," cancelled plans for a summer in Tuscany, saying: "My life is more in New York now." José Lopez Rivera, the Spaniard lacking documents to remain legally in the United States, continues to pay a lawyer to help him get a green card. Alex Bushinsky, from Russia, has started his own computer firm and Mrs. Rosalyn Morris, the Jamaican who said she was content with her rented apartment in Brooklyn, has bought some land in Florida.

Mixing new hopes with old dreams, they represent the newest seekers after the old American adventure: a better life.

Appendix
Tables and Figures

Table 1. Chronological Outline of American Immigration Policy

1788 U.S. Constitution adopted, restricts the presidency to native-born Americans and gives Congress the power to establish a uniform rule on naturalization.

1790 First U.S. census counts show a population of 3,227,000, of whom about 64 percent are British in origin, 7 percent German, 18 percent black slaves and 2 percent free blacks.

1819 For the first time, the U.S. government requires ship captains to supply a list of all passengers, indicating the age, sex, and occupation of each passenger, "the country to which they severally belonged," and the number that died on the voyage.

1875 The first federal restriction on immigration imposed, prohibiting prostitutes and convicts.

1882 Congress curbs Chinese immigration and excludes convicts, lunatics, idiots, and persons likely to become public charges. A head tax on each immigrant is also imposed.

1885 Legislation is passed prohibiting the admission of contract laborers.

1891 Ellis Island opens as an immigrant processing center. The list of excluded immigrants is expanded to include polygamists and persons suffering from loathsome or dangerously contagious diseases.

1903 List of excluded immigrants is further expanded to include anarchists and persons who believe in or advocate the overthrow by force or violence of the government of the United States.

1907 The head tax on immigrants is increased. Added to the excluded list are those with physical or mental defects that may affect their ability to earn a living, those with tuberculosis, and children unaccompanied by parents.

Gentlemen's agreement between the United States and Japan restricts Japanese immigration.

1917 Congress requires literacy in some language of those immigrants over sixteen years of age, except in cases of religious persecution. Virtually all immigration from Asia is banned.

1921 Quotas are established limiting the number of immigrants of each nationality to 3 percent of the number of foreign-born persons of that nationality living in the United States in 1910. Limit on European immigration set at about 350,000.

1924 National-Origins Law (Johnson-Reed Act) sets temporary annual quotas at 2 percent of nationality's U.S. population, as determined in 1890 census, and sets an upper limit of 150,000 upon immigration in any one year from non-Western Hemisphere countries.

1929 Quotas of 1924 permanently set, apportioning immigration slots according to each nationality's proportion of the total U.S. population as determined in the 1920 census.

1939 Congress defeats refugee bill to rescue 20,000 children from Nazi Germany despite willingness of American families to sponsor them, on the grounds that the children would exceed the German quota.

1942 Bilateral agreements signed with Mexico, British Honduras, Barbados, and Jamaica for entry of temporary foreign laborers to work in the United States under the so-called *bracero* program.

1943 Chinese-Exclusion Laws repealed.

1946 Congress passes War Brides Act, facilitating immigration of foreign-born wives, husbands, and children of U.S. armed forces personnel.

1948 Congress passes Displaced Persons Act (amended in 1950), enabling 400,000 refugees to enter the United States.

1950 Internal Security Act increases grounds for exclusion and deportation of subversives; aliens required to report their addresses annually.

1952 Immigration and Nationality Act of 1952 (McCarran-Walter Act):
—reaffirms national-origins system, giving each nation a quota equal to its proportion of the U.S. population in 1920;
—limits immigration from Eastern Hemisphere to about 150,000; immigration from Western Hemisphere remains unrestricted;
—establishes preferences for skilled workers and relatives of U.S. citizens; and tightens security and screening standards and procedures.

1953 Refugee Relief Act admits over 200,000 refugees outside existing quotas.

1957 Refugee-Escapee Act defines refugee-escapee as any alien who has fled from a Communist country or from the Middle East because of persecution or the fear of persecution on account of race, religion, or political origin.

1960 Cuban refugee program established.

1964 United States ends *bracero* program.

1965 Immigration and Nationality Act amendment of 1965:
—abolishes the national-origins system;
—establishes an annual ceiling of 170,000 for the Eastern Hemisphere, with a 20,000 per-country limit; immigrant visas distributed according to a seven-category preference system, favoring close relatives of U.S. citizens and permanent resident aliens, those with needed occupational skills, and refugees;
—establishes an annual ceiling of 120,000 for the Western Hemisphere, with no preference system or per-country limit.

1975 Indochinese Refugee Resettlement Program begins.

1976 Immigration and Nationality Act amendment of 1976:
—extends the 20,000 per-country limit and the seven-category preference system to the Western Hemisphere;
—maintains the separate annual ceilings of 170,000 for the Western Hemisphere.

1978 Immigration and Nationality Act amendments of 1978 combine the ceilings for both hemispheres into a worldwide total of 290,000, with the same seven-category preference system and 20,000 per-country limit uniformly applied.
Congress passes law excluding and deporting Nazi persecutors.

1980 Refugee Act establishes clear criteria and procedures for admission of refugees.

Table 2. Immigration to the United States, 1820–1980

Year	Number of Persons	Year	Number of Persons	Year	Number of Persons	Year	Number of Persons
1820–1980	49,998,965	1861–1870	2,314,824	1901–1910	8,795,386	1941–1950	1,035,039
1820	8,385	1861	91,918	1901	487,918	1941	51,776
1821–1830	143,439	1862	91,985	1902	648,743	1942	28,781
1821	9,127	1863	176,282	1903	857,046	1943	23,725
1822	6,911	1864	193,418	1904	812,870	1944	28,551
1823	6,354	1865	248,120	1905	1,026,499	1945	38,119
1824	7,912	1866	318,568	1906	1,100,735	1946	108,721
1825	10,199	1867	315,722	1907	1,285,349	1947	147,292
1826	10,837	1868	138,840	1908	782,870	1948	170,570
1827	18,875	1869	352,768	1909	751,786	1949	188,317
1828	27,382	1870	387,203	1910	1,041,570	1950	249,187
1829	22,520	1871–1880	2,812,191	1911–1920	5,735,811	1951–1960	2,515,479
1830	23,322	1871	321,350	1911	878,587	1951	205,717
1831–1840	599,125	1872	404,806	1912	838,172	1952	265,520
1831	22,633	1873	459,803	1913	1,197,892	1953	170,434
1832	60,482	1874	313,339	1914	1,218,480	1954	208,177
1833	58,640	1875	227,498	1915	326,700	1955	237,790
1834	65,365	1876	169,986	1916	298,826	1956	321,625
1835	45,374	1877	141,857	1917	295,403	1957	326,867
1836	76,242	1878	138,469	1918	110,618	1958	253,265
1837	79,340	1879	177,826	1919	141,132	1959	260,686
1838	38,914	1880	457,257	1920	430,001	1960	265,398
1839	68,069	1881–1890	5,246,613	1921–1930	4,107,209	1961–1970	3,321,677
1840	84,066	1881	669,431	1921	805,228	1961	271,344
1841–1850	1,713,251	1882	788,992	1922	309,556	1962	283,763
1841	80,289	1883	603,322	1923	522,919	1963	306,260
1842	104,565	1884	518,592	1924	706,896	1964	292,248
1843	52,496	1885	395,346	1925	294,314	1965	296,697
1844	78,615						
1845	114,371						

Year	Number	Year	Number	Year	Number	Year	Number
1846	154,416	1886	334,203	1926	304,488	1966	323,040
1847	234,968	1887	490,109	1927	335,175	1967	361,972
1848	226,527	1888	546,889	1928	307,255	1968	454,448
1849	297,024	1889	444,427	1929	279,678	1969	358,579
1850	369,980	1890	455,302	1930	241,700	1970	373,326
1851–1860	2,598,214	1891–1900	3,687,564	1931–1940	528,431	1971–1980	4,836,327
1851	379,466	1891	560,319	1931	97,139	1971	370,478
1852	371,603	1892	579,663	1932	35,576	1972	384,685
1853	368,645	1893	439,730	1933	23,068	1973	400,063
1854	427,833	1894	285,631	1934	29,470	1974	394,861
1855	200,877	1895	258,536	1935	34,956	1975	386,194
1856	200,436	1896	343,267	1936	36,329	1976	398,613
1857	251,306	1897	230,832	1937	50,244	1976, TQ	103,676
1858	123,126	1898	229,299	1938	67,895	1977	462,315
1859	121,282	1899	311,715	1939	82,998	1978	601,442
1860	153,640	1900	448,572	1940	70,756	1979	526,000
						1980	808,000

SOURCE: U.S. Immigration and Naturalization Service, *1976 Annual Report*, p. 39, *as reprinted in* U.S. Congress, Senate, Committee on the Judiciary, Select Commission on Immigration and Refugee Policy, *U.S. Immigration Law and Policy: 1952–1979*, 96th Cong., 1st sess., May, 1979. For 1977–1980, unpublished INS data and projections of INA data. From 1820 to 1867, figures represent alien passenger arrivals; from 1868 through 1891 and 1895 through 1897, immigrant alien arrivals; from 1892 through 1894 and 1898 to the present time, immigrant aliens admitted. Since July 1, 1868 the data is for fiscal years ending June 30. Prior to fiscal year 1869, the periods covered are as follows: from 1820–1831 and 1843–1849, the years ended on September 30—(1843 covers 9 months); from 1832–1842 and 1850–1867, the years ended on December 31—(1832 and 1850 each cover 15 months). For 1868, the period ended on June 30 and covers 6 months. The transition quarter (TQ) for 1976 covers the 3-month period July–September, 1976.

Table 3. Comparison of Number of Immigrants Admitted, Fiscal Years 1978 and 1965

Country of birth	Number		Percent change
	1978	1965	
All countries	601,442	296,697	+202.8%
Europe	73,198	113,424	−35.5
Austria	467	1,680	−72.2
Belgium	439	1,005	−56.3
Czechoslovakia	744	1,894	−60.7
Denmark	409	1,384	−70.4
France	1,844	4,039	−54.3
Germany	6,739	24,045	−72.0
Greece	7,035	3,002	+134.3
Hungary	941	1,574	−40.2
Ireland	1,180	5,463	−78.4
Italy	7,415	10,821	−31.5
Netherlands	1,153	3,085	−62.6
Norway	423	2,256	−81.3
Poland	5,050	8,465	−40.3
Portugal	10,445	2,005	+420.9
Romania	2,037	1,644	
Spain	2,297	2,200	+4.4
Sweden	638	2,411	−73.5
Switzerland	706	1,984	−64.4
U.S.S.R.	5,161	1,853	+178.5
United Kingdom	14,245	27,358	−47.9
Yugoslavia	2,621	2,818	−7.0
Other Europe	1,209	2,438	−50.4
Asia	249,776	20,683	+1,107.6
China and Taiwan	21,315	4,057	+425.4
Hong Kong	5,158	712	+624.4
India	20,753	582	+3,465.8
Iran	5,861	804	+629.0
Japan	4,010	3,180	+26.1
Korea	29,288	2,165	+1,252.8
Pakistan	3,876	187	+1,972.7
Philippines	37,216	3,130	+1,089.0
Thailand	3,574	214	+94.0
Vietnam	88,543	226	+39,078.3
Other Asia	30,182	5,426	+456.2
North America	220,778	126,729	+74.2
Canada	16,863	38,327	−56.0
Mexico	92,367	37,969	+143.3
West Indies	91,361	37,683	+143.1
Cuba	29,754	19,760	+50.6
Dominican Republic	19,458	9,504	+104.7
Haiti	6,470	3,609	+79.3
Jamaica	19,265	1,837	+928.7
Trinidad and Tobago	5,973	435	+1,131.5
Other West Indies	10,441	2,888	+337.2
Other North America	20,187	12,850	+57.1
South America	41,764	30,962	+34.9
Argentina	3,732	6,124	−39.1
Brazil	1,923	2,869	−33.0
Colombia	11,032	10,885	+1.4
Other South America	25,077	11,084	+126.2
Africa	11,524	3,383	+240.6
Oceania	4,402	1,512	+191.1
Other countries	—	4	—

SOURCE: U.S. Immigration and Naturalization Service, *Statistical Yearbook, 1978*, p. 2.

Table 4. Countries with the Greatest Number of Active Immigrant Visa Applicants, January 1, 1980, by Preference Category [a]

	1st	2nd	3rd	4th	5th	6th	Nonpreference	Total
Mexico	2,412	59,207	19	11,059	26,904	1,556	173,681	274,838
Philippines	912	32,914	32,266	14,830	165,776	3,138	1,111	250,947
China	431	10,538	633	9,692	81,093	3,469	5,681	111,537
Korea	19	4,008	198	144	67,953	1,174	835	74,331
Dominican Republic	217	16,491	.....	186	4,677	67	13,419	35,057
India	7	2,480	4,798	69	21,109	684	2,553	31,700
Vietnam	32	6,232	11	74	13,980	63	245	20,637
Colombia	38	3,856	9	149	4,895	343	9,834	19,124
Cuba	427	1,904	.....	2,243	11,751	1	838	17,164
Jamaica	249	5,594	6	577	3,892	346	6,436	17,100
Italy	63	917	30	970	11,044	330	522	13,876
Canada	252	532	496	741	3,151	876	6,097	12,145
Other countries	1,266	31,414	2,484	4,884	91,531	18,562	59,457	209,590
TOTAL	6,325	176,087	40,950	45,618	507,756	30,609	280,709	1,088,054
TOTAL APPLICATIONS, BY PREFERENCE, AS OF JANUARY 1, 1979, WERE:	5,909	145,881	51,397	33,487	285,783	28,217	363,691	914,365

SOURCE: U.S. Select Commission on Immigration and Refugee Policy, *U.S. Immigration Policy and the National Interest* (Washington, D.C., 1981), p. 146, as computed from unpublished data released by U.S. Department of State, Visa Office.

[a] 1st Preference: Unmarried sons and daughters, 21 years of age or older, of U.S. citizens (20 percent).

2nd Preference: Husbands, wives, and unmarried sons and daughters of permanent resident aliens (20 percent).

3rd Preference: Professionals and persons of exceptional ability in the sciences and arts, who will benefit the economy, culture, or welfare of the U.S. (10 percent).

4th Preference: Married children of U.S. citizens (10 percent).

5th Preference: Brothers and sisters of U.S. citizens 21 years of age or older (24 percent).

6th Preference: Skilled or unskilled workers needed in the U.S. labor market, who will not displace citizens or legal alien workers (10 percent).

7th Preference: Refugees from Communist or Communist-dominated countries, the Middle East, or areas struck by national disasters (6 percent).

Any visas not needed for the seven preferences are available for other potential immigrants.

In recent years, the United States has accepted about 500,000 immigrants and refugees each year. Most enter under one of the seven preference categories under a fixed numerical limit of 290,000 per year. The others are exempt from the limits, and they include husbands, wives, and minor children of U.S. citizens the parents of adult U.S. citizens, and refugees admitted under the parole authority of the attorney general.

Table 5. Applicants for Refugee Status, First Six Months of Fiscal Year, 1981

Country of Birth	Applications for Fiscal Year 1981			Country of Birth	Applications for Fiscal Year 1981		
	Filed	Approved	Denied		Filed	Approved	Denied
Afghanistan	3,587	2,180	140	Israel	235	23	195
Albania	63	22	0	Jordan	8	2	0
Angola	68	64	4	Kuwait	4	0	0
Bangladesh	2	0	0	Laos	13,980	13,476	29
Bolivia	9	0	0	Latvia	40	41	0
Brazil	1	1	0	Lebanon	181	175	0
Bulgaria	96	44	14	Libya	4	3	1
Burma	9	0	0	Lithuania	6	6	0
Cambodia	11,612	11,058	569	Macau	24	24	2
Cameroon	1	0	0	Malawi	2	0	1
Chile	8	0	0	Malaysia	1	0	1
China	1,383	261	613	Morocco	3	0	0
Congo	2	0	2	Mozambique	6	2	4
Cuba	1,408	1,196	9	Namibia	3	3	0
Cyprus	14	14	0	Nicaragua	11	0	0
Czechoslovakia	1,037	552	91	Nigeria	1	0	0
El Salvador	17	0	0	Pakistan	20	0	4
Estonia	5	5	0	Palestine	11	11	0
Ethiopia	1,483	938	165	Philippines	1	0	1
Finland	1	0	0	Poland	995	254	77
France	9	9	0	Romania	2,241	1,567	71
Ghana	15	0	1	Singapore	6	0	0
Greece	219	214	0	Somalia	4	0	1
Guinea	1	0	0	South Africa	4	3	1
Hong Kong	588	531	72	Spain	26	21	0
Hungary	478	192	71	Sri Lanka	1	0	0
India	4	1	0	Sudan	11	4	3
Indonesia	22	1	11	Syrian Arab Republic	363	301	2
Iran	575	307	8	Thailand	1	0	1
Iraq	1,470	898	39	Tunisia	1	0	1

Table 5. (continued)

Country of Birth	Applications for Fiscal Year 1981		
	Filed	Approved	Denied
Turkey	351	345	2
UAR (Egypt)	62	55	2
Uganda	2	0	1
Uruguay	3	0	0
USSR	7,081	6,111	49
Vietnam	31,143	29,887	1,269
Yugoslavia	106	19	34
Zaire	4	3	0

SOURCE: Refugee Resettlement Information Exchange Project, *Refugee Reports*, (biweekly publication), American Public Welfare Association, Washington, D.C., May 1, 1981, p. 8.

Figure 1. The Five Countries with Highest Levels of Immigration, by Decade, 1821–1978[a]

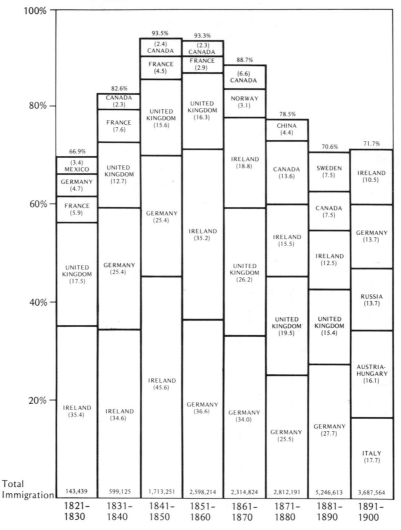

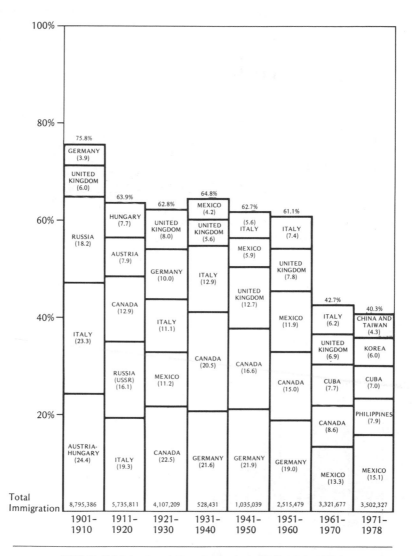

	1901–1910	1911–1920	1921–1930	1931–1940	1941–1950	1951–1960	1961–1970	1971–1978
	75.8%	63.9%	62.8%	64.8%	62.7%	61.1%	42.7%	40.3%
	GERMANY (3.9)	HUNGARY (7.7)	UNITED KINGDOM (8.0)	MEXICO (4.2)	(5.6) ITALY	ITALY (7.4)	ITALY (6.2)	CHINA AND TAIWAN (4.3)
	UNITED KINGDOM (6.0)	AUSTRIA (7.9)	UNITED KINGDOM (5.6)	MEXICO (5.9)	UNITED KINGDOM (7.8)	UNITED KINGDOM (6.9)	KOREA (6.0)
	RUSSIA (18.2)	GERMANY (10.0)	ITALY (12.9)	UNITED KINGDOM (12.7)	MEXICO (11.9)	CUBA (7.7)	CUBA (7.0)
	CANADA (12.9)	ITALY (11.1)	MEXICO (13.3)	CANADA (16.6)	CANADA (15.0)	CANADA (8.6)	PHILIPPINES (7.9)
	ITALY (23.3)	CANADA (20.5)				MEXICO (13.3)	MEXICO (15.1)
	RUSSIA (USSR) (16.1)	MEXICO (11.2)					
	AUSTRIA-HUNGARY (24.4)	ITALY (19.3)	CANADA (22.5)	GERMANY (21.6)	GERMANY (21.9)	GERMANY (19.0)		
Total Immigration	8,795,386	5,735,811	4,107,209	528,431	1,035,039	2,515,479	3,321,677	3,502,327

SOURCE: U.S. Select Commission on Immigration and Refugee Policy, *U.S. Immigration Policy and the National Interest* (Washington, D.C., 1981), p. 96.

[a]Reporting of immigration via U.S. land borders with Mexico and Canada was not fully established until 1908.

Figure 2. Average Total Annual Immigration by Decade, 1871–1979

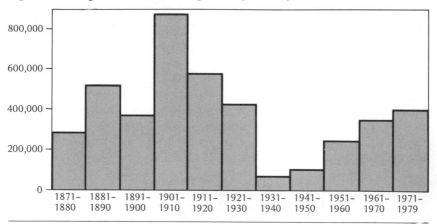

SOURCE: "Immigrants: How Many?" U.S. Select Commission on Immigration and Refugee Policy, *U.S. Immigration Policy and the National Interest* (Washington, D.C., 1981), p. 92.

Figure 3. Annual Immigration as a Percentage of Population Size

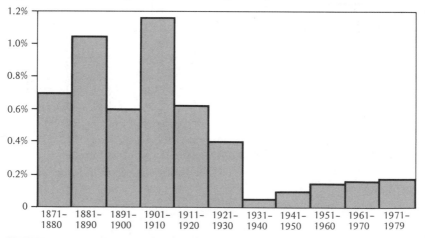

SOURCE: "Immigrants: How Many?" U.S. Select Commission on Immigration and Refugee Policy, *U.S. Immigration Policy and the National Interest* (Washington, D.C., 1981), p. 92.

Figure 4. Immigration, 1976–1981, by Selected Categories

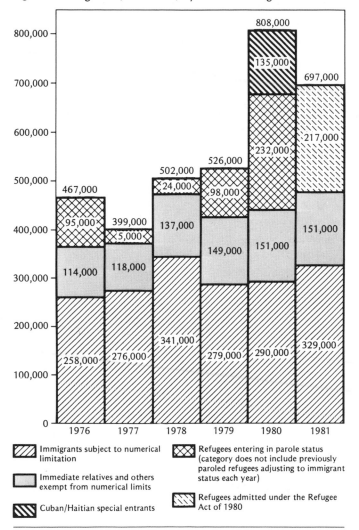

SOURCES: U.S. Immigration and Naturalization Service, *Annual Reports, 1976–78*, and unpublished INS data 1979; INS reports of aliens paroled and special entrants admitted, 1976–80; State Department field visa issuance reports and projections based on previous totals in certain categories for 1980 and 1981. *Reprinted in* U.S. Select Commission on Immigration and Refugee Policy, *U.S. Immigration Policy and the National Interest* (Washington, D.C., 1981), p. 93.

Bibliography

INTRODUCTION

The sources below are for the reader who is looking for more information on modern immigration. Not intended to be a comprehensive survey, the list includes several titles with excellent, detailed bibliographies.

No definitive treatment of current immigration exists but Stephan Thernstrom and Ann Orlov, eds., *Harvard Encyclopedia of American Ethnic Groups* (Cambridge, Mass., 1980) is an invaluable, if uneven, guide. It includes essays on some 121 immigrant and ethnic groups, as well as several thematic pieces, bibliographies, and tables. Standard textbooks in American immigrant history include: Maldwyn Allen Jones's classic, but dated, *American Immigration* (Chicago, 1960); Maxine Seller's *To Seek America* (Englewood, New Jersey, 1977), a fine interpretive work with exhaustive, critical bibliography; James Stuart Olson, *The Ethnic Dimension in American History* (New York, 1979), a well-defined and broadly detailed survey; Leonard Dinnerstein, Roy L. Nichols, and David M. Reimers, *Natives and Strangers* (New York, 1979), which attempts to weave the history of America's immigrants into the larger fabric of American history. Arthur Mann, *The One and the Many: Reflections on the American Identity* (Chicago and London, 1979) casts a seasoned and perceptive eye on the tensions inherent in a pluralist society. Nathan Glazer and Daniel Patrick Moynihan, *Beyond the Melting Pot: The Negroes, Puerto Ricans, Jews, Italians, and Irish of New York*, 2nd ed. (Cambridge, Mass., 1970) is an important, although dated, study. John Higham, *Strangers in the Land: Patterns of American Nativism, 1860–1925* (New Brunswick, N.J., 1963) is a classic work on the tangled roots of America's restrictionist immigration policy.

Several general guides and bibliographies are available: John D. Buenker, *Immigration and Ethnicity: A Guide to Information Sources* (Detroit, 1977); Wayne C. Miller, *A Comprehensive Bibliography for the Study of American Minorities*, 2 vols. (New York, 1976); Research Institute on Immigration and Ethnic Studies, *Recent*

Immigration to the United States: The Literature of the Social Sciences (Washington, D.C., 1976).

United States government publications make a great deal of information on immigration easily accessible. Among the most useful are: various reports of the Select Commission on Immigration and Refugee Policy, in particular, United States Select Commission on Immigration and Refugee Policy, U.S. *Immigration Policy and the National Interest: The Final Report and Recommendations of the Select Commission on Immigration and Refugee Policy to the Congress and the President of the United States, March 1, 1981* (Washington, D.C., 1981). Statistical summaries prepared by the Immigration and Naturalization Service are published in the *Annual Report*. Although not yet available when we were working on this book, the population reports resulting from the census of 1980 will yield important information for the study of immigration.`

CHAPTER 1: INDOCHINESE

Several useful studies on the Indochinese refugee migration are available. They include an overview of the first wave of refugees by Gail Paradise Kelley, *From Vietnam to America* (Boulder, 1977); a longer-range analysis by Daniel Montero and Marsha Weber, *Vietnamese Americans: Patterns of Resettlement and Socioeconomic Adaptation in the United States* (Boulder, 1979); and from a policy perspective, Judith Vadalia Taft, David S. North, and David A. Ford, *Refugee Resettlement in the United States: Time for a New Focus* (Washington, D.C., 1979). Frank Snepp's iconoclastic report on the complexities of the American evacuation from Vietnam, *Decent Interval* (New York, 1977) is an interesting and absorbing account. The Refugee Resettlement Information Exchange Project, *Refugee Reports*, a biweekly newsletter published by the American Public Welfare Association, Washington, D.C., contains helpful information on the placement, settlement, and accommodation to American life of the growing number of refugees.

CHAPTER 2: ILLEGALS AND UNDOCUMENTED

Much of the literature on illegal or undocumented immigration can be found in newspapers and journals, especially the *International Migration Review* and *Migration Today*. Most of the books that consider ways to restructure the country's immigration policy spend considerable time on the question of entries outside the law. Barry R. Chiswick, "Immigrants and Immigration Policy," in William Fellner, ed., *Contemporary Economic Problems* (Washington, D.C., 1978) is one example of many attempts to assess the economic impact of immigration, legal and otherwise. Among the many useful government reports on the subject of illegal immigration, see: Report to Congress by the Comptroller General of the U.S., "Smugglers, Illicit Documents and Schemes are Undermining U.S. Controls over Immigration." (Washington, D.C., 1976).

CHAPTER 3: PERUVIANS

Dwight B. Heath and Richard Adams, eds., *Contemporary Cultures and Societies of Latin America* (New York, 1965) is a reader in social anthropology of Central and South America and the Carribean. It includes two articles of particular interest on Peru: Oscar Nunez del Prado, "Aspects of Andean Native Life," and William P. Mangin, "Role of Regional Associations in the Adaptation on Rural Migrants to Cities in Peru." Two general histories with material on Peru are: J. H. Steward and L. C. Faron, *Native Peoples of South America* (New York, 1959) and Paul Radin, *Indians of South America* (New York, 1942). More specifically on Peru, see Thomas E. Weil, *et al.*, *Area Handbook for Peru*, (Washington, D.C., 1972) and Robert V. Master, *Peru in Pictures*, (1965, Reprint: New York, 1972).

CHAPTER 4: KOREANS

No definitive study of Korean immigration exists, but the following works may be consulted: Hyung-chan Kim and Wayne Patterson, eds., *The Koreans in America, 1882–1974* (Dobbs Ferry, N.Y., 1974); Hyung-chan Kim, ed., *The Korean Diaspora: Historical and Sociological Studies of the Korean Immigration and Assimilation in North America* (Santa Barbara, Ca., 1977); Bong-youn Choy, *Koreans in America* (Chicago, 1979). Two helpful articles on the Koreans are: Monica Boyd, "The Changing Nature of Central and Southeast Asian Immigration to the United States: 1961–1972," *International Migration Review* 8 (Winter, 1974), 507–20 and Euiyoung Yu, "Koreans in America: An Emerging Ethnic Minority," *Amerasia* 4 (1977), 117–31.

CHAPTER 5: IRISH

General studies of Irish immigration to the United States include: Carl Wittke, *The Irish in America* (New York, 1956); William V. Shannon, *The American Irish* (New York, 1966) and Andrew M. Greeley, *That Most Distressful Nation* (Chicago, 1973). On population changes in Ireland and the effect of these changes on emigration, see Robert E. Kennedy, *The Irish: Emigration, Marriage and Fertility* (Berkeley, 1973). Oscar Handlin's *Boston Immigrants* (Cambridge, Mass., rev. ed. 1959) is a classic study of the Irish in an eastern American city.

CHAPTER 6: SOVIET JEWS

There is a vast literature on the history of the Jews in Russia. Three of the most readable books available are: Salo Baron, *The Russian Jew Under Tsars and Soviets* (New York, 1964); Solomon Schwarz, *The Jews in The Soviet Union* (Syracuse, N.Y., 1951); Lionel Kochan, ed., *The Jews in Soviet Russia Since 1917* (New York,

1970). Hedrick Smith, *The Russians* (New York, 1976) provides a fine overview of contemporary life in the USSR. The noted author, Elie Wiesel, offers a moving first-hand account of Jewish life in Russia in *The Jews of Silence* (New York, 1966). On the earlier immigration of Russian Jews two outstanding books are: Irving Howe, *The World of Our Fathers* (New York, 1976) and Moses Rischin, *The Promised City* (Cambridge, Mass., 1962). Joseph Edelman, "Soviet Jews in the United States: A Profile," *American Jewish Yearbook* (New York, 1977), pp. 157–81, should also be consulted.

CHAPTER 7: WEST INDIANS

The entire issue of *International Migration Review* 13 (Summer, 1979) is devoted to Caribbean migration to New York. It includes an overview by Roy Simón Bryce-Laporte and several other articles on Dominicans, Garifunas, and Haitians. An important monograph on the earlier period is: Ira Reid, *The Negro Immigrant* (1939; Reprint: New York, 1970). Nathan Glazer and Daniel Patrick Moynihan, in *Beyond the Melting Pot: The Negroes, Puerto Ricans, Jews, Italians, and Irish of New York*, 2nd ed. (Cambridge, Mass., 1970) explore some of the differences between West Indians and American blacks in New York City. Ransford W. Palmer, "Decade of West Indian Migration to the United States, 1962–1972: An Economic Analysis," *Social and Economic Studies* 23 (December, 1974), pp. 571–87 explores the professional qualifications of recent immigrants.

CHAPTER 8: ITALIAN

On Italian backgrounds before emigration during the years of mass exodus, see Robert E. Foerster's classic, *The Italian Emigration of Our Times* (1919, Reprint: New York, 1968). General studies, bringing the subject up to date, include: Alexander DeConde, *Half Bitter, Half Sweet: An Excursion into Italian American History* (New York, 1971); Luciano J. Iorizzo and Salvatore Mondello, *The Italian Americans* (New York, 1971); and Joseph Lopreato, *Italian Americans* (New York, 1970). On Italians in New York, see Thomas Kessner, *The Golden Door: Italian and Jewish Immigrant Mobility in New York City, 1880–1915* (New York, 1977); Silvano Tomasi's study of Italian parishes in New York, *Piety and Power* (Staten Island, 1975). Richard Gambino's interpretive *Blood of My Blood* (Garden City, 1974) includes many of the author's New York experiences and observations.

CHAPTER 9: CHINESE

Louis J. Beck, *New York's Chinatown* (New York, 1898) gives a colorful picture of the area in the 1890s. Betty Lee Sung, *Mountain of Gold: The Story of the Chinese in America* (New York, 1970) is a readable, popular history. The same author's

Statistical Profile of the Chinese in the United States, published by the Manpower Administration, U.S. Department of Labor (Washington, D.C., 1975) brings together materials on the Chinese as reported in the 1970 census. Rose Hum Lee, *The Chinese in the United States of America* (Hong Kong, 1960) is an important sociological study. Chia-ling Kuo, *Social and Political Change in New York's Chinatown* (New York, 1977) explores the shift in power from the old associations to the new organizations, which are supported by government funds.

CHAPTER 10: GREEKS

The outstanding scholar of Greek immigration, Theodore Saloutos, has been responsible for several books and articles on the topic. His *The Greeks in the United States* (Cambridge, Mass., 1964) and *They Remember America* (Berkeley, 1956), a study of Greek repatriates, are both very helpful. An important early work is Henry P. Fairchild, *Greek Immigration to the United States* (New Haven, 1911). Also useful are two more recent books: Charles C. Moskos, Jr., *Greek-Americans: Struggle and Success* (Englewood Cliffs, N.J., 1980) and Evangelos Vlachos, *The Assimilation of the Greeks in the United States* (Athens, 1968).

CHAPTER 11: HONDURANS

In addition to general works on Central America, see Howard Blutstein *et al., Area Handbook for Honduras* (Washington, D.C., 1971) and Ken Weddle, *Honduras in Pictures* (New York, 1972). On the Black Caribs, see an article by Eduard Conzemius, "Ethnographical Notes on the Black Caribs (Garif)," *American Anthropologist* 30 (1928), 183–205. A bibliography of books and articles on New York's Hispanics can be found in David Lowenthal, "New York's New Hispanic Immigrants," *Geographical Record*, 66 (1976), 90–92.